MORE
ENTERTAINERS

Henry Ainley, on the left, with George Alexander in 'If I Were King' at London's St. James's theatre. The play ran from 30 August 1902 to 13 March 1903.

by
Ronnie Barraclough
and
David Reekie

Published by Zodiac Publishing International.

Zodiac Publishing, USA
#4 Herndon House, Canon Creek Air Park,
Rt. 18, P.O.Box 589, Lake City,
Florida 32025, USA.
Tel: 386 754 6527
e-mail: general@zodiacpublishing.org

Zodiac Publishing, FZ LLC, UAE.
Bld 8, Office 302, Dubai Media City,
P.O.Box 502127, Dubai, UAE
Tel: 0971 4 - 3903505 Fax: 0971 4 - 3908238
e-mail: general@zodiacpublishing.org
www.zodiacpublishing.org

Zodiac Publishing, UK.
#3 Carlyle Court, Chelsea Harbour,
London SW10 0UQ, UK.
Tel: 020 7352 8910 Fax: 020 7376 4271
e-mail: general@zodiacpublishing.org

First published 2003   ISBN 1-904566-00-6

Copyright: Ronnie Barraclough and David Reekie

Other books in the series:

Now & Then Abu Dhabi by Christine Nowell & Nick Crawley	ISBN 0-9533033-3-0
Now & Then Bahrain by John J. Nowell	ISBN 0-9533033-1-4
Now & Then Dubai by Simone Nowell & Robert Nowell	ISBN 0-9533033-3-0
Jetz & Dam Dubai by Simone Nowell & Robert Nowell	ISBN 0-9533033-6-5
Now & Then The Emirates by John J. Nowell	ISBN 0-9533033-0-6
Now & Then Oman by John J. Nowell	ISBN 0-9533033-5-7
Jetz & Dam Oman by John J. Nowell	ISBN 0-9721589-7-9
Now & Then Sharjah by John J. Nowell & Robert Nowell	ISBN 0-9721589-3-6
*ADay Above Oman by John J. Nowell	
*ADay Above The Emirates by John J. Nowell	
A Day Above Yemen by John J. Nowell	ISBN 0-9533033-2-2

* These books are published by Motivate Publishing

An Artist in Conservation by David Shepherd OBE, FRSA, FRGS and Gava	ISBN 0-9533033-9-x
My Painting Life by David Shepherd OBE, FRSA, FRGS and Gava	ISBN 0-9533033-7-3
Colours of Fujairah by Christopher Hurndall & Blanca Rösler	ISBN 0-9721589-2-8
Morley Entertainers by Ronnie Barraclough & David Reekie	ISBN 1-904566-00-6
The Seeds of Eden by Christopher Hurndall	ISBN 0-9721589-0-1
Qataban & Sheba by Wendell Phillips	ISBN 0-904566-02-2

All the above books are available post free in the UK, USA, and Europe by ordering online at: www.zodiacpublishing.org

Forth comming titles:

Now & Then Pakistan by John J. Nowell & Robert Nowell	ISBN 0-9721589-5-2
Colours of Dubai by Simone Nowell	ISBN 0-9721589-1-x
Now & Then Malta by Nick Crawley & John J. Nowell	ISBN 1-904566-05-7
Now & Then Cape Town by Paul Tingay & John J. Nowell	ISBN 1-904566-08-1
Now & Then — Beyond the Blue Horizon by Alexander Frater	ISBN 1-904566-04-9
Now & Then — The Quest for the Queen of Sheba by Wendell Phillips	ISBN 0-9721589-8-7
Now & Then Egypt	ISBN 1-904566-06-5
Hormuz By Christopher Hurndall	ISBN 1-904566-03-0

Cover Photograph by Capt. John J. Nowell LRPS FRGS
Design by Nick Crawley, Zodiac Publishing FZ LLC, Dubai Media City.
Printed by Lightning Source, Inc. Milton Keynes, UK

FOREWORD.

July 2002

I feel very honoured in this Jubilee year to be asked to write a foreword for this book.

Ronnie Barraclough and David Reekie have combined their obvious abilities and enthusiasm to produce this informative and fascinating account of the talent for amateur entertainment that has graced our town over the years.

The amount of detail included is a clear illustration of the depth of their study and research, covering as it does the inspiration that came from the regular use of the many stage facilities contained within Morley's chapels, church buildings and schools together with the Town Hall and our own purpose built Pavilion Theatre.

In my role as Mayor of the Morley Town Council I warmly welcome this book about Morley and wish it and its authors every success.

The Mayor of Morley
Councillor Judith M.Elliott.

Contents.

Foreword by the Mayor of Morley, Councillor Judith M. Elliott.   3
Acknowledgements.   6
Rhyme and Reason.   7
Another Rhyme, Another Reason.   8
Didn't They Do Well.   9
    Introduction by Mrs. Michelle Le M. Jenkins.   9
    Ainley, Henry Hinchliffe, Actor of Stage, Screen & Radio,   10
    Baines, James Edwin, Violinist & Local Hero.   25
    Bastow, Trevor & Geoffrey, Musicians of International Repute.   26
    Bedford, Brian, Actor & Director.   28
    Booth, John, Pianist and Man of Many Talents.   30
    Burrow, Renee & Harry, Actors & Entertainers.   31
    Bywater, Jim, Actor & Composer.   34
    Currie, Elaine, Dancer.   35
    Dews, Peter, Producer, Director & Actor.   40
    Fryer, Phil., "Just to be Frank" (Sinatra).   42
    Green, Phyllis, Cellist.   45
    Haigh, Verna, Singer, Dancer & Accordionist.   47
    Inman, Alfred, Violinist.   48
    Jenkins, Tom, Violin Virtuoso.   50
    Kirk, John T., Actor, Producer & Theatre Manager.   58
    Kitson, Jean, Actress.   59
    Mulchrone, Vincent J., Newspaper Reporter & Feature Writer.   62
    Popplewell, Jack, Songwriter & Playwright.   67
    Rooley, Anthony, Lutenist & Authority on Early Music.   69
    Stead, Robert, BBC Producer & Controller.   71
    Wiseman, Ernest....."Ernie Wise".   73

Entertainments Through the Centuries.   76
Early Entertainments.   98
The Temperance Hall.   106
The Victoria Music Hall.   108
The Town Hall.   110
The Alexandra Palace Theatre.   112
The New Pavilion Theatre.   114
The Picture House.   116
The Views of an Offcomed-un.   118
A World Premier in Morley.   124

The Morley Vocal Union.   128
The West Riding Singers.   133
Tingley Methodist Sylvians.   137
An interlude.   139
Morley Grammar School & The Old MorleiansAmateur Dramatic
Society.   142
Morley Technical Institute Amateur Operatic Society.   148
 The Young Generation.   148
 The Four Generations.   152
 The Pavilion Years.   152
 Curtain Up.   155
 Stage Whispers.   159
 The Pavilion cat.   165
 The Power of Advertising.   165
 More Stage Whispers.   168
 Curtain Down.   175

The Revellers.   181
The Show that Hitler Cancelled.   188
How Carrol Levis Discovered Morley's Talent.   190
The Morley Top Town Team.   192
Pantos, Pews and Revues.   198
4th March 1955.   209
It's a Small World.   211
The Morley Music Society.   213
Epilogue.   219
Subscribers.   220
Index.   222

The New Pavilion Theatre, this photograph was taken during the week commencing Monday 29th June 1914 when a variety show was the attraction.

Acknowledgments.

This book would not exist but for the encouragement and the essential assistance willingly given by the people of Morley.

The authors are indebted to all those who voluntarily offered wonderful reminiscences of their involvement with Morley's amateur entertainments and who loaned photographs from their personal collections.

A special mention must be made of David K. Atkinson's kindness in allowing the authors to delve freely into his photographic archives and special mention must be made of his painstaking work in proof reading and editing and also for his perceptive comments.

The final piece of the jigsaw fell into place when John Nowell, grandson of David James Collins (Pavilion Manager 1913/1914), visited the Barracloughs in the spring of 2002.

The eventual outcome was that a group of subscribers paid in advance, in trust, for their copies. It is to these Morley folk, listed on page 220, who most deserve our thanks, for without their faith, this book would not be available for the enjoyment of all.

Ronnie Barraclough and David Reekie

An itinerant with his performing bear outside the Church Street branch of the Morley Cooperative Society in about 1908. (see page 98)

Rhyme and Reason

A publicity shot of David Reekie for his part of Billy Bigelow in 'Carousel' which was staged at the Pavilion Theatre, Morley in 1960.

S trangely this book came about because Ronnie Barraclough and I had never met. Our paths had crossed many times in the past, it was just that we were never on the same path at the same time. Then we happened to be together in the same room, (or rather the same marquee) to celebrate the 80ᵗʰ birthday of Renee Burrow, that doyenne of Morley's amateur entertainment world. Renee together with her late husband Harry, were among the mainstays of the Operatic Society. Their contribution remains supreme, with service spanning so many years of major change and development. As Joint Secretaries and performers, their talents knew no bounds.

It was a truly inspiring evening with friends gathered from all over the country. Ronnie Barraclough was there with his wife Margaret, and still we did not meet. As he came in one door, I left by another with impeccable timing. I can only liken our movements to the cast of a Whitehall farce where the characters central to the plot are destined not to come face to face until that final moment of hilarious denouement.

The omission of years was soon to be corrected. He and I had each written and self-published books concerning Morley. At long last here was the catalyst for us to meet and exchange copies of our precious efforts. Ron's wonderful compilation covering the history of The New Pavilion Theatre Morley coming so soon after Renee's celebration was to kick-start this particular literary effort. I discussed the idea with the Barracloughs during a visit to their home in Churwell in the late summer of 2000. Both Margaret and Ronnie warmed to the idea and our partnership was sealed.

None of us are getting any younger, and it is important that the stories that follow are not lost in the mists of time. The physical face of Morley has changed considerably in recent years, and those changes are portrayed so well in the photographs and writings of local historians.

Here the firm of Barraclough and Reekie hope to save for posterity the human stories that are the very essence of a cultural revolution that was to sweep aside the habits of generations and alter the face of amateur entertainment in the town. This anthology is a salute to the past and a tribute to those who today carry on the old traditions.

David Reekie 2002, Bedale, North Yorkshire
'The offcomed-un.'

Another Rhyme, Another Reason

My wife, Margaret, and I have many happy memories of the wonderful musical shows staged by the Morley Amateur Operatic Society at Morley's own Pavilion theatre. We remember well those delightful times when we were entertained by the performances of David Reekie in the principal roles of shows such as 'Carissima', 'Showboat', 'Desert Song' and, of course, 'Oklahoma'.

When my friend and local historian David Atkinson mentioned that David Reekie was making enquiries regarding my book 'The History of the New Pavilion', I lost no time in taking this as an excuse to contact him at his home in Bedale. This coincided with the time he was putting the finishing touches to his book 'Don't Go Down the Mine Dad' for which he had been unsuccessfully searching for the words of the song of the same name. Margaret and I were able to provide them, the book about the life of David as a Bevin Boy in wartime Morley was completed, and David and I exchanged our respective tomes.

This contact resulted in the forming of a valuable friendship with David and his wife Mavis, and led to our collaboration on this joint project which, after many meetings, telephone calls and dozens of emails has come to fruition.

It is hoped that the readers of this book find it both interesting and enjoyable and that it is retained as their record of a significant part of the history of this old, proud and independently minded former mill town of Morley.

Ronnie Barraclough. 2002.
Morley.

DIDN'T THEY DO WELL.

This first section of the book consists of a collection of biographies of the men and women of Morley who were involved in the world of music, acting and entertainment and whose various achievements on and off the stage gained wide recognition. It is a small tribute to, and a record of, some remarkable Morley people.

Mrs. Michelle Le M. Jenkins kindly contributed the following introduction, coincidentally on the 50th anniversary of her first meeting with Tom Jenkins.

A phone call in 1952 changed my life. I had done well at school, earned a scholarship to music college and been welcomed as a student in Paris. I was in the London music circuit. Then came the phone call. My professor said that Tom Jenkins was auditioning for a flute player for his Scarborough season, with the promise of five months employment. Light music by the seaside sounded very pleasant.

And so I found myself in Yorkshire and the North of England for the first time. With two full programmes a day of music I had never seen, seven days a week (Saturday mornings off) I began to question the word 'light'. Scarborough prided itself on its library, so the same piece took at least a month to come round again. My flute began to wilt and so did I. I was given 24 hours compassionate leave to return to London and my professor. "You have forgotten how to breathe", he said.

Back with the orchestra I pulled myself and my playing together, and started to look around. Tom the Musical Director was leading effortlessly from his violin, at home on the platform, never tiring, with an easy rapport with the audience, and always retaining his superb musicianship. How did he do it? I started to understand: Tom was a Yorkshire man through and through, faithful to his Morley background that never let him down.

Now we learn about the other artists who came from the same roots each one with the same strength and purpose and achieving so much. We are able through this excellent book to acknowledge the pleasure and inspiration they have given us; I would like to say thank you to the authors for making this possible.

Michelle Jenkins. East Sussex.
April 2002.

Henry Hinchliffe Ainley.
1879 - 1945

Actor of Stage, Screen and Radio.
Theatrical Manager and The Head of an Acting Dynasty.

Henry Ainley as 'Bishop of Chelsea' in 'Getting Married' at the Haymarket theatre, 12 May to 11 July 1908.

Contrary to popular belief Henry Ainley was not born in Morley, but in Leeds on 21st August 1879. His parents lived in Belle Vue Terrace and the family did not move from the city until shortly after baby Henry was christened at St George's Church in Leeds, where his parents had taken their marriage vows. His father, Richard was born in Horbury and his mother Ada (nee Hinchliffe) originated from Cragg Vale. Henry Hinchliffe Ainley owed much to his father who was a remarkable man in many ways.

At ten years of age his father, like many of his generation, was put to work underground in the coal industry. At nineteen he was unable to read or write, and a sudden desire to educate himself at evening classes, perhaps stemmed from the influence of the Mrs. Ainley to be. The transformation from an illiterate manual worker to a mill owner and cloth manufacturer was startling. Henry was still only a baby when the family moved to their new home in Victoria Road, Morley and within two years Richard was a cloth finisher, employing 21 men and 26 boys. Together with his partner and friend Mr. Stephenson, Crank Mill, Morley was acquired, (this was the first steam powered woollen mill in West Yorkshire) and the family moved to a new home, 'North View', Rooms Lane, Morley, a house that is still occupied today. In 1893 Henry's sister, Beatrice, was born and the family, along with a maid servant, lived in the house for over 20 years although in the early years of the 20th century a live-in maid was not employed and Richard's sister-in-law Lily Horsfall, a school mistress, lived with the family.

Richard Ainley was soon to become a leading figure in the town, having interest in charities concerned with health and education. He was a churchwarden at St. Peter's Parish Church and an associate of Alice Cliff Scatcherd; together they served on several committees. Ainley was Treasurer for the Nursing Association of Morley for a long period. His reputation as a lecturer grew. In March 1882 he spoke to the Young Men's Improvement Society at St Peter's New School on the subject of 'Advertisement and Advertising.' Samples of advertising artwork were displayed around the room along with several exhibits borrowed from local shopkeepers. These ranged from a giant teapot and huge boot, to the figure of an'Ethiopian boy' so loved by the tobacconists of the day. Fifteen years later his influence was such that he presented a paper at the Priestley Hall, Park Row Leeds, upon 'Education and The State.'Richard Ainley's gift for oratory and his ability to hold an audience was to be echoed in his son Henry. To celebrate King Edward VII's Coronation in 1902, Richard organised Morley's carnival procession, for which there were over one hundred entries.

During his formative years the boy attended St Peter's school only yards from his Morley home, but was later enrolled as a day pupil at Mr Bundle's College situated at Morley Grange, Churwell. As befits a Yorkshire man, Henry developed a love of cricket. His great hero was Churwell born Robert 'Bobby'Peel, the famed record-breaking Yorkshire and England all-rounder. Peel also resided in Rooms Lane, and years later Ainley would proudly recall how Bobby Peel had allowed him to carry his bag from the railway station to his home. Never losing his love of the game, Henry later played for a Thespians Eleven under the captaincy of C. Aubrey Smith, who was to achieve Hollywood stardom as the epitome of an English gentleman.

Ainley began life in his father's office, but this was to last only a few weeks. Even so he left a lasting impression upon the lady employees. Many years later one elderly Morley lady who had known him at Crank Mill is recorded as saying *"he was a heart throb even then"*. In 1897 Henry was a bank clerk in Leeds when he joined the Casuals Amateur Dramatic Society and, although his mother frowned on his histrionic ambitions, Sir George Alexander gave encouragement by giving him a walk on part for a week during his company's production of 'The Masqueraders' whilst it was in Leeds. A move to a Sheffield bank was quickly followed by a step into stocks and shares with Messrs. Staniforth & Hall, Brokers, High Street, Sheffield. Once more he was acting in his spare time with a local amateur group, and was good enough to again impress the famous actor-manager of the day, Sir George Alexander. Ainley was invited to join the company but unfortunately Henry's parents again strongly objected to the proposals, and the opportunity was lost.

Nevertheless the lure of the stage was to prove too strong, and at twenty years of age Henry deserted the world of commerce and joined Mr. Frank R.Benson's Shakespearean Company in Birmingham and made his debut as a messenger in 'Macbeth'. At that time it was the best known of all the

Young Henry Ainley the matinee idol.

provincial touring companies. Mr. Benson, who formed the company in 1883, tended to rant and rave in his Shakespearean parts but his was the best school of acting at the time. In 1920 he could boast that seventy old 'Bensonians' were playing prominent parts in the West End, nearly all the star Shakespearean performers of the age learned their business under Benson. For Henry Ainley it was a new career for a new century. He toured the country with Benson and then made his first appearance on the London stage at the Lyceum on 15ᵗʰ February 1900 in 'Henry V' followed by two years of Shakespeare, one year at the Lyceum and a further year at the Comedy. Sir George Alexander was, however, not to be denied. It was he who discovered Ainley in the truest sense of the word. In March 1902 he launched Henry Ainley into the title role of Paolo in Stephen Philip's tragedy 'Paolo and Francesca'at the St. James's theatre. He was an instant success, lionised by society. His glorious hypnotic voice, his commanding stage presence, piercing brilliant eyes, thick black hair and Grecian nose made him the envy of his contemporaries. Later in 1903 he travelled to America and made his first appearance in New York at the Empire theatre, playing the part of Sebastian in 'The Pretty Sister of Jose' as leading man to Maude Adams. He then toured America as the Reverend Gavin Dishart in Barrie's 'The Little Minister.' Returning to London in 1904 he played a wide variety of leading roles. There was a brief visit to Paris in December 1905 to appear at the Opera Comique as Romeo in the balcony scene from 'Romeo and Juliet'. In June 1909 he appeared at Stratford-on-Avon as Shylock in 'The Merchant of Venice'. He was now established as a prominent actor of the British stage and, of course, had many leading ladies. He could be an outrageous flirt both on and off the stage. Cathleen Nesbitt said that as she waited to meet him for the first time at a rehearsal of 'A Winter's Tale'to be staged at the Savoy theatre in 1912, she wondered what he would be like. She mused about how he had taken London by storm, how countless young women had been in love with him and how he had loved them and left them. He was married but his reputation was Bohemian to say the least. She described Henry Ainley as a stockily built, solid young man with a ruddy face and unruly black hair and before the reading was over realized she was fortunate enough to be in the company of a really great actor, *"his eyes and his voice were so magnetic one was held in fascination."* Miss Nesbitt later wrote, *"I shall never forget him at the dress rehearsal, pacing up and down like a tiger, his eyes blazing, his magnificent kingly robe of crimson and gold flaring about him, his voice resounding through the theatre."* She rhapsodised about that voice and said the only one she ever heard again quite like it was that of Richard Burton. Cathleen fell for the Ainley charm. There were invitations, in Garrick Club envelopes, to dine after the play, and roses with a card attached "Oh my rose of the world, my dark rose, my Irish rose." She visited his house in Regent's Park and they read sonnets before the fire. Eventually his domestic problems got in the way and there was a

Henry as 'Faust' at His Majesty's theatre, 5th September to 12th December 1908.

fond farewell in a dark corner of Rules restaurant. In her memoirs Miss Nesbitt's final words on the subject had a sad ring. *"I didn't realize it then but he was already beginning to take refuge in drink. It was many years before it dimmed his talent but in the end it destroyed him and robbed the theatre of a great actor."*

He had a great range and his repertoire encompassed Shakespeare, Shaw, Du Maurier and Arnold Bennett. In 1915 he created the character role of Joseph Quinney's, the antique dealer in H A Vachell's play 'Quinney's.' Four years later he was in the film version.

Henry Ainley was the top matinee idol of the day and had many admirers, among them the young Lady Elizabeth Bowes Lyon (who became our Queen and later a much loved Queen Mother). Ainley sent her a letter, together with a signed photograph, offering theatre seats. It is dated 19th March 1916.

"I hope the play may come up to your expectations and I shall myself look forward with keen pleasure to Friday evening, and at the end of the first act I shall raise my eyes to that part of the house where you and your friend will be seated and may I hope to meet a smile of appreciation and pleasure. May I touch on one other point which is necessarily a somewhat delicate one. Please remember whatever my feelings appear towards other members of the cast they are purely and simply the attitude of an actor and not my real self."

Lavinia Spencer wrote to Elizabeth, *"...you secured such a trophy, I am*

Mr. Henry Ainley as 'Dandy' in 'The Dawn of Tomorrow' at the Duke of York's theatre from 20th June to 23rd July 1910.

awfully glad you still admire Henry, he is quite the best actor of the day."

His universal appeal to the opposite sex is demonstrated in one of the verses of the popular Music Hall song of the day, 'I'm Getting Such a Big Girl Now':-

What father says is always right,
And I have got to be good somehow
And I musn't gaze insanely
Anymore at Henry Ainley
'Cos I'm getting a big girl now.

In 1916 Ainley acted in five films before joining the army as a gunner, obtaining a commission and serving in France and Italy. On his return to civilian life in 1919, he toured the country with his own company as Edward Graham in 'Uncle Ned' and he then formed an association with Gilbert Miller in the management of the St James's Theatre in London. In the ensuing years among some of his notable productions were:-

A A Milne's 'The Dover Road', St John Irvine's 'The First Mrs Fraser', and James Bridie's 'The Anatomist'. It was, however, appropriate that Mr. Ainley commenced his theatre management with his own production of the play 'Reparation', a Russian drama by Count Leo Tolstoy, which he staged at the Grand Theatre, Leeds on Monday 18th August 1919, for six nights and a Saturday matinee. This opening in Leeds was its first production on any stage prior to its presentation at the St. James's Theatre in London, where it ran from September 1919 to January 1920. Henry played the character Fedya and it was reported at the time that he again showed a rare power of acting and that he received a reception in Leeds that obviously touched and gratified him. Two other notable events connected with this visit to Leeds were the celebration of his 40th birthday on the Thursday and his introduction of a young actor called Claude Rains who Mr. Ainley coached to stardom and who is now remembered as the Hollywood movie star in the 'Invisible Man' and 'The Phantom of the Opera'. Rains, himself, was later to develop another promising young actor, John Gielgud.

Ainley's greatest triumph must surely be as Hassan in the lyrical play by James Elroy Flecker. This production, with music by Delius and ballet by Fokine, was presented by Basil Dean at His Majesty's Theatre from 20th September 1923 to 24th May 1924. It was a sensation, acclaimed by the critics for its spectacle, music and colour, and the ecstatic performance of

Henry Ainley. Basil Dean thought that no one could speak the words of the poet Flecker better than Henry Ainley. In his memoirs Dean gave a pen-picture of the actor: "*His panache and love of the grand manner would keep the rather loosely constructed play firmly under control. If only he would keep away from the drink! This handsome man of noble voice and mien, with an infallible ear for the music of words, a cool intelligence and a sly humour, needed a core of steel to hold his many gifts within bounds. But alas! He was a mass of uncoordinated impulses that created vicissitudes and eventually destroyed him.*" Dean found it impossible to lead or drive him and had to enter into an amiable conspiracy with Ainley's

Miss Wish Wynne, as 'Janet Cannot' with Henry Ainley as 'Ilam Crave' in 'The Great Adventure' at the Kingsway theatre from 25th March 1913 to 7th November 1914.

second wife, Elaine, to keep temptation away during the trying weeks of rehearsal. Cathleen Nesbitt, now married and expecting her first child, was Yasmin in the production and she wrote: *"Ainley was Hassan the confectioner, rotund with moustache, turban and greasy grey dress and about forty. How wonderful it was to suddenly hear from that dumb, domestic bird, the magical voice of Ainley."* Hassan had to fling her down in a rage and say *"Oh thou stupendous harlot! Get thee gone!"* and would murmur *"For God's sake mind the baby, that child will pop out on the carpet one night moaning, "Allah, Allah!""*

In July 1924 he toured the provinces with the play 'Snobs' and in 1925 took over the management of the New Theatre but after playing 'Macbeth' in 1926/7 he was, because of ill-health, absent from the stage for over two years making his reappearance at the Haymarket in July 1929 in 'Hamlet', which was selected for the Royal Command performance.

Henry Ainley himself became one of the first stage actors to appear in film. He played in twenty-one silent movies, from 'Henry VIII' in 1911 to 'Sally Bishop' in 1924. He refused many lucrative offers to appear in Hollywood, declaring he would rather play Shakespeare than anything else. One of his greatest assets, his voice, could not be heard in the films of that era. With his golden speaking tones, handsome features and impressive six-foot physique, there is no doubt that 'the talkies' would have found in him true Hollywood star quality.

In 1932 after his Drury Lane performances and during the filming of J B Priestley's 'Good Companions,' Ainley was taken seriously ill and for two months he hung between life and death in hospital. He could not continue with the film, but his voice was used to record the prologue.

He was able to join his eldest son Richard in 1936 to film 'As You Like It' and in 1941 he was the commentator for the film 'Battle of the Books.' Unfortunately this was to prove his swan song in film, while he also remained terrified he may break down on stage were he to return to the theatre.

During a long convalescence in Ilkley there was some improvement in his health, which he attributed to his native air and the visits of old friends from Morley and Leeds. He listened to Yorkshire dialect saying *"the sound of it is a tonic."* He was able to broadcast from time to time for the B.B.C., including in 1937 a radio version of 'Hassan' and in 1939 as Jean Valjean in 'Les Miserables'. Also in 1939 Henry celebrated his 60th birthday in Ilkley, and he expressed a hope of being able to return to the stage, *"all I want is the doctor to say yes."*

The hoped for recovery was not to be, and his war years were spent in a stoic fight against ill health, the battle being finally lost on Wednesday 31 October 1945 when Henry Ainley died at his residence in Princess Gardens, West Acton, Middlesex. One of the greatest figures of the English theatre made his final exit in his 66th year.

A memorial service was held at the Church of St. Martin-in-the-Fields on Tuesday 13th November 1945. It passed almost unnoticed by the majority of the press, although a host of well-known actors, actresses and managers attended the service. Laurence Olivier and Lewis Casson read the lessons

Crank Mill, Morley, the first steam powered woollen mill in West Yorkshire. Acquired by Richard Ainley for his woollen business, it is where Henry worked in the office for a short time after leaving school. The building still stands but is no longer a mill.

and Frederick Ranalow sang a solo from Elgar's 'Dream of Gerontius.' Hubert Beaumont MP represented the Borough of Morley.

Henry's parents had left Morley many years earlier and retired to the Sussex coastal resort of Bognor, so severing the 'Ainley'link with Morley. But both father and son had in their own way brought undoubted credit and fame to the town. The two generations that were to follow, are also worthy of mention, for this is the stuff of dreams, where fantasy becomes truth, and truth becomes stranger than fiction.

Henry Ainley was married to two American ladies, Susanne Sheldon and Elaine Titus Fearon both marriages being dissolved. He also had a partner, Baroness Bettina von Hutten, who was born Bettina Riddle in Pennsylvania in 1874, and who became famous for her first novel 'Pam'and a number of successful sequels. She married a German baron but when she returned to England she was interned as an enemy alien during the first World War. In 1932 their daughter Henrietta Riddle was engaged to Alistair Cooke (of 'Letter from America' fame).

Another daughter Patsy did not originally have any interest in an acting career until she discovered a desire to perform with her father. She completed her training at RADA but to the great disappointment of both father and daughter the decline in his health prevented the projected appearance from materialising.

Henry's eldest son, Richard Riddle Ainley, was born on 22nd December 1910 at Stanmore in Middlesex and he died in London on 18th May 1967. He was married and divorced three times, to Ethel Glendinning (actress), Betzi Beaton (actress) and finally to Rowena Woolf. He made his theatrical debut in 1928 and to avoid accusations of nepotism, he billed himself as Richard Riddle. His first film appearance was with his father in the 1936 production of 'As You Like It', detailed later. In 1940 he was signed to a Hollywood contract by Warner Bros. and spent most of the time playing stereotypical 'Brits', usually gentlemen of leisure. During the war Richard

'North View', Rooms Lane, Morley the house occupied by the Ainley family for some 25 years. It is still occupied

served with the United States mechanised cavalry and was wounded in Germany. He ended his movie career in 1949 to concentrate on his stage work, after performing in 10 films in the 1930's and 12 in the 1940's.

Anthony Ainley, Richard's son and Henry's grandson, was born in London on 20th August 1937. When he left school Anthony was employed for a while as an insurance clerk and then joined RADA before becoming an actor, in the tradition of both his father and grandfather. He did, however, appear earlier as a small child in the 1941 film 'The Foreman Went to France'. In 1973 he was a regular in the TV programme 'Upstairs Downstairs' as the character Lord Charles Gilmour. In 1980 he took over from Roger Delgado as The Master in 'Dr. Who,' which he played until 1988. His films include 'A Man For All Seasons'and 'The Land that Time Forgot' in which he played the character Dietz.

Henry Ainley's second son, Henry junior, led a most interesting and extraordinary life. Born in 1918 he completed his education at Eton and Oxford before sailing around the world, in 1937, on a Finnish windjammer. On returning to England he studied for the theatre but when war was declared in 1939 he joined the Merchant Marine, followed by service in the Royal Navy. After leaving the navy he had a range of occupations from deep-sea trawling to stage-managing in the West End. He was both a member of the cast and the stage manager for the play "The Rivals" which ran at the Criterion Theatre from 25th September 1945 to 16th February 1946. The following year, 1947, he left England when he was appointed the French correspondent for a London Sunday newspaper. In 1950 Henry Junior, motivated by anti-communist views, made his own way to Sidi Bel Abbes in North Africa to enlist in the French Foreign Legion. At the relatively older age of 32 he completed the famous regiment's gruelling and rigorous training schedule and was soon promoted and posted to Indo China, where he fought in the campaign leading up to the Vietnam conflict. When he was eventually invalided out of the regiment he wrote a book that was published in 1955 with the title "In Order To Die." The reviews of the book are self-explanatory, *"An English Legionnaire's experiences with the French Foreign Legion in French Indo China during the early 1950's, prior to Dien Bien Phu. A heroic and tragic tale. A personal story of the son of a famous English actor. The whole confusion and drama of the Indo China war is brought vividly into focus. From the steamy paddy fields and the rank jungle come the tales of devilish guerrilla warfare. The graphic inside story of men waging war which had already been lost through infiltration, corruption and bribery."*

There follows details of Henry Hinchliffe Ainley's appearances in London theatres along with his film appearances.

Mr. Henry Ainley's London Stage Performances.

Theatre Dates Title Character

P = Performance. MP = Matinee Performance

1900

Theatre	Dates	Title	Character
Lyceum	15/2–21/2	Henry V	Duke of Gloucester
Lyceum	1/3-14/3	Hamlet	English Ambassador
Lyceum	15/3-5/5	Richard II	Sir Stephen Scroop
Lyceum	23/3-28/3	Twelfth Night	Curio
Lyceum	29/3-4/4	Antony & Cleopatra	Agrippa

1901

Theatre	Dates	Title	Character
Comedy	2/1-14/1	The Taming of the Shrew	Servant
Comedy	13/2-25/2	Coriolanus	Cpt of the Volscians
Comedy	27/2-11/3	As You Like It	Jaques
Comedy	13/3-25/3	Richard II	Bushy
Comedy	27/3-8/4	Hamlet	Rosencrantz
Comedy	29/3 (1MP)	The Bennets	Mr. Denny

1902

Theatre	Dates	Title	Character
St. James's	19/3-17/7	Paolo & Francesca	Paolo
St. James's	30/8-13/3/03	If I Were King	Noel le Jolys

1903

Theatre	Dates	Title	Character
St. James's	19/3-17/7	Old Heidelberg	Von Wedell
Imperial	7&8/6 (2P)	The Golden Rose or The Scarlet Women	Student
His Majesty's	8/6&20/6 to 26/6	Flodden Field	Donald Grey

1904

Theatre	Dates	Title	Character
Duke of York's	8/9-15/12	Merely Mary Ann	Lancelot
His Majesty's	8/11(1MP)	Trilby	William Bagot

1905

Theatre	Dates	Title	Character
Terry's	9/3&11/3(2MP)	The Merchant of Venice	Bassanio
His Majesty's	20/3,3/4&10/4(3P)	Trilby	William Bagot
Shaftesbury	8/4-5/5	Othello	Cassio
Haymarket	18/5(1MP)	Shakespeare vs Shaw (Review) Mr. Branbound	(G.B. Shaw also in the cast)
Adelphi	4/7-15/7	Aylmer's Secret	The Creature
Comedy	21/8-23/9	The Duffer	Paul Martin
Terry's	25/9-21/10	The Duffer	Paul Martin
Scala	23/9-7/10	The Conqueror	Sir Beauvise of Degrevant
Scala	10/10-11/11	For the Crown	Constantine Brancomir
Scala	26&27/11(2P)	Dodo:A Detail of Yesterday	Jack Broxton
St. James's	27/12-13/1/06	Beside the Bonny Brier Bush	Lord Hay

1906

Theatre	Dates	Title	Character
St. James's	9/1-27/1	As You Like It	Orlando
Scala	28/1&29/1(2P)	Lady Inger of Ostrat	Nils Lykke

Court	27/12-16/3(6MP)	Pan and The Young Shepherd	Neanias
Court	12/3-24/3	Electra	Orestes
Court	26/3-6/4	Hippolytus	Hippolytus
Savoy	18/4-10/5	The Bond of Ninon	Chevalier de Bellorme
Comedy	12/5-3/4/07	Raffles the Amateur Cracksman	A.J. Raffles
Savoy	12/5-26/6	The Shulamite	Robert Waring
Lyric	17/5-27/6	Othello	Cassio
Court	9/7-15/9	You Never can Tell	Valentine
Drury Lane	20/9-5/12	The Bondman	Michael Sunlocks

1907

Adelphi	5/1-23/2	The Bondman	Michael Sunlocks
Duke of York's	4/3-26/4	The Great Conspiracy	Cpt. Roger Crisenoy
Duke of York's	4/5-7/6	ARoyal Family	Prince Victor Constantine
Adelphi	17/6-26/6	ATragedy of Truth	Michael Hennessy
Royalty	27/6(1MP)	The Heart of the Machine	Jim Estcourt
St. James's	29/7-13/9	The 18th Century	Ensign Rupert Trevor
St. James's	14/9-19/10	The School for Scandal	Joseph Surface
His Majesty's	7/10-3/1/08	As You Like It	Orlando

1908

Queen's	1/2-22/2	Stingaree, the Bushranger	Greville Dare
Playhouse	19/3-10/4	Marjory Strode	Jean Vicomte de Selac
Haymarket	12/5-11/7	Getting Married	Bishop of Chelsea
Haymarket	16/6-26/6(6P)	The Chinese Lantern	Tikipu
His Majesty's	5/9-12/12	Faust	Faust
		(H.Beerbohm Tree as Mephistopheles)	
His Majesty's	8/12-12/2/09(6MP)	Hanneles Himmelfahrt	Stranger

1909

Garrick	19/1(1MP)	Kiddie	Only 3 in cast
His Majesty's	26/1-4/2(4MP)	The Admirable Bashville or Constancy Unrewarded	Bashville
Criterion	25/2-27/3	The Real Woman	Hugh Graham
Aldwych	1/5-25/5	One of the Best	Dudley Keppell
His Majesty's	14/5-20/5(3MP)	Light O'Love	Fritz Lobheimer
Adelphi	15/6-25/6(6MP)	The World and His Wife Don	Julian
Hicks (Globe)	6/7-9/7(4MP)	His Borrowed Plumes	Basil Delaine K.C.
Hicks (Globe)	15/7-21/7(8P)	His Borrowed Plumes	Basil Delaine K.C.
His Majesty's	14/9-6/11	False Gods	Satini
His Majesty's	8/11-24/11	Trilby	William Bagot
His Majesty's	25/11-11/12	Beethoven	Anton Schindler
His Majesty's	25/11-26/12	ÀRussian Tragedy	Paul Vanoff

1910

His Majesty's	24/1-29/1	Beethoven	Anton Schindler
His Majesty's	1/2-19/3	The O'FlynnTale of Love & War	Philip Defford
His Majesty's	28/3-19/4	The Merry Wives of Windsor	Master Fenton
His Majesty's	2/4-23/4	Julius Caesar	Cassius
His Majesty's	7/4-30/4(6P)	Twelfth Night	Feste
His Majesty's	11/4-23/4(3P)	Hamlet(no scenery, tapestry only)	Laertes

His Majesty's	25/4-30/4(4P)	The Merchant of Venice	Bassanio
His Majesty's	27/4-28/4(2P)	Richard II	John of Gaunt
Duke of York's	20/6-23/7	The Dawn of a Tomorrow	Dandy
Criterion	14/7(1MP)	An Idyll of Seven Dials(2 in cast)	Herbert Greencroft
His Majesty's	15/7(1MP)	The Unlucky Family	Papuan Chief
His Majesty's	1/9-8/4/11	Henry VIII	Duke of Buckingham
Aldwych	18/11(1MP)	APageant of Great Women	Prejudice
Globe	31/12-25/1/11	Beau Brocade	(The Producer)

1911

Aldwych	29&30/1(2P)	The Passing of Talma	Talma
Lyceum	1/3-20/5	The Prisoner of Zenda	Rudolf Rassendyll
Drury Lane	17/5(1P)	Money	Waiter
Covent Garden	23/5(1MP)	Beethoven	Anton Schindler
Comedy	7/6-1/7	The Crucible	Mark Melstrode
Duke of York's	28/8-19/10	The Concert	Gabor Arany
Queen's	11/11-9/12	AButterfly on the Wheel	Roderick Collingwood
Savoy	26/11(1P)	Pains & Penalties :	
		The Defence of Queen Caroline	George IV

1912

Aldwych	12/3-19/4	Proud Maisie	Neil MacAlpine
Haymarket	16/4(1P)	The Sixth Commandment	Martin
Lyric	7/5-29/6	The Five Frankforters	David
Savoy	21/9-28/11	The Winters Tale	Leontes
Savoy	15/11-15/3/13	Twelfth Night	Malvolio

1913

| Kingsway | 25/3-7/11/14 | The Great Adventure | Ilam Crave |
| St. James's | 27/6(1MP) | London Assurance | Max Harkaway |

1914

His Majesty's	22/5(1MP)	The Silver King	Samuel Baxter
Covent Garden	5/11(1MP)	Philip The King	Philip II of Spain
Kingsway	25/11-30/1/15	The Dynasts	Reader

1915

Covent Garden	2/2(1MP)	The School for Scandal	Joseph Surface
Kingsway	13/2-27/3	Fanny's First Play	Juggins
Haymarket	20/4-8/12	Quinney's	Joseph Quinney
His Majesty's	5/7(1MP)	Henry VIII	Earl of Surrey
His Majesty's	23/7(1MP)	Peter Ibbetson	Col. Ibbetson
Haymarket	9/12-8/4/16	Who Is He?	Mr. Parker
Queen's	14/12(1P)	The Dumb & The Blind	Joe

1916

Court	26/3&27/3(2MP)	Youth	Cecil Wainwright
Haymarket	22/4-13/5	The Mayor of Troy	Mjr. Solomon Hymen Toogood
Drury Lane	2/5(1MP)	Julius Caesar	Mark Antony
Drury Lane	2/5(1MP)	AShakespeare Pageant	Malvolio (Twelfth Night)
His Majesty's	19/5(1MP)	Hoops (music by Ivor Novello)	Producer

Haymarket	30/5-12/8	Fishpingle	Benoni Fishpingle
Covent Garden	7/6(1MP)	AShakespeare Pageant	Antonio
Opera House	23/6(1MP)	The Admirable Crichton	Thomas
Prince of Wales	18/12-27/1/17	The Happy Family	Manager & Extra
Daly's	23/12-3/2/17	Young England	Prologue

1917
Drury Lane	24/2-24/3	Young England	Prologue

1918
Drury Lane	27/9(1MP)	Pageant of Drury Lane Theatre	Apollo

1919
St. James's	26/9-3/1/20	Reparation	Fedya
		(transferred from the Grand Theatre, Leeds).	

1920
St. James's	9/1-20/3	Julius Caesar	Mark Antony
St. James's	27/3-8/5	Uncle Ned	Edward Graham & Mgr.
St. James's	16/4(1MP)	APantomime Rehearsal (Burlesque)	Manager
St. James's	17/8-11/12	His Lady Friends	Manager
St. James's	20/12-31/1/21	Peter Pan	Mr. Darling

1921
Aldwych	1/2-12/3	The Tempest	Prospero
Ambassadors	30/5-29/10	If	John Beal
Palace	29/12(1MP)	Trilby	Svengali

1922
Haymarket	7/6-13/1/23	The Dover Road	Mr. Latimer

1923
His Majesty's	29/5-28/7	Oliver Cromwell	Oliver Cromwell
His Majesty's	20/9-24/5/24	Hassan:And How He Came To Make	
		The Golden Journey To Samarkand	
		(Poetic Prose) Hassan Music Frederick Delius	

1924
Adelphi	2/6(1MP)	The Ware Case	Member of the Public
Drury Lane	3/6-5/7	London Life	Simon Blackshaw
Apollo	18/9-17/1/25	The Fool	Daniel Gilchrist

1925
Adelphi	21/3-1/7	Iris	Frederick Maldonado
Adelphi	11/5(1MP)	My Lady's Dress	Ivan
New	24/9-28/11	The Moon and Sixpence	Charles Strickland
New	2/12-30/1/26	Quinney's	Joseph Quinney

1926
New	5/2-6/3	Much Ado About Nothing	Benedick
New	23/3-26/6	Prince Fazil	Prince Fazil

Princes'	24/12-19/2/27	Macbeth	Macbeth

1929

Haymarket	2/7-10/1/30	The First Mrs. Fraser	James Fraser also Henry Oscar
Haymarket	25/10(1MP)	Henry V	Henry V

1930

Haymarket	22/4-19/5	Hamlet	Hamlet
		(chosen for a Royal Command Performance)	

1931

Westminster	21/7-26/1/32	The Anatomist	Robert Knox
Westminster	21/12-13/2/32	APair of Spectacles	Uncle Gregory

1932

Westminster	9/3-21/5	Tobias the Angel	Archangel Raphael
Drury Lane	3/5(1MP)	Bardell v Pickwick	Mr. Pickwick
Drury Lane	7/6(1MP)	Shall We Join the Ladies?	Mr. Gourlay

1945

Westminster	21/7-26/7	'This Sceptred Isle'	
		Dramatisation of Shakespeare's Call to Gt.Britain in Time of War	

The 24 English Films which featured Mr. Ainley:-

Henry VIII. 1911.

She Stoops to Conquer. 1914

Called Back. 1914

A Batchelor's Love Story. 1914.

Sweet Lavender. 1915.

The Prisoner of Zenda. 1915.

The Outrage. 1915.

A Man of His Word. 1915.

The Great Adventure. 1915.

Brother Officers. 1915.

The Marriage of William Ashe. 1916

The Manxman. 1916

Iris. 1916

Rupert of Henzau. 1916.

Sowing the Wind. 1916.

Quinneys. 1919.

Build Thy House. 1920.

The Prince and The Beggar Maid. 1921.

Money. 1921.

The Royal Oak. 1923

Sally Bishop. 1924.

The First Mrs. Frazer. 1932.

The Good Companions. 1933.

As You Like It. 1936.*

Battle of the Books 1941 (Commentator)

* The 1936 version of 'As You Like It' is available on video & DVD.

Henry played the 'Exiled Duke' and his eldest son Richard played 'Sylvius'.

This adaptation of Shakespeare's 1600 comedy marked Laurence Olivier's first screen appearance in a Shakespeare role. John Laurie (of Dad's Army fame) was also in the cast.

Mr. Herbert Henry Asquith, Morley's most famous son, was born at Croft House, off Church Street, on 12th September 1852. He became the Home Secretary in the Liberal Government of 1892 to 1895 and later held the highest office of Prime Minister from 1908 to 1916.

Mr. Asquith officially opened Morley Town Hall on 16th October 1895 and received the Freedom of the Borough on 24th July 1913.

He was created Earl of Oxford and Asquith and died at Sutton Courtney, Oxfordshire on 15th February 1928.

The Right Honourable H.H. Asquith's connection with Morley entertainment is a tenuous but interesting one; in a number of ways he shared common ground with Henry Hinchliffe Ainley, for in addition to their Morley origins they shared the name Henry and also the initials H.H.A. and they both appreciated the good life including a fondness for good wine. Mr. Ainley was on the fringe of the Asquith's circle, perhaps when they met there was some reminiscing about their roots in a West Riding Mill Town. Was there something in Morley's sooty atmosphere that was responsible for developing the land's premier actor, producing the country's Prime Minister and growing the World's best rhubarb?

Here are a few of the interesting public statements made by Mr. Ainley.

"I would rather play in Shakespeare than anything else".

"I am proud of my Yorkshire parentage and I love to speak the dialect".

"It would be a pity if dialects were to die out. They keep the English speech virile and individual and save it from becoming emasculated".

"I pray I shall never be called upon to act for my living on a Sunday". (1930).

"Smoking should never be allowed in the theatre". (1939).

"You could roll me out into a Yorkshire pudding". (1939).

The Final Curtain.

Mr. Ainley, who was described as a charming man with good looks and a mellifluous voice, was taken seriously ill in 1932 whilst rehearsing for the film "Good Companions", after which his only stage appearance was a brief one in 1945, just three months before he died on 31st October 1945.

James Edwin Baines
Violinist and Local Hero.

James Edwin Baines was not only a fine violinist, but also one of the town's forgotten heroes. On Tuesday 9th May 1911 there was a disastrous fire at the Empire Palace Theatre, Edinburgh where Mr. Baines was a member of the theatre's orchestra. The fire broke out during the evening show resulting in the loss of ten lives.

The stage illusionist, known as 'The Great Lafayette', was performing in one of his elaborate scenes when flames suddenly burst out. Within a few minutes the whole stage became a roaring furnace. The fire-curtain was rung down and the theatre orchestra continued to play in a successful effort to calm the audience who were able to evacuate the building without mishap.

Backstage it was a different story. Everything was destroyed leaving only bare walls. Among the ten people who died were 'Lafayette' and several members of his company. In his act the illusionist had employed a lion and a horse; both animals perished. 'The Great Lafayette' had made his escape and reached the street without injury but he returned into the flames telling bystanders he must save his lion. He was to die in the attempt. Two 'midgets' named Coats and Dale were also among the fatalities and they were returned for burial to their home city of Sheffield.

James Baines remained in his place with the orchestra until the audience had safely left the building. Instead of leaving the theatre, Mr. Baines heroically battled his way through the flames beyond the auditorium in an effort to rescue artistes trapped in the conflagration. Regrettably he too perished in the valiant effort. His body was found together with his Yorkshire friends Coats and Dale. He had the two 'little people' clutched in his arms.

James Edwin Baines lived with his wife and three daughters at 10, Wordsworth Square, Albert Road, Morley. He was a professional musician well known to the people of Morley and Ardsley, and his body was conveyed from Edinburgh by train to Woodkirk station for a hero's funeral at Woodkirk Church. Several thousand people congregated to pay tribute to a very brave gentleman.

Trevor and Geoffrey Bastow.
Musicians of International Repute.

The musical achievements of two Morley brothers, the sons of Horace and Edith Bastow, life long residents of Churwell, is remarkable not only for the scale of their respective successes, but for the fact that so few local people know of this family's attainments.

The elder brother **Trevor** was born in Morley on the 20th February 1945, and attended Churwell Primary School and later Batley Grammar School. His professional music career began in the 1960's, playing piano in and around the Leeds area with the Pete Hurley Trio. The band also had regular summer seasons at various Butlin's Holiday Camps and American bases on the continent. Trevor later accompanied many stars of the day at the Batley Variety Club and the Wakefield Theatre Club before taking a resident job as pianist and arranger with the Denis Langfield Orchestra at the Leeds Mecca Locarno Ballroom (where Sir Jimmy Saville started his career as manager). Here **Trevor** made his first television appearances in the form of the 'Come Dancing'series, and provided many of the orchestrations.

In the 1970's he joined his younger brother Geoff in London as a member of the Johnny Howard Orchestra and also began to work regularly in the London recording studio scene as pianist-arranger and conductor for many stars of the day including Charles Aznavour, Tom Jones, Gilbert O'Sullivan, Shirley Bassey, and many more, even including The London Symphony Orchestra.

In 1975 he became pianist and later musical director for Tom Jones, accompanying Tom on his world tours visiting Lake Tahoe, Las Vegas, the London Palladium and various venues in South America, Japan and the Far East.

In the 1980's, Trevor stopped touring and returned once more to the London studio scene. Here he worked as composer/arranger/keyboard player, appearing on numerous television shows, including 'The Benny Hill Show', the Tom Jones TVseries and arranging for pop artists including Boy George's Culture Club. He was for many years resident pianist with Des O'Connor on TV, and continued well into the 1990's.

In the 80's and 90's Trevor played on numerous successful film scores including many by the noted film composer Jerry Goldsmith: 'Alien', 'Basic Instinct', 'Supergirl', 'Gremlins', 'Legend', 'Medicine Man' and 'Poltergeist'.

Trevor continued working until his untimely death in June 2000.

Born in Morley on 20th May 1949, **Geoff Bastow** attended Churwell

Primary School and later Morley Grammar School. Like Trevor, Geoff began his musical career in the 1960's, playing in and around the Leeds area with the pop band 'The Beathovens'. He then took a resident job as pianist and later guitarist with the Graham Warner Orchestra at the Mecca Locarno Ballroom in Bradford. It was here that he had his initial experience with television in the form of the BBC 'Come Dancing' series, for which he provided many musical arrangements. In 1970 he accepted a job with the Ray McVay Orchestra at the Lyceum in London. His brother later joined him and they both became active in the London recording studio scene.

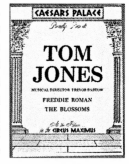

Programme showing Trevor Bastow as Tom Jones's Musical Director at Caesars Palace in Las Vegas in the early 1950's.

Geoff later joined Trevor in the Johnny Howard Orchestra as guitarist, and together they accompanied many of the day's top artists, including Lulu, Bruce Forsyth and Frankie Laine.

Geoff appeared on, and orchestrated, many pop records of the day by such artists as Gilbert O'Sullivan, Tom Jones, Daniel Defoe, Barry Manilow, David Dundas, Tina Charles and Biddu, occasionally orchestrating for the film composer John Barry.

In 1973 Geoff began touring America and Japan as guitarist with Englebert Humperdinck, appearing in Las Vegas, New York, Lake Tahoe and many of the top US venues, whilst also on occasion accompanying Bob Hope on his TV show in Hollywood, with the Les Brown (and his band of renown) Orchestra.

He later returned to the London recording scene and played on many TV shows of the day including the Miss World Contest until the late 70's. At that time he moved his base to Munich, where he worked for many European and International artists such as Donna Summer, Boney M., Kurt Edelhagen and Jennifer Rush. As a composer he produced numerous television and radio advertising jingles for BMW, Time Life, Microsoft and others.

His compositional credits include the 1985 Austrian Eurovision Song Contest entry 'Children of the World' which achieved 8th place (a hit by Austrian standards, since they often come last). Other compositions include songs for Eric Burdon, Elton John and Charlene (Dallas) Tilton and several other international artists.

Geoff still lives in Munich and continues to write and play for advertising, film and record productions.

We sincerely thank Mr & Mrs Bastow for providing the details of their two most talented sons.

Brian Bedford.
Actor and Director.

Mr. Brian Bedford.

Born in Morley on 16th February 1935, Brian Bedford lived with his parents and older brother Vincent in Britannia Road, Morley.

When he left school he was employed as a warehouse worker until he was accepted at the Royal Academy of Dramatic Arts, where his contemporaries included Peter O'Toole, Albert Finney and Alan Bates. He was so outstanding during his final year at the Academy that the Liverpool Repertory Company gave him a year's contract. After only six months, and at only 21 years of age, he played the title role in 'Hamlet', remarking at the time *"I'm probably the youngest Hamlet in the business"*. During this period in Liverpool, in the year of 1956, an unknown Brian Epstein, later of the Beatles' fame, spent much of his spare time with Mr.Bedford. Mr. Epstein had aspirations to become an actor himself. He enrolled at R.A.D.A. but soon returned to Liverpool to find fame in another direction.

Mr. Bedford's appearances at Liverpool led him to highly successful performances in London's West End and at Stratford-on-Avon, where he worked with Sir John Gielgud and Peter Brook. This was the start of a distinguished, successful and long career in England, Canada and the United States.

Among his many stage successes were 'Five Finger Exercise', 'The Knack', 'The Misanthrope', 'Private Lives', 'Hamlet', 'The School for Wives', 'Jumpers', 'London Assurance', 'The School for Scandal' and 'Roundabout'. Mr. Brian Bedford earned five Tony nominations for his work on Broadway and he won the Tony Award for his performance in 'The School for Wives'. Other awards include the Obie and New York Drama Desk Awards for his role in 'The Knack', a Drama Desk Award for 'Two Shakespearean Actors' and the Los Angeles Drama Critics Award for 'Equus'.

As a Shakespearean actor he has long been a mainstay of the Stratford Festival of Canada in Ontario. He made his debut there in 1975 and over the years has played numerous leading roles including Tartuffe, Richard III and Macbeth. His directing credits include 'The Winter's Tale', 'Waiting for Godot,' 'Equus,' and 'Titus Andronicus', 'Coriolanus' and Racine's 'Phèdre'.

His one-man Shakespearean evening, 'The Lunatic, the Lover and the Poet' (*quotation from "A Midsummer Night's Dream"*) has taken him around the world. *(This one-man tour-de-force on the life of William Shakespeare, told through his poetry, prose and sonnets, compiled and performed by Brian Bedford, is available as an audio tape recording published by the Canadian Broadcasting Corporation).* Mr. Richard Wilbur, Poet Laureate of the United States, is quoted as saying *"Brian Bedford is the best actor of poetry I know of"*. Mr. Bedford still finds time for visits to acting workshops and classrooms and his lecture entitled 'Speaking of Shakespeare' is always well received.

He has recently directed and starred in 'The School for Scandal' and during the 2001 season at Stratford, Ontario he directed and held the starring role in 'Private Lives' by Noel Coward.

In addition to a distinguished stage career Brian Bedford has appeared many times in films and television including 'Miracle in Soho' (1957), 'Winter-set'(1958), 'The Angry Silence'(1960), 'Edgar Wallace Mysteries No. 6'(1962), 'The Punch and Judy Man'(1963), 'Grand Prix'(1966), 'Pad and How to Use It' (1966), 'Coronet Blue' (1967), 'Androcles and the Lion' (1967), 'Robin Hood' (1973, animated film, the voice of the title character), 'The Walt Disney Comedy and Magic Revue'(1985), 'The Last Best Year' (1990), 'Scarlett' (1994), 'Nixon' (1995), 'More Tales of the City' (1998).

He made notable T.V. guest appearances in 'Alfred Hitchcock Presents', 'The Equaliser', 'Cheers' and 'Murder She Wrote'.

Mr. Bedford's mother's maiden name was O'Donnell and he has many relations in Chicago from that side of the family. He became a naturalised citizen of the United States and has resided there for over forty years. In 1997 he was inducted into the American Theatre 'Hall of Fame'.

John Booth.

Mr. John Booth.

Born in Morley in 1947, John Booth lived in Peel Street with his father, Norman, and his mother, Connie. Norman was the organist at the Brunswick Primitive Methodist Chapel. One of the highlights each year was the rendition of the Messiah sung by the augmented chapel choir accompanied by Norman on the organ.

John Booth was Head Boy at Batley Grammar School before continuing his education at Reading University and at the John Hopkins University School for Advanced International Studies in Bologna and Washington DC.

Mr. Booth is a music lover, a pianist and a member of the London Bach Society. He is also a photographer and a member of the National Portrait gallery. A keen sportsman, he was coached by Jack Charlton at soccer and Johnny Lawrence at cricket, playing with Morley in the Yorkshire Council. Being a life-long cyclist, his hero as a youngster had to be, and was, Beryl Burton, the many-times world champion who rode with the Morley Cycling Club. An excellent cricketer he captained his school side, played at Reading University and over the years has enjoyed playing for many teams.

A self-employed freelance journalist, John Booth was introduced to the newspaper business by Mr. Vincent Mulchrone, the Morley-born feature writer for the Daily Mail. His reporting career began with the Durham Advertiser and Aycliffe Chronicle and then the Evening Advertiser in Swindon, subsequently working for the Yorkshire Post in Leeds, the Washington Post in Washington DC., the Financial Gazette in Harare and then the Guardian, the European and the Observer newspapers in London. He has since worked as a freelance for the Daily Mirror, the Guardian, Lloyd's List, Financial News, the Observer and the Times Educational Supplement. He teaches journalism and writes regularly for the Tribune and has also collaborated with the journalists John Pilger and Paul Foot.

John Booth, joined the Labour Party in 1970 and stood for Parliament in 1974 when his opponent was Nicholas Ridley. He was again unsuccessful in the 2001 election when, as a "Genuine Labour" candidate, he stood against Peter Mandelson at Hartlepool.

The Burrow Factor.

Renee Burrow with the awards recognising her long and distinguished service to amateur theatricals.

Mr. Harry Burrow.

Renee Burrow and her late husband Harry feature so much in the local theatrical scene that it seemed right to dedicate a whole chapter to their contributions.

Members of the OMADS, Yorkshire Electricity Players and Morley Amateur Operatic Society they performed in many different types of productions and venues, including Armley Jail and Harewood House, and in front of a very wide variety of audiences – more of that later.

They are best known for their numerous and varied roles with Morley Amateur Operatic Society or Morley Technical Institute Amateur Operatic Society as it was known back in 1937 when Renee joined. A year later Harry strode onto the Pavilion stage and into Renee's heart as the Red Shadow in Desert Song. Unfortunately with the outbreak of War the Society was temporarily disbanded but Renee and Harry's relationship wasn't, it blossomed as they both became involved with a number of different groups entertaining the Morley public and the troops stationed nearby during the war years.

The OK Concert party, the OMADS and The Revellers, led by Leo Leathley, entertained with sketches, singing and dancing. Renee was an OMADarling dancer and Harry a soloist until leaving to join the forces himself in 1941.

The entertainers travelled all over Yorkshire but always in secret under the auspices of VESNC (Voluntary Entertainment Services of the Northern Command) and the venues ranged from the canteens of Gun stations and Army marquees to the Theatre Royal in York and ball rooms of Stately homes which were being used as hospital wards for injured officers. The audiences - whether there were just 50 gunners or over a thousand servicemen and women - were always very appreciative particularly when the high kicking OMADarlings took the stage. Facilities ranged from the best the stately homes could offer - afternoon tea with Baroness Beaumont at Carlton Towers - to a bucket behind a tent!

One memorable occasion was visiting Armley Jail to entertain the inmates where Renee recalls that Emily Fletcher's rendition of 'Bless this House'

was the hit of the evening! Entertaining the 'babes in the wood' was memorable for another reason. Taken secretly to a well-camouflaged location in the middle of a forest, Renee and fellow entertainers learned afterwards that the

Omadarlings in the revue 'What Now'staged at the New Pavilion theatre in December 1946. (Renee is 2ⁿᵈ from the left).

troops they had entertained left for Normandy and the D-Day landing within a few days of their show.

It was around this time that Renee took to drink! On a particularly cold day, having waited ages for transport at that well known Morley spot, The Prospect Hotel, fellow entertainer Jack Popplewell suggested something to warm them up. Into the Prospect they went where a large rum was produced. Renee doesn't remember much about the performance that day - just that a warm glow stayed with her!

There was another longer lasting warm glow for Renee and Harry. It hadn't been a case of 'out of sight out of mind'whilst Harry was away in the RAF but 'absence making the heart grow fonder' and in June 1942 he managed to get sufficient leave for them to be married at Back Green Methodist Chapel, Churwell on the 27th of the month.

After the War when the Operatic Society shows restarted Renee and Harry starred in many roles becoming extremely well known locally – particularly during 'show' week. As well as romantic leads including Chopin in 'Waltz Without End', Harry took on more senior roles such as Cap'n Andy in 'Showboat' and the 'Red Shadow's father' when the Operatic Society again did 'Desert Song' whilst he was also a most villainous Jud in 'Oklahoma'. Altogether he was in 20 main shows between 1938 and1974 and appeared in numerous Concerts and Music Hall performances during the same period.

Renee was also in many of the latter as well as in 13 main shows between 1937 and 1958, often as the soubrette delighting audiences with roles such as Ellie in 'Showboat', Lady Jane in Rose Marie and later and most challenging of all Aunt Eller in 'Oklahoma'.

Inevitably she has many memories of various parts some of which bring tears to the eyes – literally! A dance sequence in Showboat provides one of the most painful: Co-star Leslie Bielby failed to catch his spinning partner at a crucial moment and she landed inelegantly on the floor. He was to regret his careless hands later in the show. In the next scene Renee was supposed to accompany him on stage and start her solo: unfortunately she was being treated for a bruised posterior backstage and Leslie suddenly realised he was alone on the stage. Like a real trouper he gamely started to sing the opening words only to be attacked by a whirlwind. Having heard the music of her song from the bowels of the Pavilion Renee forgot her pain, rushed onto the stage, pushed Leslie out of the way and yelling *"Don't you dare sing my song"* she took over where he thankfully left off.

One of Harry's most demanding roles, and one never forgotten by grateful co-stars was on the opening night of 'Waltz Without End'. Jean Lloyd his leading lady lost her voice completely with only hours to go before the performance. Delia Broadley from Pudsey was brought in at literally the last minute and met her leading man for the first time as they waited in the wings for their first entrance. As Delia said afterwards, Harry's advice was for her to play the moves exactly as she had done at Pudsey and he would follow her lead. Amazingly this worked perfectly and later, with makeup and wigs removed, Delia was talking to Renee and Harry expressing her gratitude to Chopin for the way he had helped her. Just as Harry was about to say *"it had been a pleasure"* Delia continued with *"I must find him to thank him"*. She had no idea the man she was talking to had been her leading man for the previous 3 hours!

Not content with treading the boards with the Operatic Society they took on several official duties – Joint Secretaries, Business Managers and Patrons' Secretaries both becoming Honorary Vice presidents and Life members. When Harry finished his term as Society President in 1979 Renee as the first lady President succeeded him. Harry's final role on stage was in Orpheus in the Underworld in 1974.

Renee and Harry's contribution to another Society should also be mentioned. In 1950, Renee was asked by the Area manger of the Yorkshire Electricity Board (for whom she worked) to form a Drama Group to take part in the annual Area Drama Festivals. This she did and she and Harry performed in many of the plays between 1952 and 1976. As well as taking part in the drama festival in which both of them won individual awards, the group also put on regular plays at Leeds Civic Theatre.

Since Harry's death in 1980 Renee has continued to be actively involved with the Society and in 1997, she was awarded the National Operatic and Dramatic Association Diamond Bar in recognition of her 60 years service - the first member of the Society to receive this. She celebrated with a return to the stage taking on the glamorous part of 'Slave of the Ring' in Aladdin in 1999. She enjoyed it so much she couldn't resist a repeat performance in 2001 when she appeared as 'Queen of the Deep' in Robinson Crusoe. Whatever will this Octogenarian thespian get up to next?

Jim Bywater.
Actor and Composer.

Mr. Clifford Bywater was a well-known Morley trumpet player who performed in many venues in the area including the Pavilion Theatre where he entertained on at least two occasions. On 16th September 1945 he acted as compere for the 'Hot Spots' variety show, in addition to performing a cornet solo. On Sundays 10th and 31st March 1946 he was an entrant in the Carroll Levis 'Search for the Stars'competition when he was described as *'Cliff Bywater, trumpet player, glassblower, 4, Birch Street, Morley'*.

Mr. Bywater's son, Jimmy, whilst still at Morley Grammar School, was a member of the Teenage Ramblers Skiffle Group that is included in the story of the 1958 Morley Top Town Team. Another member of that group, Tony Rooley has also done well in the entertainment world, (see Anthony Rooley, Lutenist).

Jimmy Bywater became a television presenter for children's programmes, actor and composer. Among his achievements are a number of television appearances including, 'Ready When You Are Mr. McGill' (1976), 'Accidental Death of an Anarchist'(1983), also in 1983 a guest appearance in 'Up in Smoke' (one of 'The Bill' series), as Wilf Starkey, the barman in 'Coronation Street' (1985) and in 'A Killing Kindness' (1997), (one of the Dalziel and Pascoe series).

Jim Bywater is credited as Composer for 'Accidental Death of an Anarchist' (1983) and for the television series 'Driving Ambition'(1983).

Elaine Currie
Dancer

(The following story is written by the lady herself and is unedited. It is a wonderful example to any young person today who feels that their chosen career is not worth striving for).

Elaine photographed on Llandudno Pier in 1961 whilst performing at the Pier Pavilion in 'Double Your Money' with Hughie Green.

Between leaving school at 16 in 1953 and becoming a professional dancer in 1959, I trained, qualified and worked as a Diagnostic Radiographer whilst taking part in many shows both with Morley and Leeds Amateur Operatic Societies. The shows were my life- I could not imagine ever not being able to dance and I remember saying to my mother that if ever I could not dance, I would rather die! Rather dramatic but it seemed true at the time.

In 1959, Jean Pearce, who was the dancing mistress for Leeds Amateurs, formed a small troupe of semi-professional dancers of which I was one. As well as various functions, we had a six-week contract at Leeds City Varieties. You will remember, perhaps, how these were old fashioned variety shows but with a stripper as well. In those days, once the stripper had stripped off, she wasn't allowed to move. Very different from today and very moral comparatively. It was great fun. We did four routines per show; two shows a night and three on Tuesdays and Saturdays. We made our own costumes too and rehearsed next week's show at the same time.

I was working at Leeds General Infirmary then and fixed my half day off around the performances. I can't remember what we were paid. I know it wasn't much but none of us cared. I loved every minute, despite the occasional lecherous men outside the stage door and catcalls during the performance.

Later that year I answered an advert in the local paper for dancers to take part in the forthcoming pantomime at Leeds Grand Theatre. (I was becoming restless and an alternative career option was to move to Lausanne in Switzerland as a Radiographer via a colleague at work. The audition came up first. I often think how different my life would have been,

Elaine, 2nd from the right, whilst in pantomime with Charlie Chester at Southsea in 1962.

had I taken the other option).

The audition was very cursory - basically, if you could do high kicks, you were in - so I was in. I handed in my notice and we had three weeks of rehearsals in Leeds before opening on Christmas Eve for a twelve week run, six nights a week and matinees on Wed and Sat. I think I was paid £4.10s.0d a week.

There were other dancers beside we locals —'proper professionals' and they were paid more so it was in the company's interests to employ local talent. The pantomime was 'Goldilocks and the Three Bears' with Ronnie Hilton as the star. He was a very nice, unassuming person and gave each dancer a signed address book, which I still have, as a last night gift.

I was always devastated on the last night of any performance week and grieved for at least a fortnight afterwards or until I got stuck into the next show. The end of this run was worse than anything I had previously experienced, due to the length of the run and the camaraderie, which had built up between cast members, particularly the dancers. We had become a sort of family - now we were all going off in different directions - it was awful. In order to get another dancing engagement, it was necessary to move to London where all the auditions were held and so I left home to live in the wicked city. My parents, understandably I suppose, were rather concerned for my safety, having the not untypical Northern view of the South.

I had obtained a post as temporary Locum Radiographer at New Cross Chest Clinic, south of Elephant and Castle, which included a bedsit for rent in the nurses'home. I used to put in lots of evening overtime so that I could dash up to the West End in my lunch hour for auditions, which were advertised each week in 'The Stage'. This involved a long bus and underground journey and I was often late back, having had no lunch. Fortunately, my boss was very understanding and interested. I was very lucky there.

Two other girls from the pantomime shared a bedsit in a large hostel in Queensway where other theatrical people stayed. Gerry Dorsey, now Engelbert Humperdinck, was there at the time. I sometimes stayed over with the girls at weekends -3 of us in a double bed, a slot meter for the heater and a single ring cooker. It was very cold and none of us had much money. Lots of boozy parties and bedroom swopping went on. I hated this existence and soon stopped going, preferring my own quiet bedsit in New Cross. I was developing a separate social life there anyway.

Auditions in London were quite different to the one in Leeds - definitely the 'cattle market' type. Dozens of girls turned up and were often rejected at first sight due to being too short, not blonde etc. Sometimes we would be asked to do a few high kicks or pirouettes and a short tap or ballet routine, and then lined up at the front of the stage for rejection. One by one. Soul destroying stuff!

I tried anything except auditions for topless dancers. Those jobs were easy to come by since revue bars were just starting up. One of the girls above gave in and got a job at Raymond's Revue bar. She went on to work at the Paris Lido. Once I auditioned at Murray's Cabaret Club. The manager said, *"What's a nice girl like you doing here? Give it up and go home."* Good advice perhaps but not what I wanted to hear. I tried to get a job advertising stockings, nail varnish, shampoo etc. TV ads hadn't come along yet. I remember being shown a picture of wonderful legs or beautiful hands and nails and being asked *"How do your legs / hands match up to these?"* Mine never did and I would slink out, embarrassed and humiliated again. Why did I carry on, I wonder? This was, however, all good training in developing a pretty hard shell to protect against constant rejection and dubious offers around.

In the end, I was accepted as revue dancer for Butlin's holiday Camp in Ayr, Scotland -a four month contract; two shows a night, six days a week plus 15 hours Redcoat duty to cover accommodation and food, preceded by two weeks rehearsal plus costume fittings in London on minimum pay. We travelled up to Scotland on the train and my parents came to see me briefly as we passed through Leeds.

It was a very small camp situated in picturesque surroundings next to the beach and we all lived in tiny 2-berth chalets with old-fashioned spring-based bunk beds. It was a lottery as to who had the top bunk. The one on the bottom would often get hair all tangled up in the springs above.

The show cast did not include anyone well known and was a typical review of its time a tenor and soubrette, a comedian, a speciality act and the dancing girls. Great fun again but not great stuff. However, we were celebrities with the campers who used to wait at the stage door for autographs. On Saturdays, changeover day, we were all on duty all day in reception standing around for hours in high heels, part of the Redcoat uniform. It didn't do my circulation any good at all.

Life in camp was just like 'Hi-de-Hi' and watching that programme always brings back fond memories of that very happy and unique time, before the days of mass foreign travel. As a Redcoat too, we were 'somebody special', especially on ballroom duty when anyone who could dance was in great demand. Other duties were as Bingo callers, supervising Snooker or Table Tennis competitions or taking campers on guided walks on the beach. We could swap our duties around and I always opted for the walks on the beach if I could. Meals were taken in the great food hall. Each of us had our own table and group of campers for the week.

At the end of the summer, I went back to London as a Locum Radiographer, this time to University College Hospital (UCH), as it was closer to the West End. I came home to Morley in December to take part in the Pantomime again but this time as a proper professional dancer, having now acquired my Equity card. As the job was still very low paid, I also worked as a Locum Radiographer at Leeds Chest Clinic –a pattern of working two jobs at once that was to become a typical part of my life in the future.

The pantomime this time was 'Aladdin' with Jimmy Clitheroe as Wishy Washy. This production had come directly from the London Palladium and had wonderful scenery and costumes. The score was based on 'Scheherezade' - very evocative and the choreography was quite special. I was lucky enough to be chosen as one of six dancers with extra special routines. We had a group of male dancers too and they were great fun. It was a laugh a minute. One of them, Lindsay Kemp, was to become famous in his own right as a mime artiste and to create his own company, which now travels the world. Back in London, after the panto ended and back in my old job at UCH, I did the rounds of auditions again and this time landed a much better job in a Harold Fielding production (a well respected impresario) at Llandudno Pier Pavilion, destroyed by fire some years ago now. The show was 'Double Your Money'with Hughie Green and the year was 1961. The choreographer was Dougie Squires (from TV's Top of the Pops) and the routines were demanding, to say the least. One was a three minute kicking routine -a la Tiller Girls- extremely strenuous. Even though we performed this every night for ten weeks, we used to nearly collapse in the wings when we came off stage. As usual, we had two weeks rehearsal (£4.10s.0d a week, considered to be pretty good at that time) in which we had to learn six routines, as well as go for costume fittings. These were all made to measure by Bermont's THE costumiers of the West End. A regular visitor to our rehearsals was Lionel Blair -a good friend of our choreographer. I was surprised and flattered to be chosen as 'Head Girl'for our troupe of dancers. This meant that, during the run I would be responsible for taking the weekly rehearsal and for keeping up standards. It was a very high profile show with no expense spared -whether this was due to the requirements of Hughie, I don't know. He was every bit as unpleasant as the recent TV programme suggests but all other members of the cast were extremely nice people. My life now had settled into a regular pattern of Summer Season and Leeds pantomime, interspersed with Locum Radiography in London or Leeds.

The next panto was 'Sleeping Beauty,' with Morecambe and Wise as the King and Jester respectively and David Whitfield as the Prince. Another lavish production but without the satisfying choreography of the previous year, it was, nevertheless, great fun again. Although a very private person off stage, Eric Morecambe used to have us all in fits of laughter on stage as we never knew from one performance to the next what he would say or do. In the scene where all the courtiers are asleep, I had to stand by the throne on which Eric was sitting, waiting for the Prince to come and wake us all up. We were supposed to stay absolutely still for what seemed like ages. Eric tried his best to make us laugh by whispering ridiculous things (and he often succeeded), for which we were told off by the stage manager.

This was followed in 1962 by a Summer Season in Southsea, once more working for Fielding Productions and once more Head Girl. The star of the show was Charlie Chester, with a supporting cast of the Countrymen (a singing group) and Rawicz and Landauer -all really good to work with. Once again, we were in the main pier theatre -a lovely well equipped theatre, which has since been destroyed by fire. It was here that I met my future husband who was supplementing his student income by working backstage as an electrician. His father worked full time on the electrics (all levers in those days) and his mother was wardrobe mistress. To supplement my income, I now worked during the day as a Radiographer at the local hospital and stayed on there after the show ended until it was time to return to Leeds for the next panto.

My swan song was "Cinderella" at Leeds Grand with Lonnie Donegan as Buttons and Danny la Rue as one of the Ugly Sisters. Not a very happy company this time -Lonnie being a particularly unfriendly type and an atmosphere pervaded everything. I was once again working as part time Radiographer at the Chest Clinic where I unfortunately sustained a back injury whilst using an ill maintained chest stand. This brought my professional stage career to an abrupt halt as I was admitted to hospital initially, and then put out of action for a whole year, during which time I had to have osteopathy treatment and virtually learn to walk again.

Fortunately, everything turned out all right in the end and I once more changed career the following January and became an airline stewardess with British European Airways for whom I worked for six years before starting our family. I had married in 1966.

I still dance -teaching a weekly dance-exercise class on Mondays and have been learning Flamenco for the past four years. Chris (my husband) and I learn ballroom dancing twice a week and my back hardly bothers me now -a testament to the value of exercise.

Peter Dews
T.V. and Theatre Producer, Director and Actor.

Mr. John Dews, a railway officer, living at Royston Hill, East Ardsley, was post-war leader of the Labour group on Morley Town Council and Mayor of Morley for the period from November 1946 to November 1947.

His son Peter Dews, born on 26th September 1929 at Ardsley, became a most distinguished theatrical producer and director. Educated at Queen Elizabeth Grammar School, Wakefield his drama teacher, Ronald Chapman, is credited for encouraging his interest in the theatre.

At first Mr. Dews taught in Barnsley and Knaresborough and then, while acting and directing at Bradford Civic Playhouse in 1952, he wrote a play that was broadcast on BBC North.

Later he became the Artistic Director at Birmingham Repertory Theatre where his productions included 'Hamlet', with Richard Chamberlain in the cast, followed by 'Rosencrantz and Guildenstern Are Dead'. He then became the director of the Scottish Theatre Company moving on to be the Artistic Director of the Chichester Festival Theatre. Here he directed many productions including 'Julius Caesar', 'Hail Caesar' and 'Time and the Conways'.

Later still Peter Dews was involved with many theatrical productions in the West End, on Broadway and in Canada including: - 'Antony and Cleopatra', 'Othello', 'Julius Caesar', 'Much Ado About Nothing', 'As You Like It', 'Hamlet', 'Vivat! Vivat Regina!', 'Hadrian VII', 'Equus', 'Man and Superman', 'When We Are Married', 'The Pleasure of His Company', 'The Circle' and many others. In 1969 he was presented with a Tony Award for his directorship of 'Hadrian VII'.

He was connected with the Stratford Festival in Ontario, Canada from 1979 where he directed 'King John'. He crossed paths there with Brian Bedford in 1981 when Peter directed 'The Comedy of Errors' and 'The Taming of the Shrew'; the latter production being available on video.

Mr. Dews was also involved with many television presentations. He brought Shakespeare to a mass audience as the producer of the BBC Television series 'An Age of Kings' (writer William Shakespeare, music Arthur Bliss) which consisted of eight consecutive interlocking Shakespeare plays – namely 'Richard II', 'Henry IV Part 1', 'Henry IV Part 2', 'Henry V', 'Henry VI Part 1', 'Henry VI Part 2', 'Henry VI Part 3', and 'Richard III', played in one cycle (28th April to 17th November 1960) to look at 86 years of British history. The plays were divided into hour long episodes in which particular historic events were portrayed in their proper succession Among the actors were Robert Hardy and Sean Connery. It was the first time in the 20th century that all the Shakespeare histories had been done in sequence. In 1963 he produced and directed 'Julius Caesar' for the BBC Television's 'Spread of the Eagle' series, a nine part cycle based on three Roman plays by William Shakespeare. (The others being 'Coriolanus'and 'Antony and Cleopatra').

Mr. Dews's other television productions include: -

'R3'	1964	(Sci/Fi).
'Undermind'	1965	(Sci/Fi).
'The Man in Room 17'	1965	(Crime/Thriller).

For 'The Life of Henry V' (1957) he was presented with the British Academy of Film and Television Arts Award in the category 'Single Drama (Director)'.

In addition he was the producer, in 1959, of 'The Constable's Move', which featured Leonard Rossiter.

Mr. Peter Dews died in August 1997.

The cast of the Morley Grammar School 1953 production of 'The Mikado'. The photo. includes:- 2nd row from the front, from the left, Hazel Bedford, Miss Kenyon, the 2nd man is Mr. Hacking then June Rhodes, Mr. Cross, Mr. Dews, Maureen Spurr, Donald Webster, Moira Riley, Blanche Walton, Mr. D.A. Stevenson and John Barstow.

Phil Fryer.
'Just to be Frank.'

Phil. Fryer 'Just to be Frank'Sinatra.

Phil Fryer opened his Churwell barber's shop in 1986 in the old Cooperative Society's premises at the corner of Hartley Street and Elland Road. In addition to successfully catering for the tonsorial needs of his fellow villagers Phil has also continually given his time and energy to charitable causes. For seven years he organised the 'Churwell Five Miler' race that raised funds for the benefit of the Forget-me-not charity, Heart Research, the Coronary Care Unit, the Half and Half Appeal and the Candlelighters Unit based at St. James's Hospital. He has raced in events in many parts of the United Kingdom, completing the cycle marathons 'Lands End to John O'Groats Challenge' and 'Morley to Siegen' (Morley's Twin Town in Germany) and participating in the most exacting of sports, the Iron Man Triathlons (non stop swimming, running and cycling) in places as far away as Germany and Lanzarote. To enable him to participate successfully in these gruelling events much time and energy had to be given to hard training, this in addition to the obvious necessity of working for his barber's shop business. The fuel that kept his fires burning was the benefits that the very worthy charities gained from his efforts.

Whilst on holiday in 1997 Phil was persuaded to have a go at karaoke singing in a bar. This he did reluctantly but his version of a Frank Sinatra song was so well received he decided to begin singing in venues around Morley in an attempt to establish himself in the area. At that time he received good advice and correction from two friends. Ken Christian a local singer, who had the experience of singing for many years on the club circuit, took Phil under his wing and allowed him to have a spot at some of his engagements. Allan Kent, a D.J. and singer also encouraged him and taught him how to include expression and emotion into his songs. A London based 'Look-alike' company registered him on its books, Mark Richie of the Stage magazine wrote *"This young man successfully adopted the look and sound of Sinatra,"* and the first year culminated in an engagement to sing at the Jaguar S type car launch at Hessle.

In 1999 Phil's singing career gradually advanced further, enabling him to gain more experience and polish. There was a performance at the Leeds Irish Centre with Bobby Knutt. Together with engagements in quality hotels and restaurants in the Yorkshire Dales and the Lake District. He auditioned for the BBC Children-in-Need competition, entitled 'Bears in Their Eyes', attaining a position in the last five and singing live on television for the first time. After the ordeal of sitting all day waiting his turn he was shaking from head to foot. That year he became the resident singer at the Crystal Room (Ex. Batley Variety Club). His staunch local supporters were not forgotten and there were well-supported engagements at venues in Churwell, Morley and the surrounding area.

The year 2000 saw Phil form his own trio and there were engagements as a supporting act to Ken Dodd at the Frontier Club, Batley, to Les Denis at the Princess Theatre in Blackpool and then as the main act at the Civic Hall, Leeds before the Lord Mayor of Leeds, Bernard Atha. On 15th August Phil was filmed by Yorkshire TV and the next day he was interviewed live with Christa Ackroyd and featured in the Sun newspaper under the heading 'The New Frank', following in the next few days with interviews on Radio Aire and Magic 828, when his CD was played. Between 28th October and 4th November Phil, accompanied by his trio and a Yorkshire T.V. crew, flew to the United Arab Emirates to fulfil bookings in Dubai, Al Ain and Abu Dhabi. The resultant 30-minute documentary, entitled 'Just to be Frank', was broadcast on Yorkshire T.V. and in the Border Regions. There were gigs at top class restaurants and then on 15th December he sang live on Yorkshire T.V. with his trio and the Wakefield College Choir.

There were more engagements in 2001. A documentary shown on Granada T.V. in January, the Yorkshire T.V. programme repeated in February and in March Phil was the guest speaker at the Joseph Priestley College Award evening. He was booked to perform at Pontins, Blackpool every Tuesday throughout the whole of the summer season at the 'Sinatra Tribute Night'. At this time Phil experienced one of the personal highlights of his career so far when he had the privilege of a meeting with Mr. Frank Sinatra Junior who wished him good luck with his career, gave his autograph and graciously allowing himself to be photographed with Phil. This event left Phil quite overwhelmed and the photograph is now one of his most treasured possessions. There was a major step later in this year when a big band was formed, with the assistance of his pianist Matt Stacey, who became his musical director and arranger. Before the end of the year there was the opportunity to stage three big band performances culminating in a wonderful evening at Morley Town Hall on Thursday 13th December 2001. Phil took the financial risk of booking the expensive hall with the hope there would be sufficient people willing to purchase tickets, and the people of his home town did not let him down. Every seat was taken and the lucky people in the audience that night will not forget the experience for a long time. The swinging band accompanied Phil on some 25 numbers that evening resulting in a thunderous standing ovation at the completion of the performance. The occasion was used to successfully launch Phil Fryer's charity CD 'Just to be Frank' with all the profits being donated to the 'Oliver Brooke Appeal' for the Candlelighters.

It started with *"a few beers and a song"* said Phil who is now performing full time with engagements nationwide, working with his big band and with impersonators of Dean Martin, Sammy Davis and Bing Crosby.

The first engagement for 2002 was a flying return visit to Dubai for the New Year celebrations. Phil and his band are looking forward to their many forthcoming engagements at venues all over England; the year 2002 will be an exciting one.

The tradition of Morley artistes successfully advancing into the professional world of entertainment, now has the name of Phil Fryer proudly set in lights at the start of this new millennium. He fully deserves the honour to be placed among a select band of Morley citizens who have progressed to international acclaim.

Phyllis Green.
Cellist.

Mrs. Green, a noted musician and artist, was born Phyllis Tiffany. Her earliest musical training came from her father, Mr. James William Tiffany, who played trombone both at the Leeds Grand Theatre and the City Varieties, and also with the Bradford Blue Imperial Band. He taught cornet, trumpet and trombone but Phyllis did not regard these as suitable for a girl and was more attracted to the cello. As a keen amateur artist this attraction was enhanced when she was greatly impressed by the portrait by Augustus John of the famous Iberian cellist Guilhermina Suggia playing the cello in a flowing red dress.

With the help of her father and by her own perseverance Phyllis made herself proficient on the cello and began to seek work in the orchestras which were recruited to accompany the silent films in some of the de luxe cinemas in the area. Through a Mr. Jefferson, a musical agent, she obtained work at Pontefract Lane Cinema in Leeds, where a special musical score for the orchestra came with each reel of film.

After gaining experience in the cinemas Phyllis decided that she would prefer work in which her talents would be more obvious and which had better hours. Accordingly when she heard that the cellist was leaving the trio at Collinson's café in Leeds she successfully applied for the position and played there until her marriage in 1937 to Mr. Alfred Green, Morley's famous pork butcher.

Collinson's café, in King Edward Street was noted for its excellent refreshments, mahogany décor and the high quality of the musical entertainment which patrons could enjoy with their morning coffee or afternoon tea. The trio developed an excellent rapport and became an accomplished ensemble. Phyllis particularly remembered playing at Collinson's with Arthur Percival, violinist, who became sub-leader to Laurence Turner in the Halle Orchestra. The pianist was Winifred Dixon who was an excellent teacher and accompanist and who accompanied Phyllis when they broadcast for the BBC from the Leeds studios in the early 1930's.

The trio performed at the Harrogate Prince of Wales Hotel in 1934 for a private dinner party for the Australian cricketers who were staying there during the Headingley Test Match. It was the Saturday evening when Don Bradman had just completed an innings of over three hundred runs and Phyllis was able to add the great batsman's name to her autograph collection. Her accompanist at that time was Violet Harrop who later became the first wife of Mr.Tom Jenkins the famous Morley violin virtuoso.

After her marriage Phyllis gave up professional music to assist her husband in the Green's pork butcher's business that baked the famous 'Green's Pies'. However her husband, Alfred Green, was also an accomplished pianist and, when time permitted, she continued to play the cello at home to his accompaniment. During this time she also played with the orchestras formed to accompany the productions of the Morley Technical Institute Amateur Operatic Society at the Pavilion Theatre, Morley Grammar School and at the Town Hall. It is thought she played her cello for over twenty such shows and especially remembered playing for 'Showboat', 'The Merry Widow', 'Countess Maritza', 'The Flower Drum Song' and 'Guys and Dolls'.

After the death of her husband Phyllis added painting and woodcarving to her artistic endeavours but performing music was her first love and she enjoyed playing at home with a group of friends making up a string quartet or quintet.

Verna Haigh.
Singer, Dancer and Accordionist.

Miss Verna Haigh was a versatile entertainer and a big favourite of Yorkshire audiences. She was an excellent singer, dancer and accordionist who performed at many of Morley's venues, including the New Pavilion theatre when she performed in the following shows:-

'Lets'	Monday 18th February 1935.
'Revubilee'	Monday 23rd March 1936.
'The Revellers'	Sunday 17th November 1940.
'The Revellers'	Sunday 18th January 1942.
'The Magnets' Concert Party	Sunday 16th January 1944.

Verna also sang with the popular local George Speight Dance Band.

Often billed as *'soubrette and dancer'* as well as an accordionist, she became *'Morley's Own Pantomime Star'* performing at the Alhambra Theatre, Bradford in Francis Laidler's 1940/41 production of 'Jack & The Beanstalk', with individual song, dance and accordion.

Alfred Inman.
Violinist.

Mr. Alfred Inman was a professional who never lost sight of his roots, and in retirement came back to those roots to quietly serve the community he loved. He was born in Morley towards the close of the 19th century in an age when people took a delight in making their own entertainment, in the days before radio and television. Mr. Inman was brought up in an atmosphere of family musical evenings. One of his sisters was a good singer and the other played both the piano and the banjo, so it was not surprising that his mother should buy him a half-size violin for his seventh birthday. It was one of his most treasured possessions for the rest of his life. He quickly learned to play the instrument and by the time he left Victoria Road School, at thirteen years of age, he had decided to become a professional violinist settling down to eight hours a day hard practice for the next two years, under the tuition of Mr. Fred Carr, who was the leader of his own Morley based professional orchestra. When he was fifteen years old Alfred launched his career making his debut as a solo violinist at the Dewsbury Empire Theatre, billed as *'Yorkshire'sBoy Virtuoso'*.

When the Mayor of Morley, Alderman W.L. Ingle J.P., opened Morley's New Pavilion Theatre on Saturday 25th November 1911 a Grand Opening Concert was staged, the proceeds being in aid of the Morley Nursing Association. The top of the bill that night was *'Master Inman, violinist'* and a review written at the time states *"Master Inman displayed his remarkable skill on the violin with a brilliant performance of a composition by Pagannini, which he played with great artistic taste and, in response to the inevitable demand for an encore, he performed the Intermezzo from 'Cavalleria Rusticana'."* The management of the newly opened theatre hired Mr. Carr and his orchestra to play and also to accompany the many and varied acts. It was always billed as *'The Pavilion Orchestra of Talented Musicians under the direction of Mr. Fred Carr.'* A violinist in that orchestra was Mr. Carr's former pupil, Alfred Inman. When the Pavilion had a change of policy to concentrate on dramatic productions the orchestra was not required and Mr. Inman joined the Bradford Palace Theatre orchestra.

A professional musician's life can be nomadic and this suited Mr. Inman's temperament. He obtained an engagement at Liverpool and while in that city he accepted the offer of a place with an orchestra on a Royal Mail liner, which, of course, allowed him to travel extensively.

He eventually returned to Morley and in the following years played in orchestras in almost every theatre, hall and café in the area. Among the places that echoed to his magic touch were the Queen's, the Grand and the

Empire theatres in Leeds and the Victoria Pier at Blackpool. He became leading violinist for the Leeds Scala Orchestra, one of the finest in the North. During that period he made bi-weekly broadcasts on the B.B.C. radio. He played for ten years at Field's Café on Commercial Street in Leeds and at the Theatre Royal for the pantomimes.

During the Second World War he was a member of the Scottish Orchestra, at that time one of the big five philharmonic orchestras in Britain. For many years he was a member of the Northern Philharmonic Orchestra, frequently accompanying the world famous Huddersfield Choral Society. During his long and distinguished career he accompanied numerous concert artistes and ballet stars. He played with some of the leading musicians in the country and under many world-famous conductors, including Sir Malcolm Sargent, but he always remained the average man-next-door, never being the 'arty' long-haired type of musician. He was a very professional musician whose playing career extended for over 50 years. Locally he was always known as one of the best-dressed men in Morley and, probably unique in his profession, he was a life member of a workingmen's club.

Coincidentally Mr. Inman's last full time job was with the orchestra at the Dewsbury Empire theatre - the theatre where he started his professional career all those years before. He was there when the theatre closed its doors for good. He then lived in retirement at his home in Troy Road, although in the 1950's, he played again at the Pavilion Theatre as a member of the orchestra for the Morley Amateur Operatic Society's musical shows. Most members of the society thought of Alf as an amateur like themselves. How wrong they were, and it is indicative of Alfred Inman's common touch, that he rarely spoke of his musical achievements.

There was an interesting connection between Alfred Inman and the Morley violin virtuoso Tom Jenkins. Mr. Inman did not do much teaching but in the early 1920's Tom Jenkins was one of his pupils, receiving tuition from him for a period of four years.

Tom Jenkins.
Violin Virtuoso.

Mr. Tom Jenkins the leader of The Grand Hotel Orchestra, Eastbourne, famous for its weekly B.B.C. broadcasts, in 1939, the same year that he appeared at Morley's Pavilion theatre.

Tom William Jenkins was born on 4th November 1910 at Harlech Crescent, Hunslet, Leeds, the second son of Harry Jenkins, a Wakefield man of Welsh stock. After Tom's birth the family moved with his elder brother, George Hollins Jenkins, first to Batley, then to Morley, and finally settled in 14, Highfield Crescent, Tingley, by this time with a younger brother Albert Hilton Jenkins. His father was employed as an engineman at the nearby Topcliffe Pit, while Tom's mother, Henrietta was a well-known contralto singer and player of the pianoforte, who performed regularly with the choir of the Zion Methodist Church, Batley. She was the daughter of Thomas H. Hall, renowned throughout the West Riding as an expert violinist. Tom's paternal grandfather was also an accomplished musician.

Tom was given a toy fiddle at the age of three and began to study the violin at eight. His first public appearance was in a church concert at ten, and four years later he made his first radio broadcast.

Tom is quoted as saying one of his first recollections was going to sleep to the sound of his mother singing downstairs. When only a small child his father would take him to local chapels to listen to choirs and small string orchestras. The first time he heard a violin he thought it the most marvellous sound in the world.

Eventually after much pestering, his father bought him a half-sized violin from a Morley pawnshop. The boy grew to love that instrument.

Tom's parents considered music important enough to warrant the expense of violin lessons for their son. Henrietta's long-standing involvement with the Zion Methodist Church choir led to Tom making regular appearances at the church in the 1920's. The earliest mention of a Tom Jenkins' performance is from the Morley Observer of March 1923 and concerns a concert for the Batley Co-operative Society *'A star, although not billed, was Master Thomas W. Jenkins, of Tingley. His skill on the violin surprised as well as delighted his audience, who gave him a fine reception on the occasion of his debut.'* At that time he had been receiving tuition for four years, as a pupil of Mr. Alf Inman of Morley.

During the formative years of his violin training he was an enthusiastic entrant to the major music festivals of Northern England and was invariably among the prize- winners. In his first competition in the Leeds Musical Competition Festival young Tom gained third place in the class for violinists below 13 years of age. The adjudicator said *'A real appreciation of music, shows good taste and intonation, a very intelligent performance, he is to be congratulated on his success.'*

There were also dozens of appearances at local concerts and recitals. The press and people of the area took great pride in Jenkins's prodigious talent, and there can be little doubt that the strong local traditions of popular live music provided fertile ground for the development of his abilities. Many of his performances in 1924 were given in aid of local charitable causes, particularly those associated with the Wesleyan and Baptist Chapels.

He also performed at the New Pavilion, Morley, on Sunday November 30th 1924, in aid of the Morley and District Corps of the St. John's Ambulance Brigade. *'He played the violin solo Admiral's Galliard very skillfully and was enthusiastically encored.'*

A letter to Jenkins from the violinist Robert Slater of Morley, dated February 1925, said he was so impressed with a performance at Morley Town Hall, that he offered the gift of his violin, and he closed the letter with *'How proud I should feel if you were my grandson.'*

In 1923 the West Riding County Council awarded Jenkins a County Minor Scholarship enabling him to leave Westerton School and attend Morley Grammar School. The master in charge of music there was Arthur Gower, on whom the young violinist made a deep impression, as can be seen in a letter to Tom's parents, dated December 1924. *'Tom has done much for me, and it is for his enterprise and desire to ever give me of his best that I would just like to pay my sincere thanks to his parents. You need have no doubts as to our desires re. his musical work at the school.'*

Jenkins became a pupil of Edward Maude, leader of the Leeds Symphony Orchestra, under whose expert tuition he won first prize in the Junior Violin class at the Hull Musical Festival in 1924. Tom was soon to have the chance to take part in his first radio broadcast, which took place in November 1925. It was a lecture recital in a series called 'With the Classics'broadcast from the Leeds-Bradford Radio station.

Tom was now advanced enough musically to play regularly with Edward Maude's String Orchestra. He appeared with the Malton White Star Band giving 'Sacred Concerts' of popular classical music. In 1927 he played his first full concerto in public, giving a full rendition of Bach's 'Violin Concerto in A Minor' with his tutor's String Orchestra at the Leeds Church Institute.

He began an association with Cecil Moon a pianist from a well-known Morley musical family, whose famous Royal Baths Quartet played at the Pump Room and the Winter gardens in Harrogate. In May 1929 he took part in a radio broadcast from Leeds as a member of the Cecil Moon Trio and began a two-year professional engagement with the Royal Baths Quartet. At the same time he took up the position of solo violinist with the Harrogate Central Cinema Orchestra having in earlier years played with cinema orchestras in Thirsk and Batley.

In the summer of 1930, Tom Jenkins was asked to join the Hastings Municipal Orchestra at the White Rock Pavilion. By early 1932 his virtuosity had gathered a local following and he was receiving rave notices in the local press. When the spa towns such as Harrogate were out-of-season, he played with orchestras at coastal venues such as Blackpool, Scarborough and Whitby. He spent several summers at Scarborough with Alick McLean's band, and the summer of 1933 with 'Toni' Hopkins's North Pier Orchestra in Blackpool, his first engagement as leader of an orchestra.

The summer seasons of 1935 and 1936 saw him leader and deputy conductor of the Whitby Municipal Orchestra at the Spa Pavilion under Frank Gomez, an orchestra famous for its weekly radio broadcasts. It was a remarkable achievement for so young a man to be leader of a broadcasting orchestra.

By this stage Jenkins had married Violet Harrop, from the well known Harrogate family, the Cholmondeley-Harrops. Violet was herself a fine piano player. If their marriage proved a failure, they continued a partnership in J H Squire's Celeste Trio in London, with two film shorts being made by Pathé News Gazette featuring J H Squire, Tom and his wife. He also led the Celeste Octet in radio broadcasts and in recitals on tour.

After six years with the Hastings Municipal Orchestra, Jenkins decided it was time to branch out on his own and one of his earliest bookings was to star in a concert at the Prince of Wales Theatre in London in November 1936. He was billed as *'The Amazing Violin Virtuoso, Tom Jenkins, considered the Greatest British Soloist of his Generation.'*

Tom made headline news in the papers when he insured his hands for £10,000 and was covered to receive £20 a week for any period he was unable to play due to injury.

In 1936/37 a recording deal was negotiated with Louis Sterling, managing director of His Master's Voice. His first test recording was 'Songs my Mother Taught Me' also 'Brahms's Violin Concerto'.

Tom then had lessons from Carl Flesch, the greatest teacher of the violin. His terms of five guineas a lesson were reduced to three guineas after hearing Tom play. He would not take any pupil who was not in the very advanced class. Expert tuition such as this, combined with the experience gained from recital tours and broadcasts with the Celeste Octet, reinforced Tom Jenkins's position as one of the most popular performers of his era. This popularity was to result in his appointment, in 1938, to the leadership of the Grand Hotel Orchestra, Eastbourne, a position which was to bring him some of his greatest triumphs. The first broadcast from the Grand Hotel took place on 10th July 1938. There was a spontaneous acclaim to the broadcasts with Tom receiving hundreds of letters.

David McCallum, leader of the London Philharmonic Orchestra had sold Tom his own 140-year-old Gagliano violin from Italy. After hearing a broadcast from the Grand Hotel he wrote to Tom *'I did not think it could be the same fiddle. It sounded too good.'*

Although Tom was now a national celebrity he still found time to support local charities. At the New Pavilion Theatre, Morley on Wednesday and Thursday 15th and 16th November 1939, in an O.M.A.D.S. revue entitled "Odds On", he was billed as *'Tom Jenkins, violinist, famous for his broadcasts from the Grand Hotel, Eastbourne.'*

The time as leader at the Grand Hotel was cut short by the arrival of the Second World War when The Grand Hotel was commandeered to house troops and in 1940 Tom joined the BBC Salon Orchestra that evacuated to Evesham from where broadcasts were made in the 'Grand Hotel'style. This orchestra disbanded in 1942 when many of its members were called to military service.

Tom was conscripted on 15th October 1942 to the Royal Army Service Corps with the rank of private. By March 1943 he was attending an officers'training course at Wrotham in Kent and was posted to India shortly afterwards. Although his marriage to Violet Harrop was not a success, they were still legally married.

The journey to India was extremely uncomfortable in the hold of a converted meat ship and the impromptu concerts given by Tom helped to keep up the morale and made a deep impression on the homesick young men. En route he played the Mendelssohn Violin Concerto with the Durban Municipal Orchestra in South Africa.

On arrival in India he was once again in great demand for camp concerts at the Officers' Training School in Bangalore. In January 1944 he was commissioned with the rank of lieutenant into the Indian Army. He was posted to the North West Frontier Province and then to Peshawar, near the Khyber Pass. This outpost had a broadcasting station and before long Tom Jenkins's violin could be heard on the airwaves across this rugged, inhospitable part of what is now Pakistan, a far cry from the home comforts of Eastbourne.

He passed an elementary course in Urdu and remained in India for a year after the end of the hostilities. After playing a concert the Bombay Sunday Standard reported *'Tom Jenkins takes Bombay by Storm.'* He was taken under the wing of Dr. Meher-Homji of Poona who arranged for him to appear with the Bombay Symphony Orchestra. Playing in India was most difficult because of the intense heat and humidity which was not only physically draining for the performer but also had an unfortunate effect on the glue which holds violins together, but luckily Tom's Gagliano emerged from the war unscathed.

Towards the end of his military service, in March 1946, Tom wrote to the manager of the Grand Hotel but a higher rate of pay than his previous pre-war contract could not be agreed. He declined to return on the terms of his old contract but he continued to broadcast in the radio series 'Voice of the Violin'. In 1947 he joined the BBC Studio Players. Tom Jenkins's talent began to shine out again as it had pre-war. Within two years of his release from the army he stepped fully into the limelight again with the BBC 'Grand Hotel' broadcasts.

This revival of his fortunes coincided with the acquisition of a Stradivarius violin with which he was to achieve the pinnacle of his popularity on the radio. The Gagliano violin had survived the rigours of travel in India but Tom felt that his talent would be better served by the perfect tones of a truly great violin, particularly now that his performances were beginning to be preserved for posterity on gramophone records. He decided to fulfill his long-standing ambition by buying an original Stradivarius but he had to wait three years for one to become available. The one he eventually owned was in perfect condition with no sign of previous use and likely to improve with playing. On August 18th 1948 William Hill & Sons issued Tom with a certificate guaranteeing the genuine provenance of the instrument, giving a detailed technical description, including the fact that it still bore the maker's label *'Antonius Stradivarius Cremonencis Faciebat Anno 1667 AS'.* The instrument was prohibitively expensive and Tom had to ask a relative to help in meeting the cost. The first insurance policy for the instrument taken out in 1948 was for £1,250

In 1948 the BBC asked Tom Jenkins to take over permanently from Albert Sandler as leader of the Palm Court Orchestra. This was the time of frequent tours around Britain mainly with Reginald Kilbey (cello) and Jack Byfield (piano).

The Palm Court Orchestra produced regular recordings of popular tunes on the H.M.V. label from 1949 and attracted huge audiences.

Meanwhile Jenkins's classical recitals continued unabated. For example in 1949 he played Mozart's A Major Concerto for violin and orchestra with the Harrogate String Orchestra and also Wieniawski's Second Violin Concerto with the Northern Philharmonic Orchestra at Leeds Town Hall.

The soprano Dorothy Bond joined Tom in his appearances around the country during 1950. She was a well-known coloratura, whose purity of tone had established her reputation on the concert platform. Dorothy was also an accomplished pianist and was destined to become the second Mrs Jenkins the following year. Their partnership was tragically cut short in November 1952 when Dorothy was killed in a car accident; she was thirty-one years of age, and sadly denied the full potential of her musical career.

The happier times of their all too short partnership was during the weekday afternoons when Tom staged Palm Court Orchestra concerts at the Royal Festival Hall as part of the Festival of Britain celebrations. Also in 1951, on Saturday 3rd March, an audience of 1,000 Morley admirers packed into the Ebenezer Methodist Church to give a big welcome to Tom; he rewarded them with a brilliant performance. As a national figure there were heavy demands on his time but he willingly agreed to this return visit to his hometown. During the time he was in the church there were continual visits to the retiring room where he made everyone welcome. He had a busy time signing autographs and greeting many admirers and old friends. His programme that day included 'La Capriccioso', 'Nocturne in E Flat', 'Gypsy Airs', 'Meditation from Thais', 'Polonaise', 'Hora Staccato', 'The Londonderry Air', and 'Mazurka de Concert'. After the concert he had to hurry back to London to make preparations for his regular Sunday evening radio broadcast.

The culmination of Tom Jenkins' public acclaim came when he won the Daily Mail National Radio Award for the Most Popular Musical Entertainer two years running, in the periods of 1952/3 and 1953/4.

In December 1952 Tom began to interview musicians for the orchestra he would be taking to the Spa at Scarborough for the summer season the following year. One of the young musicians who applied was Michelle Le Mesurier Croll, a 23-year-old flautist who had previously played with the Sadler's Wells Orchestra and the Boyd Neel Orchestra. She passed her audition, and in July 1953, during the Scarborough season, she and Tom became engaged. During this time Tom's 22-year-old daughter, from his first marriage, Margaret, had taken a job as a hotel receptionist in Scarborough in order to be near her father.

Tom and Michelle were married at Kensington Registry Office in London on 7th December. The bride carried 'Roses of the South'as a reminder of the Strauss Waltz, which had become the signature tune of the Palm Court broadcasts. Along with Tom's sixteen-month-old son (by his marriage to Dorothy Bond), they settled in Streatham, South London.

In November 1953 Tom made his only television appearance when it was thought that with his quiet charisma he might become as big a star on television as he had become on radio. That winter saw another demanding schedule of concert appearances at provincial centres including a special outside broadcast of 'Grand Hotel' from the Pump Room Bath and a London Philharmonic Orchestra concert at the Albert Hall.

In February 1954 he appeared with the Hallé Orchestra at the Free Trade Hall, Manchester.

Tom Jenkins' name was now in lights across the entrance to the Spa so that it reflected in the water across Scarborough Bay Come the 1954 season he was earning £100 per week, in a seventeen-week freelance engagement with an expanded orchestra of twenty.

There were discussions with Sir Thomas Beecham about the possibility of leading the Royal Philharmonic Orchestra, but this was not meant to be. During the winter of 1954/55 the provinces were toured giving around 25 performances in a trio with his wife Michelle Croll on flute, and Gerald Gover on piano. 'The Tom Jenkins Quintet' was also formed at that time, and broadcast for the BBC on Thursday evenings and Saturday lunch times throughout that same winter.

In 1955 he also began to broadcast as leader of two new groups, The Tom Jenkins Orchestra (sometimes known as The Winter Garden Orchestra), and the Spa Orchestra. The Tom Jenkins Orchestra broadcast on the BBC Home Service on Sunday evenings, between 6.30 and 7.15 pm, beginning on 18th September 1955. It was whilst leading this orchestra that he celebrated the thirtieth anniversary of his first radio broadcast which he had given in Leeds in November 1925, at the age of fifteen. To commemorate the occasion, his orchestra played Bach's 'Air on the G String', one of the pieces he had played during the original broadcast.

The Tom Jenkins Orchestra and the Spa Orchestra continued to broadcast almost continually until July 1956 when increasing ill health forced him to abandon his leadership. In July he underwent a major operation for lung cancer, was forced to take time off for convalescence, but continued to broadcast at a reduced rate. The listening public knew nothing of his illness. In fact it was so serious that one of his lungs had been removed, and he was left in a very weak condition. In spite of this, he showed great courage and determination, and did not lose his charm or humour during what was to prove, a terminal illness.

In August 1956 he asked the BBC to be allowed to play again. It is stated the BBC would have loved him to lead the violins but he was too weak. So he took his place among the ranks. The orchestra in which he made his last two broadcasts was the London Theatre Orchestra, and the programme was 'String Songs'. The public were unaware that among the string section, played a violinist who was the most popular radio musician of his day. Tom played anonymously for he knew that this was his swan song and he was content to return to his musical roots.

According to those who played with him in his final broadcasts, he was visibly racked with pain, and often doubled up in his chair, but he still managed a joke with his fellow musicians. His last broadcasts were completed in January 1957, and Tom died on 13th February 1957, at his home at 3, Selwood Terrace, Kensington, at the age of forty-six.

At the funeral service in St. Martin-in-the-Fields, the musical accompaniment was led by members of the BBC choruses and choirs, many of whom had sung in Tom Jenkins's broadcasts over the years. There too in the church were many distinguished personalities from the BBC and the world of music in general.

Following Tom's death, the Stradivarius with which he had risen to the peak of his fame languished in a bank strong room, unable to be kept at the house of his widow, Michelle, as it was simply too valuable. However, in 1995 Michelle Jenkins decided that the violin should be sold, so that a new generation of violinists would have the opportunity to play this magnificent instrument. The sale would also allow her to commission a biography of Tom Jenkins, as a testament to his talent and the popularity he achieved during his tragically short life.

On 20th June 1995 the Stradivarius was the centrepiece of an auction of musical instruments at Sotheby's in New Bond Street, London. After some fierce bidding, it was eventually sold for £375,000, more than double the lower pre-sale estimate of £180,000.

Elisabeth Thomas purchased the violin for her ten-year-old daughter Christine. Mrs. Thomas and her husband, Hans-Josef, ran a violin dealership in Aachen, Germany. Christine was regarded as something of a musical prodigy. It was reported at the time of the sale that, as this was an early Stradivarius, it was slightly undersized compared with those made later. Certainly it was an ideal instrument for a young girl of great talent to echo the virtuosity and dedication of its previous owner.

The memory of Tom Jenkins lives on in the City of London where an award is still presented annually at the London Guild of Music in the name of this exceptionally talented musician.

(We are greatly indebted to Mrs. Michelle Jenkins for allowing the use of information contained in the book 'The Tom Jenkins Story', and for the permission of its authors Peter Pugh and Duncan Heath.

The full and most interesting biography of Tom Jenkins, entitled 'The Tom Jenkins Story', tracing his rise from a Morley schoolboy prodigy to a national celebrity, may be obtained from Cambridge Business Publishing, Grange Road, Duxford, Cambridge CB2 4QF, price £16.95 plus £3 p&p. Cheques should be made payable to 'Mrs. M. Jenkins Trust Accoun'. All proceeds go to a fund for the benefit of makers of bowed string instruments.

Mr. John T. Kirk.
Actor, Producer and Theatre Manager.

For many years Mr. Kirk, who was born in 1909, was one of the leading theatrical personalities in Morley. He was educated at Morley Grammar School and also studied at colleges in Leeds and London before gaining his LRAM (Eloc) and LGSM (Eloc) in 1939.

In 1929 he was a founder member of the Morley Adult School Players for whom his productions included Shaw's 'Candida', T.S. Elliot's 'Murder in the Cathedral' and also the world premiere of D.H. Lawrence's 'A Collier's Friday Night', which really placed Morley on the Amateur Dramatic Map.

During the Second World War Mr. Kirk served in the Royal Armoured Corps. On return to civilian life he decided to make the professional stage his career joining the Birmingham Repertory School and the Stratford Memorial Theatre to be with Sir Barry Jackson for the seasons 1946, 1947 and 1948. During the 1950's he was the Producer/Manager at theatres in Barrow and Leicester and then Drama Adviser in Central Scotland residing in Stirling.

He was in demand to teach drama and speech therapy at various schools in Scotland and then for eight years, towards the end of his career, he held the position as Assistant Manager at Leeds Grand Theatre.

Mr. Kirk was also associated with the Old Morleians Amateur Dramatic Society for which he produced four plays, all staged at the Pavilion theatre, 'The Ghost Train' in 1959, 'Cat Among the Pigeons' in 1960, 'Off the Deep End' in 1961 and 'As Long As They're Happy' in 1962.

Mr. Kirk was involved in an unusual incident during the summer of 1939 when he was in Moscow attending a drama festival. He was arrested by the police and questioned for three hours because he had taken photographs of the production of Bernard Shaw's 'The Apple Cart'. He was only released after Sir Barry Jackson, the Malvern Festival producer, had given assurances to the Russian authorities. Sir Barry was attending the festival along with a group of British supporters he had taken to Moscow at the invitation of the British Drama League.

Morley Adult School Players. The cast on stage for 'When We Are Married' in December 1951:- from left to right : Back row, John T. Kirk (photographer), Harry Trepte (parson), Gertie Kirk, Betty Fatkin (maid), Margaret Rylands, George W.Atkinson, George Gledhill, Henry Atkinson, Reg. Saville. Front row, John Anderson (kneeling), Ada Almond, Florence Thompson, Alice Hartley, Ruth Trepte.

Jean Kitson.
Actress.

Miss Jean Heather Kitson left Morley Grammar School at 17 years of age to enter the professional theatre, a world in which she had a most distinguished acting career, until abandoning the stage in 1959 to get married. Her wedding to Mr. John Alan Jennings took place at St.Peter's Church Morley on Saturday 7th March 1959. Among the guests were several actors and actresses and also Mr. Harry Hanson, the well-known producer and director of the Court Players who had travelled from his home in Brighton.

Between these two events Miss Kitson had a stage career spanning almost 14 years in Repertory Companies throughout England and Wales during which time she worked with many artistes who eventually became household names. It all began when she successfully answered an advert in 'The Stage' to become, at 17 years of age, the Assistant Stage Manager at the famous Theatre Royal in Leeds, with the opportunity to play occasional small parts such as maids and schoolgirls with 'Harry Hanson's Court Players'. On arrival at the theatre for her first day at work she found that her stage manager was none other than Peggy Mount a lady who, like

Miss Jean Kitson in 1951 when she was acting with Harry Hanson's Court Players at the Prince's Theatre, Bradford. Her photograph was featured on an advertisement for the play 'Who is Sylvia?'

herself, was not a bit interested in stage managing, both being desperate to become full time actresses. A very pretty 16-year-old girl called Billie Whitelaw, who was of course to become a famous actress, travelled from her home in Bradford to share the 'youngster' roles with Jean.

About a year later a stroke of luck came Jean's way when she was promoted to playing Juvenile Lead roles. This came about because the very nice looking girl who was originally chosen for the position, a good actress, found it quite impossible to learn her lines in the short time available to Repertory Company actors. This event occurred when the company was playing in a remote part of South Wales which meant that Jean was the only substitute available. She snapped up the opportunity when the job was offered and made it hers. She especially enjoyed her new position when shortly afterwards the company moved to the Royalty Theatre in Chester where she found herself lucky enough to be playing romantic roles opposite a young Francis Matthews. Although it was many years later that he made a name for himself in films, radio and television, the local girls considered him a great heart-throb even in those early days.

Over the next decade Jean stayed with Harry Hanson and, as he had over twenty companies in different areas, she was able to move around the country and was never out of work. The repertory actors were not paid a great deal but they did have the opportunity to play a wonderful variety of roles which would not have been available to them in the West End. During those years Miss Kitson played alongside many actors who were to become household names in later years. Her 'Dad' in numerous North Country comedies was Bryan Mosley, who much later became Alf Roberts in Coronation Street. Another good friend, colleague and excellent character actress was Elizabeth Bradley who later portrayed the Coronation Street character Maud Grimes. Jean reminisces, *"Of course there was Pat Phoenix. She joined us at the Prince's Theatre in Bradford in the 1950's, though her name was then Pat Pilkington. We shared a dressing room for more than a year, but she left in a great huff after a row with the producer. Almost the last words I heard her say as she furiously took off her make up were "I'll show him. I've played here to thousands...one day I'll play to bloody millions!" and of course she did."*

Jean writes of her early married life, *"After leaving the theatre and turning on the television back home it seemed as though half the people I had ever worked with were either popping up in a drama or advertising something. My family got used to me shouting "that's Teddy Palmer!" when there was a tubby man sucking Opal Fruits, or when a woman was advertising Omo, crying out "Oh, it's Janet Whiteside.""*

Leaving the live theatre was not, however, the end of Jean's acting career. In the early 70's she moved to Norfolk and discovered that Anglia

Television needed people with an Equity Card to occasionally play small roles. She describes this era in her own words, *"I had a great time, with tiny parts in a number of 'Tales from the Unexpected', even a little scene with Derek Jacobi, who was lovely. It was a revelation to me, having spent all my acting life in the theatre I found it difficult to tone down every reaction down to suit the camera. But the money! I would have had to work in Rep. for six months to earn a similar amount for a few days in front of the camera. Though, of course Rep. work was steady, whereas T.V. certainly is not, apart from the few big names. So I didn't make a fortune, and there has been very little work for the past couple of years but we had a lot of fun, especially during the filming 'Hi-di-Hi' which took place in Dovercourt, Essex. A crowd of us assembled there every autumn, took over the chalets and generally made ourselves useful, usually just as a part of a big crowd of jolly campers. As a final comment, I don't think viewers realise the sort of people who constitute crowd scenes in television. Some of them are fascinating. Artists who have been big stars in their hey-day and are just glad to keep their hand in and make a bit of money, ex pantomime dames, old Music Hall stars, dancers, singers even circus performers. One of these, no longer alive I am afraid, was George Formby's sister Mary. In her youth she and her husband toured the world with a circus act- one of the highlights being a match with a boxing kangaroo! They retired to Yarmouth and I gave Mary a lift many times to different television locations, and what interesting tales she had to tell."*

Jean together with her sister Millicent Hirst and her late brother Bill originally arrived in Morley under police escort. Their father was in the West Riding Constabulary.

Vincent J. Mulchrone.
Newspaper Reporter and Feature Writer.

Vincent Mulchrone was born in 1923 the son of Mr.and Mrs. Patrick Mulchrone of 42, Great Northern Street, Morley. As a boy he attended Queen Street Infants School, Cross Hall Boys' Junior School and his formal education was completed at Morley Grammar School where, in 1939, he was successful in the Northern Universities School Certificate Examination. At 16 years of age and with the outbreak of war approaching, he found employment as a window dresser at Lewis's Department Store in Leeds - but not for long. The teenager took the opportunity to fulfil his ambition to become a professional writer when he saw an advertisement for a junior reporter at his local weekly paper, the Morley Observer, and successfully applied for the position. Although this was only the first rung on the ladder it was the beginning of the climb that eventually took Mr. Mulchrone to the peak of his profession as a famous Fleet Street journalist who was much sought after by the national daily papers.

During this period most of his spare time was taken with voluntary duties in the Morley unit of the Home Guard but he did find the opportunity to

Mr. Vincent Mulchrone with Mr. & Mrs. G.W. Atkinson and the last Mayor & Mayoress of Morley Borough, Alderman & Mrs. J.S. Binks, in the Mayor's rooms on Tuesday 5ᵗʰ February 1974.

appear on Morley's amateur stage; he was a performer in a variety show entitled 'Music Hall' which was staged from the 13th to 15th February 1941 following this as stage manager for 'The Revellers' concert on 9th August 1942 - both events being presented at the Morley Pavilion Theatre.

His early days as a local reporter were soon interrupted when he joined the Royal Air Force in which he served as a pilot travelling as far away as Java. On completion of his war service it was a return to work as a reporter with the opportunity for another short spell with Morley's amateur theatricals. He again appeared at the Pavilion Theatre, this time in the Old Morleians Amateur Dramatic Society's production of the play 'Quiet Wedding', for six nights from Monday 24th November 1947 and, along with his sister Kathleen, in the O.M.A.D.S. revue 'Spring Fever', for six nights from Monday 26th April 1948.

Mr. Mulchrone soon left the Morley Observer and was employed by the Yorkshire Evening News, the Manchester Evening News, the Daily Mirror and then, in 1950, the Daily Mail in Manchester, before moving to the Fleet Street office in 1954. He was head of that paper's Paris Bureau in 1957 and then settled into his natural vocation as a feature writer and special reporter winning awards as 'Descriptive Writer of the Year' in 1964 and 'Feature Writer of the Year' in 1970. He reported in 1975 from as far away as Viet Nam.

Here are the introductory sentences from one of his typical masterpieces written about the lying in state of Sir Winston Churchill. *"Two rivers run silently through London tonight, and one is made of people. Dark and quiet as the night-time Thames itself, it flows through Westminster Hall, eddying about the foot of the rock called Churchill."*

Before the 1966 soccer cup final between England and Germany he wrote: - "If the Germans beat us at our national game today, we can always console ourselves with the fact we have beaten them twice at theirs."

Vincent was a larger than life character who brought colour to the readers of the Daily Mail, especially in the dull grey era following the Second World War and, although he became famous, he never forgot his Morley roots. He claimed with Yorkshire pride *"I and the best pork pies in the world come from Morley"*. In one article he informed the whole country of the mouth-watering attributes of Morley's pork pies which were, of course, baked and sold by Green's Pork Butchers situated a few yards from the Pavilion and only a stone's throw from his original Morley home.

Mr. Mulchrone always enjoyed a visit to his home town and on one occasion, whilst being introduced as the after dinner speaker at a local gathering, on a prearranged signal a waiter brought in a large silver salver. The lid was removed with a flourish to reveal a Green's pork pie. No one in the room found it more hilarious than Mr. Mulchrone himself.

Tom Gomersall, who was the person actually responsible for this amusing incident, has given a first hand account. *"It was probably in the mid 1960's when I was asked to propose the toast to "The School" at the annual dinner of the Old Morleians. This was while Mr. Hulbert was still the headmaster. The guest of honour at this dinner was Vincent Mulchrone, who was formerly with the Morley Observer, and at that time was with the Daily Mail. In an article Vincent had praised the culinary delights of eating Green's pork pies as a student at Morley Grammar School. In common with many other youngsters before and since, he had indulged in the mildly illicit practice of surreptitiously eating these pies on the way to school. By using the "back way", there was a slightly reduced risk of being detected in the forbidden practice of eating in the streets. I had been privileged to be a member of the Grammar School scouts at the same time as Vincent, so I felt it to be appropriate to indulge in a light-hearted dig at this nationally well-known figure. I purchased a Green's pie, smuggled it into the dining room, and arranged with the head waiter that at a given signal from me he would bring the pie in on a silver platter and present it to Vincent with my compliments."*

There was a dramatic occasion when the Morley Local History Society held its annual dinner in Morley Town Hall on Tuesday 5th February 1974, the last one before the local government reorganisation that lost the town its independence. The Mayor and Mayoress of Morley, Alderman and Mrs. J.S. Binks attended the dinner and the guest speaker for the evening was Mr. Vincent Mulchrone who, a few days earlier, had written a vitriolic article concerning the I.R.A. and this resulted in the Morley police receiving a message that an attempt would be made on his life during his visit to Morley. He was consequently shadowed by two plain clothed police officers during his stay in the town. Places were set at the dinner for the two officers with obvious bulges under their shoulders that were not just muscles. Prior to the guests taking their places for dinner the Town Hall had to be evacuated and everyone retired to a nearby car park whilst bomb squad officers from Catterick, together with police and 'sniffer' dogs, searched the building. The 'all clear' was eventually given and the dinner went ahead 50 minutes late, fortunately without any further untoward incidents.

Mr. Mulchrone was proud of his family, his wife Louie and their three sons Martin, Patrick and Michael. It was in their private company that he sought refuge between the spells of globetrotting that made him the Daily Mail's most travelled and admired writer.

Unfortunately Mr. Vincent J. Mulchrone died in 1977 at only 54 years of age. At the time of his death he was acknowledged to be the top feature writer in Fleet Street. One of his colleagues wrote *"The tragedy is that, when leukaemia struck him down he had so much more in him to write, and there is no one else who could write it in the way he would have done."*

There were many tributes paid to him including one from H.M. the Queen who said *"Mr. Mulchrone was well-known and well liked by the Royal Family and a very popular figure."*

During our researches into the life of this great newspaper writer we made reference to the excellent collection of his articles published in 1978 by the Associated Newspapers Group Ltd under the title 'The Best of Vincent Mulchrone'. Its subtitle was 'a lifetime of wit and observation of the folly and splendour of his fellow humans by the Daily Mail's finest reporter.' The authors wrote to the Daily Mail requesting permission to use their copyright material.

Twenty-four years after Vincent's death we received an immediate reply from no less a person than Vyvyan Harmsworth LVO, Director of Corporate Affairs for the Daily Mail and General Holdings Limited, which we are delighted to reproduce in full.

"Thank you for your letter dated 20th August 2001. I am delighted on behalf of the late Lord Rothermere for you to use any quotes in support of Vincent Mulchrone, which you have gleaned from the foreword to his book. He was one of our most respected journalists and much loved for the depth of his writing and his humour. He was also an energetic golfer who often played with the Chairman of Associated Newspapers and to this day we have the Vincent Mulchrone Trophy, which is played for on an annual basis. There are a few people left who knew him personally and if you wanted to be put in touch with any of them I would do so with pleasure.

Out of interest, do Green's pork pies still exist?"

Sincerely Vyvyan Harmsworth

In the next post Mr Harmsworth sent a cutting from that very day's Daily Mail. The following are the relevant extracts from John Edwards leader 'The Way It Is'under the title 'Drink, not ink, was Fleet Street's lifeblood.'

'Drink lifted the spirits and it spilled over into the words. The finest writers in Fleet Street had most of their best phrases released by whisky.

Here was the great Vincent Mulchrone of this newspaper and someone who honoured the whole profession with his class, and he got the train from Byfleet Surrey each day he was around and bought a taxi ride from Waterloo. The cab dropped him at The Harrow pub next to the office. Vincent looked up and down the street for cops. Then at 9.45am, they opened the door quickly for him and he went into the back bar. Half a bottle of Moet & Chandon was always in an ice bucket on the counter. If it was a really bad day he would take a Fernet Branca chaser as well.

Vincent walked over to the office afterwards, picked up his assignment, and outwrote everyone into early graves. Never ever was he heard to say he was going to do 50 press-ups and a little machine cycling. And he was the best, and when he went from us forever, he left a space the size of Australia.

When Vincent Mulchrone passed on, they made for him the only tribute he would have wanted. The bar he began his day in was named after him. A plaque is fixed to the wall and his picture, too.

No papers are made around there now. New customers, bankers and lawyers, ask about the name. He was the best of an era which is part of history, they usually get told.'

Morley is proud of him, and so it seems is the industry he once served so well.

Remembering Vincent Mulchrone.

Mrs. Lucy Piercy, nee Strickland and her friend Sheila, Old Morleians now living in the South of England, were friends of Vincent Mulchrone in their early days in Morley. When they learned that the London bar he had frequented was named in his honour they decided to pay it a visit for old times sake.

It was in February 2002 when the opportunity arose and, after being twice misdirected, they entered The Harrow public house at the junction of Whitefriars Street and Primrose Hill, just off Fleet Street, and ordered drinks at the bar. There appeared to be no sign of any Vincent memorabilia and when they made enquiries a young barman overheard the conversation and said "they want the Vincent Mulchrone room". He immediately picked up their drinks and suggested they follow him, whereby he escorted them back through the door into Whitefriars, then around the corner and re-entered the premises by another door situated in Primrose Hill. A small corridor led to another door bearing the sign "The Vincent Mulchrone Room" and this opened into a small secluded bar which was actually situated behind the main bar and adjacent to a function room. The room contains a small bar, two bench seats and a couple of tables. On the wall above a fireplace there are two good sized photographs of Mr. Mulchrone along with one framed testimonial from Mr. Harmsworth and another one which records how well liked and respected he was by all the journalists who knew him, not just the ones at the Daily Mail.

The ladies felt pleased to have been able to visit this memorial, (still maintained 25 years after his death), to the memory of a well-liked and respected Morley man who reached the top of his profession.

Jack Popplewell
Songwriter and Playwright

For many years rhubarb growing was an important industry in the area south of Leeds. In addition to the farms, sheds and acres of land used for rhubarb growing, most gardens also had a rhubarb patch for domestic use.

Jack's father, Walter Popplewell was a local rhubarb farmer at the Manor Farm, Churwell, where part of the farm house on Old Road, dated back to 1605. Walter Popplewell was also the president of the Rugby League and took the first British team to Australia.

Jack Popplewell took over the responsibility of the farm from his father and continued its successful operation, producing two harvests each year, forced rhubarb in winter and green-top in summer, thus providing all year round employment for hard working Churwell people. Unfortunately, along with local independence, most of the rhubarb fields have gone, often to make way for the housing developments required in a dormitory area.

Whilst conducting his farm business Jack Popplewell led another completely different life which brought him into contact with famous musicians, singers, actors and show business personalities. He became a successful songwriter for the stars. Over forty of his songs and compositions were published, including the huge hit of the 1940s, 'If I Should Fall in Love Again,' which was performed and recorded by many artistes. One of the most popular of its recordings was by Gracie Fields. Jack Popplewell's songs were recorded by many of the great stars of the era, including Vera Lynn, Geraldo, Ambrose and Anne Shelton. Bing Crosby recorded Jack's composition 'My Girl's an Irish Girl' and his song 'Tonight Beloved'was recorded, in Italian, by Gigli.

As if these achievements were not sufficient, Jack Popplewell then turned his talents in another direction to become a famous playwright. His first play 'Blind Alley', for which he also composed the music, opened in 1953 and was made into a film in 1958 entitled 'Tread Softly Stranger', starring Diana Dors and George Baker. His next play was 'Dead on Nine' which opened in 1955 at the Westminster Theatre, London and ran for nearly 200 performances, starring Andrew Cruikshank and Griffith Jones. A smash hit in 1957 was 'Dear Delinquent' with David Tomlinson, Anna Massey and Patrick Cargill. More successes followed; 'A Day in the Life Of....'(1958), 'And Suddenly its Spring' (1959) and 'Busybody' (1964), which did a world tour.

Jack Popplewell wrote 'Breakfast in Bed' in four weeks and allowed this play to be staged by the Old Morleians Amateur Dramatic Society at

Morley's New Pavilion Theatre on 1ˢᵗ December 1958 and again on 27ᵗʰ April 1972, when it was performed at Morley Grammar School. He attended both productions. Five of his successful plays were produced in five years. At the request of Wilfred Pickles he adapted the Harold Brighouse play 'Hobson's Choice' into a musical.

Jack Popplewell eventually moved just over the Churwell boundary, where he resided with his wife Betty and daughters Juliet and Vanessa at 'Vaynol Gate', Rooms Lane, Morley, a former mill owner's house. He entertained at his home celebrities from the stage and musical world. One of his friends was Vera Lynn who, during one of her visits, became intrigued with the skills of rhubarb growing. She returned home to Surrey with some Churwell rhubarb roots in an attempt to grow them in the South. No doubt this would not be very successful as rhubarb only seemed to flourish in the sooty soil of the old mill towns.

Mr. Popplewell was a private person who shunned publicity but he did appear in person to assist Morley's local amateur performers in their war efforts to provide much needed entertainment for both the civilian population and the troops. He appeared on the stage of the New Pavilion on Sunday 17ᵗʰ November 1940, when 'The Revellers', staged a show in aid of a 'British Legion Treat for Local children', which included *Jack Popplewell introducing his song success, with Emily Fletcher as vocalist'*. The song was the hit number 'If I Should Fall in Love Again'. On Sunday 16th January 1944, 'The Magnets' concert party presented a revue which included Jack Popplewell billed as *'Morley's own composer of popular songs with an interlude on the piano, assisted by John Goodson as vocalist'*. He played a number of his own compositions including 'If I Should Fall in Love Again', 'Only You' and 'Really and Truly'.

Also during the war years Jack was a popular member of the Morley concert party 'The Revellers' which travelled throughout the North of England providing much appreciated entertainment at Army depots and RAF stations. During 1940 he was introduced to the audiences as the 'News Chronicle' £50 song contest winner.

Mr. Jack Popplewell, a real celebrity, was born in1909 and died on 16ᵗʰ November 1997. His remains were 'buried at sea'.

Anthony Rooley.
Lutenist and Authority on Early Music.

Mr. Anthony Rooley

The Teenage Ramblers Skiffle Group was a popular act with the successful Morley Top Town Team; they are both mentioned elsewhere in this book, along with Jimmy Bywater one of its members. Another of the boys in the skiffle group to become famous was the self-taught guitar player Tony Rooley. Born on the 10th June 1944, the son of Madge and Henry Rooley, he left Morley Grammar School at 16 years of age to work for a while in Leeds before attending the Royal Academy of Music.

Having risen from a Morley skiffle player he became Anthony Rooley L.R.A.M. (Performers) i.e. Licentiate of the Royal Academy of Music and, in 1990, Hon. F.R.A.M. i.e. Fellow of the Royal Academy of Music.

Mr. Rooley now enjoys an international reputation as a lutenist, discovering and playing forgotten masterpieces from the Renaissance. In 1969 he founded the 'Consort of Musicke' and, as its director, has steered the group from strength to strength. The Guardian reported, *"Few have done as much to revive the sensibility and thereby the stature of early English music as Anthony Rooley and his 'Consort of Musicke.' This renowned ensemble is dedicated to the research and performances of the vast repertoire of music for voices and instruments from the sixteenth and seventeenth centuries. Perhaps one of the greatest contributing factors to the group's success is the consistency of its personnel. Despite their individual careers the members have continued to work together to create an ensemble in which the singers know each other's voices intimately. Sopranos Emma Kirkby and Evelyn Tubb, alto Mary Nichols, tenors Joseph Cornwell and Andrew King, and bass Simon Grant form the nucleus of all the Consort's work, spending much of the year touring at home and abroad. The group has an abundance of recordings many of which have been made for 'Musica Oscura', the record label established in 1993 by Anthony Rooley in partnership with Arjen Terpstra."*

Mr. Rooley's ventures into television and radio include 'Banquet of the Senses', featuring the 'Consort of Musicke' performing exotic madrigals by Claudio Monteverdi in the setting for which they were written, 'The Palazzo Te in Mantu'. He was also credited with the musical research for the 1983 B.B.C. T.V. film of 'The Two Gentlemen of Verona'.

In 1982 he wrote the 'Penguin Book of Early Music'and in 1990 Element Books published his work 'Performance: Revealing the Orpheus Within'. This achieved worldwide readership and was translated into Japanese.

Anthony Rooley has also been involved with Radio 3 projects including 'Perfect and Endless Circles'. Created with the novelist Russell Hoban, to mark the 350th anniversary of the death of William Lawes, it has been described as a *"delicious mix of music and speech"* and its poetry has even been compared to Dylan Thomas's 'Under Milk Wood'. As a highlight to Purcell's tercentenary year, Anthony was involved in a bold and progressive reworking of Henry Purcell's and Thomas D'Urfey's musical play 'Don Quixote'. He collected together the original scores and scoured source material for incidental music resulting in the musical weaving together of the 1690's and the 1990's.

In addition to all his many activities Mr. Rooley still manages to teach and also to perform concerts in many corners of the globe, both as a soloist and in small ensembles.

It has certainly been a steep climb from his boyhood days in a Morley skiffle group to a leading authority on early music and expert lute player.

Robert Stead.

In 1854 Mr. Samuel Stead established Morley's first printing press in a building near Morley Bottoms. He eventually considered the Morley public would support a local weekly paper printed in the town for the benefit of the townspeople. He launched the Morley Observer in 1871 and the Stead family ran it for the following 85 years. The paper is, of course, still in existence.

Mr. Robert (Bob) Stead, who was the grandson of Samuel, was born in Zoar Street in 1909. On leaving Morley Grammar School he went to work on the family paper serving as chief reporter and then news editor. He especially enjoyed reporting the Morley Rugby Union matches.

He was the youngest member of Morley Town Council when he was elected a councillor in 1933. In 1939, at the outbreak of war, he was appointed an Air Raid Precaution report centre officer in Morley until he joined the Royal Navy in 1942. He served as a lieutenant on board mine sweepers and then in a naval training establishment.

When hostilities ceased in 1945 he was appointed the senior talks producer for the B.B.C. at the Manchester studios. He became a representative for the B.B.C. in Australia, New Zealand, Africa and the Caribbean until 1958 when he was appointed controller of the north region

The Wheatsheaf Hotel was situated in America Moor Lane. For many years the inn provided lodgings for theatricals engaged to perform in Morley. It is thought the two little people were performing at The Victoria Music Hall, see page 108.

of the B.B.C. Radio in Manchester. He was responsible for the start of the 'Gardeners' Question Time' which became so popular it had a 15-year waiting list for venues wishing to host the programme. Morley Town Hall was one of them.

He worked in Australia for a while with the radio network there.

For many years Mr. Stead was a member the Morley Liberal Club and he was also a founder member of the Twenty-Four Hour Luncheon Club. He was awarded the C.B.E. in 1965.

Robert Stead was well known in Morley as an active and talented member of the Old Morleians' Amateur Dramatic Society. Besides contributing to several editions of the Medical Charities' Carnival magazine 'The Rag Bag' in the early 1930's he also helped to write and produce a number of the revues presented for charities on the stage of the New Pavilion theatre. Among them were: -

Week Commencing Monday 18th February 1935.
The Revue
'Lets'
Devised and Produced by 'Bob' Stead.

Week Commencing Monday 15th February 1937.
The Revue
'Encore'
'Bob'Stead was a member of the cast.

Week Commencing Monday 1st November 1937.
Emlyn Williams's Play
'Night Must Fall'
Robert Stead's acting was "*well received*".

Week Commencing Monday 14th March 1938.
The Revue
'Choose 'Ow'
(On this occasion Mr. Stead was the compere introducing the entrants in a talent contest, which included Ernie Wise.)

Three Nights Commencing Thursday 13th February 1941.
A Variety Show
'Music Hall'
Robert Stead was a member of the cast.

Mr. Robert Stead passed away at the grand age of 92 in April 2001.

Ernest Wiseman.....Ernie Wise.

Ernie Wise kindly enclosed this photograph when he wrote to Ronnie Barraclough in 1998 with his reminiscences concerning his appearance at Morley's New Pavilion theatre in 1938.

This is not the place, nor is it necessary, to record the amazing achievements of the much loved, nationally famous, laughter-provoking duo of Morecambe and Wise as their rise to fame is so well documented. They were two entertainers who could attract T.V. audiences of up to 29,000,000 and really did "bring sunshine" into our homes.

This book can only be concerned with artistes born in the old Borough of Morley, or who spent their formative years in the area, consequently this is the story of the early days of one of this fabulous pair, Ernie Wise, who certainly qualifies, if anybody does, to be included under the heading 'Didn't They Do Well'.

Born on 27th November 1925 Ernest Wiseman arrived in Ardsley as a baby when his parents brought him to live at 12, Station Terrace, East Ardsley, a railway house which was eventually demolished for the construction of the motorway. His father, Harry, was employed by the London & North Eastern Railway Company at Ardsley but in his spare time enjoyed entertaining at local venues. He used the stage name 'Carson'and it is thought he was the 'Ted Carson'billed as *"the versatile entertainer, a lad from Morley"* when he appeared on the stage of the Pavilion on 4th January 1928, and *"for a return visit"* on 11th May 1928. On those occasions he performed between the screening of silent films. With a weekly railway wage of £2 the extra money earned in the field of local entertainment was a welcome addition to the family finances.

Ernest attended Thorpe Junior and Infant school and when he revisited there in 1990 he reminisced about the good memories he had of those days. His later education was at East Ardsley Boys'school where he professed he did not have a very happy time.

He was quite a seasoned performer by the age of nine and, as he was the only one with any show business experience, he was always asked to produce the school pantomime.

When only six years of age his father introduced him to the stages of

Working Men's Clubs in Leeds and Bradford, first as a double act, 'Carson and Kid', and then as a very popular solo boy entertainer, singing, telling jokes and dancing.

The Leeds education authorities objected to him working late in the evening and at weekends and his father was told he had to stop exploiting him. He ceased performing in Leeds and instead took up engagements in the Bradford area.

Ernest was 13 years of age when discovered by the bandleader Jack Hylton and this led to a change of name to Ernie Wise and the historic meeting with Eric Bartholomew, resulting in the formation of the legendary partnership of Morecambe and Wise which was to span over four decades and reach unprecedented heights. The forty-three year partnership ended when Eric died on Monday 28th May 1984. Ernie retired from show business in 1995 and died on Sunday 21st March 1999.

Ernie performed on the stage at Morley's Pavilion theatre, although he was the 12 year old Ernest Wiseman at the time.

The Old Morleians' Amateur Dramatic Society staged its 1938 revue 'Chuse 'Ow' at the Pavilion theatre from March 14th to 19th and a local talent contest was included in the programme. The request for entrants was worded as follows: -

A fine chance for local amateurs.

Do you want to take part in the OMADS revue?

Can you dance, croon, play a musical instrument, give impersonations or be funny? Each night of the revue, prizes will be awarded to the winners of a local talent competition.

Auditions will be held shortly to select suitable entrants

Whether you are eight or eighty, send in your names now to

Mr. Harold Leathley, "Ashleigh", New Park Street, Morley (secretary of the OMADS)

Write now!

The preliminary rounds of the contest were held on each evening during the week with the final at the Saturday performance. The entrants that did not make it to the finals were: -

Mr. W. Mountain (age 25), ventriloquist.

Carine Abbey (11), tap-dancer.

Janet Holmes (16), vocalist.

Beatrice Matthew (13) & Elsa Riva (12), song & dance artistes.

Ronnie Mitchell (6), monologist.

Edith Gaunt (16), accordionist.

James Brooke (22), song impressionist.

Brian Killerby (12), monologist.

Leonard Dickinson (24), bone soloist.

Leonard Haigh (8), singer.

Mr. H. Drummer (23), (crooner).

The Saturday night finalists were: -

Phyllis Lessons (10), comedienne, Police Station, East Ardsley.

Hetty Harris (13), song & dance, 18, Bank Terrace, Morley.

"Whirlem & Twirlem", who were A. Sykes & J. Ackroyd, acrobats.

Stella Hodgson (13), song & impersonations, 176, Britannia Road.

and Ernest Wiseman (12), comedian, 12, Station Terrace, East Ardsley.

The voting by the audience on ballot papers was close. Each of the runners up received an award of half-a-guinea (52p?) whilst an additional prize of a special course in tap-dancing, given by the Society's ballet mistress, went to Hetty Harris. The first prize of three guineas (£3.15p) was awarded to Ernest Wiseman whose comedy song and clever tap-dance routine "brought the house down".

It was reported at the time that the audience thoroughly enjoyed the competition, which provided proof of the excellent standard of talent the Morley district can produce. The company joined the audience in the singing of the National Anthem.

Mrs Janet Wood (nee Holmes), Mrs Olwyn Chew and Mr. R. Barraclough mention this occasion elsewhere in the book

Just 12 months later, in 1939, Ernest Wiseman, billed as Ernie Wise, "The English Mickey Rooney" appeared on the stage of the Empire Theatre, Leeds in Jack Hylton's show "Band Wagon". It was one of the engagements on a tour of the British variety theatres.

Janet Holmes (now Wood) on the stage at the Pavilion Theatre in March 1938 as an entrant in the OMADS talent contest. The scene is set in a radio broadcasting studio.

Entertainment Through the Centuries

A journey through the history of Morley is to re-live the musical achievements of its people. If it is true that Nero fiddled while Rome burned, the seven hills of Morley also echoed to the sound of fiddling during the 18th century. Prior to that time the town was a small rural community and little is recorded as to how the villagers made music.

The life-styles and working habits of people in those early days were very different to the change brought about by the Industrial Revolution, which saw unprecedented growth in the area. As the mill chimneys pushed skyward and coalmines sunk ever lower in greater numbers, a new breed of worker emerged demanding more of their newfound fellowship. Here was the growth of the Non-conformist chapels and a widening of church activity in general. Where people had previously been content to listen to the fiddler and join in the occasional dance, there was now a growing desire to make music of their own. So came about the slow blossoming of choirs and bands.

The history of Morley is so overflowing with people joining together to make music that we as authors are sure to have overlooked some society or individual; for this we sincerely apologise. It has been a great joy to rewrite the facts that have been drawn together by historians over the years and to unearth other little known items during our research. That so many of our contemporaries have taken the time to write and share their precious memories has been of great encouragement. Our correspondents' enthusiasm for this project has continued to motivate the authors, their voices and music sing in the ears of our imagination and the faces of those within memory appear as fleeting images of yesteryear. The past is the past, but thank God, the present is still making music upon the very foundation laid by those now long gone.

Back in the 1700's a church such as **St Mary's in the Wood**, known at the time as the Old Chapel, had no organ and relied upon a violinist, violin cello and flautist to accompany its emerging choir. When the choir was absent **John Taylor** was known as the 'Tune Striker' and the congregation would follow his lead. Mr Taylor was also the bell-ringer and the gravedigger, truly a man of many talents. A lead singer of that time was **Ananias Illingworth** who could sight read and hit perfect pitch, any music of the day be it written in tonic solfa, bass or treble clef. St Mary's first organ (although a small one) was installed in 1798.

About that time a young man was developing his skills upon the violin of whom it was said *"all musical blessings flow, as far as Morley was concerned."* This was **David Hirst** a fiddler of great merit. He was still remembered long after his death on 27th July 1865 at the grand age for those days of eighty-six. **William Smith's** book **'The History & Antiquities of Morley'** printed in 1876 sets down:-

"Countless stories are remembered by our elder villagers of Hirst and his fiddle. How our village fiddler, accompanied by Tommy Blakeley and others, would attend oratorios for miles around, and having taken too freely of Yorkshire hospitality (then generous to an extreme) would come to grief with their darling instruments through some obliquity of vision or other cause as they were plodding their way homeward."

Hirst, or 'old Dave' as he was generally called was a supreme egotist and regarded himself as a Paganini, and was disposed to fault find and be critical of his musical associates. It was generally agreed that no one could have a higher opinion of his ability than **Hirst** himself. His virtuosity was self - taught and it was known for him to practice throughout the night, if faced with a challenging piece of music.

Old Dave's other legacy was to sire three sons, all of whom became eminent members of the musical profession and local society.

Strangely this rare poster of an early concert does not relate to 'Old Dave Hirst' or any of his three sons, but to a **J. Hirst** an exponent of the pianoforte. A question mark remains as to whether he is the Joseph Hirst involved in the next story. The National School was that early seat of learning adjacent to St Peter's Parish Church, until it was replaced in 1875 by the purpose built St. Peter's School nearby. The original National School is now the Parish Hall. One can only assume that the audience that evening in 1835 represented the 'nouveau riche' of the area's fast developing industrial base. Who else could afford to pay one shilling for a 'south end' seat, let alone two shillings for the privilege of the supposedly superior seating at the 'north end.'

But let's return to the early 1800's and the **Morley Reed Band** of some twenty or so members, including a **Joseph Hirst**, together with a **Thomas Rose, David Scott, Samuel Wade and Samuel Webster.** With a name like Samuel Webster in their midst one can but imagine the group's appetite for the products of his namesake in Halifax. Like Webster's beers, **The Morley Reed Band** was a quality product, and much in demand around the area. Before secret ballots Morley people had to journey to York to vote and on one occasion

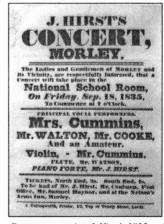

Poster announcing J. Hirst's 1835 Concert at the National Schoolroom, now St. Peter's Parish Hall.

77

the band appeared there at a Reform meeting. The journey in itself would be no mean feat in those days, let alone for a one-day gig. Years later it was recalled with pride how the band played through Tadcaster in the middle of the night during the return trip with complete disregard for the weather. The term used was *"it was raining like Old Harry."*

The band had one non-playing member of note in the shape of **John Sykes**. His official title was 'Drum Hugger', and as well as hugging the big bass drum around, he carried all the band's music in a satchel on his back. The drummer was a **Mr Fox**, and **Sykes** was so devoted to this percussionist, that during a concert he would take the weight of the drum so as not to tire the stick swinging Fox.

Later upon that very drum the date of 1848 was painted. This was the year when the band was reformed into the **Morley Brass Band**, and heralded an epoch of even greater achievement for the players. The transfer from reed to brass in that year meant a move up into the first division of the brass band world. The band won great acclaim for over a century, before they in turn were taken over by the British Legion. Some events and personalities are worthy of special mention.

Ceres Jackson was an orphan boy brought up at the New Inn, Churwell, and became a trumpeter so extraordinary in his talents, that many spoke of him as a genius. His ability to triple tongue was outstanding and accomplished with complete ease. He toured America as soloist with the Black Dyke Mills Band in 1906-1908. During the late Edwardian period he was in constant demand as soloist in the great Messiah performances. At the Leeds Coliseum with Dame Clara Butt and David Hughes before an

Morley Brass Band with Mr. & Mrs. Harry Hardy outside their home, Croft House, Town End, Morley in 1948, the band's centenary year.

audience of 3000, his rendering of 'The Trumpet Shall Sound,' so electrified the company he had to take ten curtain calls. He was engaged later to conduct local bands, but his impatience with those less talented than himself, made him a disliked master.

100 years after 'Drum Hugger' Sykes, the band had another such loyal and devoted member in **Richard (Dicky) Barker**. Barker spent a lifetime serving the band prior to the outbreak of the Second World War. Mr Barker is still remembered today, for a slight speech impediment that meant 'Dicky' sounded like 'Ditty'. Many of us will not be remembered for a single thing, but dear simple Ditty has written himself in Morley's history by his unswerving dedication to the band.

The Morley band was a power in the competitive field for over 70 years and won many prizes. **Harry Castle** was the last permanent conductor with **Arthur Hopwood** as principal cornettist. In those closing years of the band's history, other bands sought to attract such players as **R. Brooke** and **S. Osborne**, but probably the best remembered player was another **Samuel Webster**, a bass trombonist better known to hundreds of bandsmen as **'Bunk'** or **'Bunkus'** because of his great girth. The year before the band was taken over they won The West Riding Band Contest at Knottingley Town Hall, being conducted on the day by the great Bernard Behrens of Black Dyke fame.

The Morley Harmonic Society was formed in the early 1870's for the purpose of encouraging the study of vocal and instrumental music. Many influential townsmen formed an energetic committee, led by **Mr G. H. Stead** Secretary and **J. W. Bowling** of Heckmondwike, conductor. The intention was to organize an instrumental band and chorus capable of performing the best music and of undertaking concerts of a superior style. By 1876 the society had *'publicly rendered some of our greatest oratorios with credit to themselves and with satisfaction to the public.'* (The words of **William Smith**).

In 1881, the full band and chorus of 150 performed Mendelssohn's 'St Paul' at the Ebenezer Schoolroom on Tuesday 18th January.

It is likely that players involved with the Harmonic Society Orchestra, were also members of **The Morley Private String Band,** which performed around the same period. The ensemble played many halls around the West Riding and frequently in their hometown. In the 1800's visits were made to the Baptist Tabernacle, a rather grand sounding Soirée at the Co-op Hall, followed by an entertainment for The Workpeople's Treat at the same venue. When a Mr Smith gave a musical lecture, the band provided musical backup; this could have been **William Smith** the historian, for his book on Morley had only been published a few years earlier.

As Queen Victoria's reign came to an end **The Morley Concertina Band**

Morley Concertina Band c1930.

made its debut and was popular in concert and at old time dances. The band consisted of many family members such as the **Sharps**, the **Sykes**, the **Mitchells** and the **Hawkins**. The popularity of the instrument went into decline as the 20th century progressed and did not survive the opening of hostilities in 1939.

If the concertina was a bellows and button keyboard instrument, a contemporary band was all strings and plectrums. This was the **Queen Street Wesleyan Mandolin & Banjo Band.** The thirteen players performed in many parts of the West Riding and rehearsed in a house behind **Harry Roebuck's** furniture shop in Morley Bottoms. It was not believed to have survived beyond the 1914-1918 war.

The Queen Street Wesleyan Mandolin and Banjo Band standing at the front of the chapel c1900.

MORLEY PARROCK NOOK ANTHEM PRIZE BAND 1907

The Parrock Nook Anthem Prize Band of 1907, with hobbyhorse.

The dawning of the 1900's spawned numerous comic carnival bands in Yorkshire, especially in the West Riding. It is an accolade to the working classes of the early 20th century and their inherent sense of fun that we place this item proudly alongside so many instrumentalists. In the Huddersfield & Halifax area, Brighouse formed 'The Wiffen Waffen Band', and nearby Lindley 'The Waffen Fuffen Band', while Holmfirth boasted of its 'Wonderful Wiffy Wuffy Band'. It was as one moved east towards Leeds that the organizers stopped waffling and introduced some originality into the names. While reverberations echoed from 'The Silsden Underground Artillery Band, Otley slaked the dust with their 'Splashum Splushem Band'. 'The Woodbine Willies' from Meanwood threw up a smokescreen against the formidable 'Hunslet Nanny Goat Lancers', who in turn tried to run rings round 'The Hunslet Jungle Band' whose music endeavoured to drown the sound of the approaching 'Airedale Fireside Lancers'.

Amid all this jollification, one stood supreme above all other bands in the West Riding, and was the one with the longest life. **'The Morley Parrock Nook Anthem Prize Band'** was formed around 1900 and existed continuously for at least 36 years. Its longevity can be attributed to the fact that the band was supported by a few families and, as the years passed by, sons replaced fathers.

Brass Bands were usually sponsored, but the carnival bands were formed from purely working class roots, relying on simple homemade instruments. They existed to take part in carnival competitions, to raise money for local charities, and to give enjoyment and fun to their audiences. Most towns and villages in the West Riding held summer carnivals that included prize

The Parrock Nook Anthem Prize Band when sponsored by the Yorkshire Evening News.

competitions to attract the attendance of the bands that often travelled distances to take part.

The basis for the strange looking musical instruments used by the bands was the simple 'Tommy Talker' or 'Kazoo' which was inserted into an amazing variety of specially constructed tin shapes or into everyday items such as old kettles, funnels and gramophone horns. The 'Tommy Talker' is not really a musical instrument but a method of amplifying the human voice by breathing or humming against a skin or paper membrane. To deter professional musicians from taking part in the competitions there was a rule that the instruments had to be home made. For band members fancy dress was the rule of the day together with a painted face if the character demanded further embellishment.

As can be seen from the two or three surviving photographs the band had a collection of the most bizarre shaped instruments, some of which were made at **'Tinner Taylors',** a long established and well-known Morley hardware trader. If the instruments themselves were strange, what about the name chosen for the band; there seemed to be no connection with the Borough of Morley. There is a Parrock Nook Congregational Church at Rishworth, near Sowerby Bridge. Perhaps people from Morley had seen an earlier band in that area and were impressed enough to start one of their own using the name Parrock Nook, but that is conjecture. The use of the word 'prize' in the name simply reflected the band's success. Over the years the band was a prodigious winner in competitions throughout the area. It was only beaten on one occasion before the 1st World War, by the Allerton Bywater Pit Band.

The Parrock Nook Anthem Prize Band

Anthems were an important part of the band's programme and were readily available from 'Service of Songs', a popular book of the time.

An extensive repertoire included the marches 'Georgia' and 'Belfiga.' Contrastingly 'John Brown's Body', was a typical comedy number, while the tragic 'If I Should See a Little Soldier Marching as to War', was intended to be a tear-jerker. ' Recitations from Shakespeare were often used in the sketches. A popular request was the **'Lee Fair Anthem'** for which the words of the first verse and chorus are :-

My Father's house above,
Oh when shall I be there,
To sing of thy redeeming love,
And all its glory share?

Yonder is my house and portion fair,
My treasure and my heart are there,
And my abiding home,
For me my elder brethren stay,
While angels beckon me away,
And Jesus bids me come,
And Jesus bids me come,
And Jesus bids me c-o-m-e,
While angels beckon me away,
And Jesus bids me come.

On entering competitions the bands usually had to agree to take part in a parade through the town or village and a prize was given for the best band in the procession. As a rule the band competitions were held in a local park and points awarded for the way they marched into the ring whilst playing. Each band performed a different set of numbers, and points were lost if a player took his instrument out of his mouth. Adjudication was based on smartness, upon a comic sketch performed to music and for a twenty minutes concert. In some instances it must have been acceptable for bands to perform similar sketches. There was an occasion when the Holbeck Jungle Band defeated the Parrock Nook Band because the judges decided that the Holbeck conductor 'died better' than the Morley leader during a performance of 'The Death of Nelson'.

For many years the band had its headquarters at The Cross Keys Hotel in Britannia Road, where landlord **Luke Crosby** was a keen advocator at all their performances. **J. Willie Spurr** was Morley's conductor and his costume was often a clerical garb. The organiser of its events was **Mr. J.W. Steel** of Rock Terrace, Albert Road, Morley but the accepted leader was **Billy Commons** who dressed as a dancing donkey. On other occasions **Capper Woodward** was the donkey and **Johnny Blackie** appeared as a bear complete with chain and attendant, **John Land**. John was also a female impersonator. As he marched **Jimmy Kelly** carried a mock gas lamp, fitted with a 'Tommy Talker' that he played while winding a handle as another bandsman climbed up and down the lamppost. **Joe Holroyd**, who was in the band as a youngster, performed a sketch with his father, which ended with the son pulling his staggering parent out of a pub while the band struck up with 'Father, Dear Father, Come Home With Me Now'. A hobbyhorse was featured in the 'Parrock Nook Band'and this, along with the quaintly painted faces, suggests a connection with much earlier English traditions

The 'Parrock Nook' was essentially a marching carnival band but it did perform on a Morley stage on at least one occasion. In December 1921 it played at the Pavilion accompanying the competitors in a contest for the best impersonator of Charlie Chaplin. At that time the Pavilion was a cinema and the event was to support the showing of the silent film 'The Idle Class', starring the great comic himself.

It was a sad loss to Morley when the **Parrock Nook Anthem Prize Band** ended in about 1936, although a small group stayed in existence until 1939.

The authors are indebted to the late Mr. George Atkinson for the many details of Morley's Parrock Nook as set down in his unpublished personal papers, and to David K Atkinson for allowing us to draw from his father's material.

The Morley Juvenile Band formed in 1910 by **Jim Issacs** under the patronage of **George Edwin Baines** of Britannia Mills met the same fate. Mr Baines, a great champion of music for the working classes, was also President of the Morley Vocal Union. In the few short years of their existence the band performed many times in Dartmouth Park and other towns around the West Riding.

June Watkins, a publicity sitting for the Morley Amateur Operatic Society's presentation of 'Carousel' at the Pavilion Theatre, Morley in 1960.

From the Morley Observer dated 15th January 1909 is a reference to **Fred Carr's Premier Orchestra.** This was also the earliest mention we can find of **The Morley Amateur Operatic Society** whose members were staging 'The Mikado' at the Town Hall. The advertisement heralded the *'special engagement of Fred Carr's Premier Orchestra'* and *'Fred Carr's professional band has been engaged.'* It gives the impression that the orchestra was a greater attraction than the music of Sullivan or the words of Gilbert, or indeed the society members who were due to perform.

Fred Carr was a music teacher living at 21 Pawson Street Morley, and he formed his professional orchestra to undertake engagements at various venues in the area. As well as musician, it would appear that he was an excellent publicist and a PR man living way before his time.

When the New Pavilion Theatre opened in December 1911, the

Fred Carr with his 'Pavilion Orchestra of Talented Musicians'. Mr. Carr is seated holding the baton. This photograph was taken at the entrance to the Townend National School, only a few yards from the Pavilion Theatre's stage door.

GEO. GLOVER'S
FAMOUS
ORCHESTRA.

HIGH-CLASS ENGAGEMENTS, CONCERTS, BAZAARS,
AT HOMES, &c.

TERMS:
GEO. GLOVER, 23, KING STREET, MORLEY, LEEDS.

Mr. George Glover taken in 1914 when he resided at 25, King Street, Morley

management hired Carr and his musicians to form the theatre's resident orchestra. They were always billed as *'The Pavilion Orchestra of Talented Musicians under the direction of Mr Fred Carr.'*

The Theatre suffered a fire in 1913 and pending the necessary repairs and refurbishment, dramatic productions took the place of variety. Fred's orchestra was no longer required and their last appearance was to provide backing music to the silent film 'The Mysteries of Paris'. For five weeks the Pavilion presented films while the stage area was rebuilt for stage productions. A contemporary of Fred Carr was **George** an insurance agent and musician. In 1905 he lived at 5 King Street Morley, but moved higher up the road to number 25 in 1914. He advertised *'Geo. Glover's Famous Orchestra. High Class Engagements, Concerts, Bazaars, At Homes, etc.'* Not quite the razzamatazz of Fred Carr, but perhaps Mr Glover did seize the opportunity of filling a vacuum when the Premier Orchestra went full time at the New Pavilion theatre after it opened in 1911.

Many top class musicians originated from Morley and **Mr. Alfred Inman** was a violinist 'out of the top drawer.' His full story is featured elsewhere under 'Didn't They Do Well?'

There was a direct connection between **Alfred Inman** and **Tom Jenkins**, Morley's truly great violin virtuoso. Mr. Inman did not do much teaching, but in the early 1920's Tom Jenkins was one of his pupils for a period of four years.

A contemporary and life-long friend of Alf's is featured next. Both were elected life members of **Fountain Street Working Mens' Club**, a distinction of which they were truly proud. One wonders if the officials of that time, fully appreciated what a great position the club was in; for a workingman's club to have one distinguished professional musician as a member would be remarkable, but to have two is probably unique.

The contribution made by **Norman Hartley** to local music during the greater part of the 20th century would be difficult to exaggerate, for he is still remembered as Morley's **'Mr Music Man'.** His influence spanned the years with the same ease that his fingers covered the octaves and danced the keys, for here was a pianist who quietly combined musicianship with an imposing stage presence. Not for him the candelabra and sequined suits of

'Liberace', he possessed a black dinner suit, which he occasionally varied by wearing a cream jacket when appearing with **George Speight** in their act of 'Four Hands in Harmony'. Norman's name appears so many times within this book, it had been decided to leave this entry at the last full stop, but later Ron Barraclough intervened, *"oh come on David, he was your father-in-law, tell us something about the man that others are not likely to know."* So here goes.

Norman Hartley at the organ.

*"I sometimes find it difficult to relate to Norman as my 'father in law,' because he was my pal and musical advisor long before I married his youngest daughter. In my singing efforts, he was always there to help, and on more than one occasion his uncanny skills as an accompanist saved me from disaster. He could recognise the key I was **not** supposed to be singing in, and transpose the accompaniment to suit; he would know why I had left out the second verse and anticipate that the missing words would emerge from my inconsistent mouth somewhere between that omission and our arrival at a unanimous conclusion. I knew I was wrong, and he knew I was wrong, but he never said so. The audience, thinking the performance to be faultless would be as generous as ever, but it was Norman who deserved the plaudits.*

To not have him at the keyboard always created in me a feeling of 'there being something missing' in my performance. On the other hand he could be the very devil if he so chose. Norman possessed a sense of humour almost as wicked as my own, and we would feed off each other. One of my regular numbers was 'The Sergeant Major's on Parade', which involved quite a bit of business between the verses and chorus. One of his favourite tricks was to improvise and depart from the set music. This would involve a 'staged confrontation' between the two of us. The trouble was I never knew what he was going to play; it could be anything from 'the Laurel & Hardy' theme, to the 'Dead March from Saul'. If he thought the occasion appropriate he would play an obligato completely foreign to what I was singing just to see if I could stay on course, and acknowledge my pleading glances toward the keyboard with a look of assumed innocence and complete rapture.

On leaving school he was put into the printing trade as an apprentice, but little is known within the family of those early days. His marriage lines (1921) record him to be 'a printers journeyman', and later documents dated 1927, list him as 'a professional musician'. It would appear that throughout his working life he combined his printing work with that of a pianist, although during the heyday of the silent screen his playing became a fulltime occupation.

He was 17 years old when he gave his first performance at the Palace Cinema, Morley, and later worked at the Town Hall, which also showed films and variety acts between screenings. Norman had to play for them all. The seats were 1d, 2d and 3d. Moving on, he worked for the New Century Picture Company in Leeds, where he covered 12 cinemas. He also played the Queen's Theatre, Holbeck with a small orchestra.

It was after the collapse of silent films that he returned to his work as a printers' compositor. To plot his precise movement in the workplace is difficult because Norman was a fiercely independent in all things except his home life, here his wife Linda nurtured and spoilt him to an extreme.

What is known is his dedication to provide the needs of a young family. During the slump in the late 1920's and early 1930's he was out of work and had to put his piano playing talents to work in an area where he disliked performing. He played in pubs and clubs in order to provide the essentials for the growing family.

Then came the war, and though too old to be conscripted, he took war work as a government official checking the quality of the armaments coming out of Fairburn, Lawson, Coombe & Barbour at their Kirkstall Road factory in Leeds. He was later moved to the George Cohen works at Stanningley. Whenever possible he devoted much of his leisure time to the Voluntary Entertainment Services and was widely travelled in and around Yorkshire. Most Saturday evenings he would be at the keyboard with George Speight and his band, playing for the ballroom dances held at the Morley Town Hall; it was here in the Alexandra Hall that I first saw him and met his two daughters, Muriel and Mavis.

After hostilities he returned to his old trade of printers compositor and worked until his retirement for Tillotson & Firth just off Church Street. One of his regular assignments was the racing calendar for the Bookmakers' Protectiom Association. A BPA calendar was always hung at home to record and monitor his many gigs and engagements. The family always knew when there was racing at Fontwell Park, although no one had the least interest in 'the horses'. What they did need to know was where Norman was gadding off to on his many evening and weekend engagements, and Linda needed to have a shirt washed and ironed. Norman was most particular about his appearance and would spend a considerable time cleaning and polishing his shoes. He would be horrified by today's 'trainer' generation.

He had a vocabulary all of his own and many of his words are still in regular daily use within our home. Norman would never use an expletive or be profane, so he invented his own method of swearing; 'jiplops' and 'chelbs' were much to the fore in times of difficulty.

In winter his fingertips were prone to damage and would crack open. I know that these fissures were most painful for both his types of work (sorry no pun intended). He would bandage his fingers for typesetting, and revert to flesh coloured plasters for his stage work. In his later years he also suffered from bronchitis, which finally ended his long association with the Operatic Society. Their shows were always in the depth of winter and the long stint of sitting in the orchestra pit for six nights proved too much for a man now in his seventies. I am convinced that his music ability came from deep within his soul, and perhaps, from some previous existence. Norman was the master of his trade and yet largely self-taught, his only period of training having lasted just one year.

Following the death of his wife Linda, Norman tried to carry on his life in Morley, but he was now in his eighties and did not find life easy. During their 51 years of marriage, Linda did everything for Norman except eat his food and put him to bed. As a result, Norman found difficulty in providing for himself. The family joke was 'Dad can't even boil an egg'. Sadly the patriarch had to give up his independence and love for Morley and move to Leeming in North Yorkshire where Mavis and I ran 'The Willow Tree Inn'. He was not wanting for company, but did not seek it, and even stopped playing during his final months. The piano in his room remained silent.

He entered the Friarage Hospital Northallerton for a minor operation, but alas he contracted pneumonia. Mavis was so upset by his laboured breathing and the prognosis we had been given, that I persuaded her to go home.

The man I had first met in 1944 died peacefully in November 1979 at the grand age of 84. Even in approaching death there was a moment of pure farce; not funny at the time, but looking back on the incident, I know Dad would have enjoyed the moment. The Sister in charge had offered to move him into a small private room, which I thought a good idea. We were all in one accord, except for the bed, which proved to be of non-standard width, and would not meet the rigid requirements of the door. Having got poor Norman along the corridor, I had to help tilt the bed at an alarming angle to gain access into our quiet haven. Norman remained unconscious, but knowing him, he would have overseen all the kerfuffle with much amusement.

He seemed to like his new quarters, for his breathing settled down, and he seemed to be at peace. In musical terms it was his final diminuendo, and within a couple of hours he was gone. I was able to hold his hand during that time, just as he had held mine on stage."

Billy Theaker & His Orchestra alias Willie Theaker and his New Variety Orchestra, alias Billy Theaker's Variety Band, alias Billy Rekeath & his New Variety Orchestra

The following details are the unedited words of **Mr Joe Tetley** of Churwell, to whom we extend our sincere thanks.

*"I started to learn to play the violin in 1939 when I was seven years of age. My teacher was **Mr Billy Theaker** who, at that time, lived in Commercial Square and worked at Jackson's, Peel Mills, but prior to that he had been the musical director at a number of theatres and cinemas throughout the north of England.*

I progressed with the instrument sufficiently to be invited by Mr Theaker to play in his various orchestras. In those days boys did not wear long trousers until they were 13 or 14 years of age, which meant I was the only musician, clad in short trousers and long stockings, no matter how prestigious the venue.

I remember playing between three and four hours at various Morley 'Mayoress at Home'functions when the orchestra provided Palm Court type music.

During the war years the citizens of Morley, and the troops stationed in the town, needed entertainment to help them through those hard dark times, and the Pavilion Theatre provided it with many Sunday night concerts, always to support charitable causes. Billy Theaker's Orchestra was the mainstay of many of the amateur companies that staged these shows. The 'OK's', the 'ATC 's', 'Happy Landings', 'Leeds Sylvians', 'Northern Commanders', 'Northern Spotlights', 'Smilers', 'Victory', 'Hotspots', 'Rockets'and others were all concert parties of that time.

Mr Theaker occasionally changed the name of his orchestra to add variety. It was also know as Willie Theaker and his New Variety Orchestra, Billy Theaker's Variety Band, also Billy Rekeath & his New Variety Orchestra (ie Theaker in reverse). Coincidentally there was a magician who performed in some of these concerts under the stage name of 'Maharg', this being his surname Graham in reverse.

When the orchestra played at the Pavilion Theatre it was seated in the old orchestra pit amongst the dust, old orange peel and paper wrappers until the musicians rebelled and were allowed to play on stage behind the performers. This became modern practice in theatres and on television.

I remember Mr Arthur Spencer, who was the manager of both the Picture House and the Pavilion played the drums, and Willie Sibley was the first violinist. I was the fifth violinist, but only 10 years of age.

I especially recall the shows produced by the Rockets Concert Party, and staged by permission of Japa Paper Products Ltd of Churwell, with the proceeds being donated to the Japa Service's Welfare Fund and to St Dunstans. The group was organised by Winnie Cheesman, who became very deaf and had to lip read; she always wore trousers and ruled her concert party with a rod of iron.

We all had plenty of fun on the occasions of the Sunday concerts, rehearsals were held on the afternoons, prior to the evening show. As a 10 year old I thought I was in a different world and would not have missed those times for anything."

Herbert Johnson was the first Morley pianist to achieve more than local fame and made many appearances with the first Choral Society between the wars. He became a fine accompanist and interpreter of songs for leading singers of his day. A noted exponent of Chopin's work, he gave many recitals around the UK.

Sidney Johnson, who was born at Mount Pleasant on Albert Road, became a well-known cinema organist with a flair for interpreting the classics upon the giant wurlitzers of the day. His wife was the daughter of the famous Leeds surgeon Dr Maxwell Telling and after her sudden death, Sidney went to America to display his mastery of the cinema organ.

Emerging from the chaos of the Second World War Morley was privileged to enjoy the emergence of several young musicians. **John Barstow,** now Professor of Pianoforte at the Royal College of Music in London; **Paul Trepte,** currently organist and choir-master at Ely Cathedral; while **Anthony Rooley and Trevor & Geoff Bastow** are featured elsewhere in this book in the chapter **'Didn't They Do Well?'**

Another young pianist and organist who stayed within the town and has given long and loyal service to the Morley Music Society, is **Geoffrey Dunn.** Geoffrey's parents are remembered for their services to the **Tingley Sylvians,** with father **Harold** being a particularly fine tenor who took many principal roles within Gilbert & Sullivan shows and church music. Geoffrey's mother always provided support from the chorus and encouraged her son into a love of music. Geoffrey has been a Hon Accompanist to the **Morley Music Society** since 1958, and at the time of writing is fast moving toward his golden jubilee in that office.

The post war years heralded a golden age of young singers of great merit, the girls always having to endure fierce competition should they aspire to principal roles in any of the local societies. To add to their musical prowess many of these young ladies, had a wonderful stage presence and acting ability; thus some quality singers were sidelined because of their lack of presentational skills.

There were several contraltos of outstanding quality and ability. Top of the tree here stood **Jean Scott, Nancy Sykes and June Rhodes**. The last named was not as serious in her ambitions towards acting, preferring the concert platform. She did enjoy a professional singing career with The Cliff Adam's Singers and has now returned to the area to live. The 'off-comed-un' does have one gloriously funny memory of June when we were in prison together. **'The Revellers'** were visiting Wakefield Prison to provide an evening of entertainment to men serving long-term sentences for a variety of offences. It was June's first visit to one of HM establishments, but she did not allow her youth and ebullient approach to life to be overawed by the sombre surroundings. June had taken a tape recorder and asked where she could plug it into the mains. A prison officer offered to help, but found that the plug on the machine was incompatible to the prison's circuitry. So a 'trustee' knowledgeable in these things was summoned to put things right. He proved to be a taciturn and abrupt member of the congregation (we were in the chapel), and obviously wished to be left to get on with job unhindered. June stood over the poor man dressed in her best evening dress. She did look quite stunning as the unfortunate chap set to work on his knees, while June engaged him in unwanted conversation. Her many questions remained unanswered until she finally over stepped the mark by asking *"what are you in for then?"* There was a deathly silence as our electrician stopped working, laid aside his screwdriver and slowly looked up into June's eager face and replied in

a menacing voice *"RAPE."* That fault was never remedied, but the electrical one was, and the show recorded to June's satisfaction.

Jean Scott was truly the 'Kathleen Ferrier' of Morley's contralto world. Like her family, she was a member of Queen Street Wesleyan Methodist Chapel and of course she sang in the choir. Jean remained a

An artists impression, drawn in 1886, of the choir at The Old Chapel (St. Mary's Church) as it was one hundred years earlier, in 1786. Old John Chappel played the violincello, John Bilborough the left handed fiddle and the un-named flautist was said to play a 'wretched' flute. (see page 76)

loyal member of the choir in spite of her many successes on the concert platform. There was a period when she had to rest her voice because of problems with her vocal chords; this must have been exasperating for her, but she never showed annoyance or indulge in self-pity. In her later years Jean has not enjoyed good health, but like her sisters, the **Scotts** are remembered for their talent, their warmth and their ability to laugh at whatever life threw at them.

Nancy Sykes progressed into the world of the professional artiste with ease, for she was the one who dealt with the technical side of singing with consummate ease. In her retirement she does not want to become involved with this history, which is a great pity because many people remember her wonderful voice and the pleasure she gave to so many audiences. Her wishes are respected.

In the realm of the soprano voice, Morley's cup 'truly ranneth over' during the mid twentieth century, and many young ladies had to compete with an awesome collection of talent were they interested in playing a leading role in local societies. The authors walk a tightrope here and apologise in advance for any omission and failure to recall those voices that have (and still do), give melodious service to the choirs and societies of the district. In living memory the doyen of the local soprano world was **Emily Fletcher**, or to adopt the more respectful terms of address used until the advent of the Second World War, **Madame Emily Fletcher**.

Emily and her husband **Albert**, were a delightful pair who shared a sense of humour that carried them through life on the crest of a wave. If you are partial to the power of an operatic diva akin to that of Montserrat Caballe the Spaniard who sang that memorable duet 'Barcelona' with the late Freddie Mercury, then you would have loved Emily's singing. Not only had she the gift to sing and entertain on the concert platform, but an inherent talent to encourage and teach the young singers with whom she came in contact. The 'off-comed-un' had the great privilege to be taught by this lady, and it was she who added quality to a voice of limited range. The Fletchers lived just beyond Victoria Road School in Asquith Avenue, and Madame Fletcher was in fact the Spirella Corset Company's representative for the area, and had her fitting room at her house. It was literally a case of fat ladies calling to 'have it all taken in,' while us singers visited to 'let it all come out.' Emily was a lady of great influence, and it was a sad day when she and Albert retired to Kendal to be with their daughter Grace, who was married to Robert Cooper (another Thespian) who ran Pickard's Chemist shop on Scatcherd Hill for many years.

A group photograph of the Morley Top Town team that took part in the Ossett contests in 1958. Back row from the left:- Norman Hartley, pianist. The men in the check shirts are Alan Rhodes and Ron Whittam. The young men in white were the "Morley Five" skiffle group, Peter Austerfield, Barry Normington, Tony Smith, Maurice Lees and Keith Robinson. The two ladies are Gloria Mundy and Blanche Walton and between them is David Reekie and then George Speight, pianist. Third row from the left:- Norman Stevenson, Vernon Sykes, Fred Dale, Dennis and Stella Scargill, Brian Scott and Leo Leathley. The row of ladies has the two commeres Pat Ross on the left and Anthea Topham on the right, flanking the eight "Debutantes". The front row from the left:- Freddy Pickstone, Barry Collins and his sister Brenda extreme right. (see page 192)

Jocelyn McGough first hit a wider public in the Operatic Society's first post war production of 'The Vagabond King' and whilst she was later to leave Morley, it is a delight to her many friends that she keeps in contact from her home in Buckinghamshire. Here not only was a voice that stopped conversation, but one that flowed from an actress of natural ability.

Jean Lloyd achieved many leading roles with the Operatic Society, but was not the most fortunate of actresses, for things had a nature of going wrong whenever Jean was around. But no one can deny she was a most talented young lady.

Blanche Walton started her days with The Tingley Sylvians and the concert platform; she later played demanding roles on The Pavilion stage with a natural charm that gave the impression of *"I'm not acting, this is me for real"*.

Stella Scargill was a performer of all-round talent. Soubrette, comedienne, impersonator, soprano, pianist and actress; the 'off-comed-un' can feel her presence as I type, for she is saying *"what are you doing putting me among the Sopranos?"* My reply is simply *"who played The Merry Widow then?"* Her marriage to **Dennis Scargill** after he came home from war service in the Far East created a musical duo, which was unrivalled for its originality and entertainment value. With Stella at the piano and Dennis expertly strumming a ukulele, their voices combined to the popular music of the day; their teamwork was much in demand. Dennis took a home-study course to become qualified in the Chartered Institute of Secretaries and worked in that capacity for Sir Harry Hardy at Rods Mills, and continued as manager after the business was taken over by Rentokil. The pair eventually moved to Filey and ran a holiday apartment block for a while, and Stella became involved as accompanist to The Filey Fishermens'Choir. At that time their son **Martin** (an accomplished pianist & musician) was teaching at the Hunmanby School and today is wholly occupied in teaching pianoforte at his home near Driffield. Both he and his wife **Joan** are still much involved with Morley affairs.

There were several voices that did not make the 'big-time'in the amateur world and who can say why. One such who was always a joy to be with whether on a concert platform or not, was **Christine Brook**. Christine sings on today in the ranks of the **Morley Music Society** and she does it for the pure joy that song can bring to the inner person. More young people should try it.

Of the young men around at that time, it was the likes of **Harry Burrow, Clifford Barrass** and **Harold Dunn** who successfully strode the huge gap caused by the Second Great War. Local baritone soloists who were prepared to dress up in tights were at a premium, and it was easier to find a volunteer among tenors. **John Goodson, Noel Jelly, Tony Roberts** and **Roland Smith** come to mind, with one very fine alto voice in the shape of **Harry Fearnley**. Among the choirs their were many fine bass voices, who seem to have little inclination towards going it alone, but one particular young man's performance at The Town Hall stands clear in memory. He was very young, very tall and as immature as his singing voice as he sang 'Asleep in the Deep'. The occasion was to promote National Savings, 'the offcomed-un'together with Delia Broadley, were asked to judge an array of young entertainers. The basso-profundo was unplaced, and I received my come-uppance from the boy's mother who belayed me about with a rolled umbrella; *"call yourself a singer? You*

In 1960 Tony Roberts performed in 'Carousel'.

Margaret Nowell (now Bunney), is the young lady at the back right of the photograph, which was taken at the top of the stairs at the New Pavilion Theatre for the 1960 production of 'Carousel'. The young man in the centre is Peter Powell.

couldn't recognise a musical note from an elephant's xxxx.' She was right of course, and I decided there and then never to sit in judgment again.

Let us not forget those responsible for comedy and dance. Where does one start and at what point can one finish. In comedy roles the most prolific of players over many years was **Peter Powell**. Such was success that neighbouring societies sought his services and at the height of this man's remarkable career, he would be involved in several shows at the same time. Perhaps this explains why he remained a bachelor. Offstage Peter is an inveterate teller of tales guaranteed to keep everyone in stitches of laughter. He later served backstage as a Dresser for many of the post-war stars playing The Grand Theatre Leeds.

Some consider the soubrette the 'all-rounder' of any production. They were judged upon their ability to sing, dance, act and be funny all in the one package, and few met the criteria. **Annie Peel** played such roles before the war and in The Vagabond King in 1947, and continued to be a mainstay behind the scenes with husband **Sam Peel,** for many years. **Rene Burrow** who has made such a huge contribution to the local stage is featured along with husband **Harry** in the early chapters of 'Didn't They Do Well'. **Barbara Holliday** too continues to achieve so much for the Operatic Society, and progressed from a dancer, to performing small specialty parts, to playing leading roles. **June Watkins, Marjorie Firth, Beth Pashley** and her sister in law **Margaret Pashley** are all prime examples of timed performance and splendid moments of comedy.

Terpsichore was the goddess of dance, and she provided Morley with

The principals in 'Oklahoma' at the New Pavilion theatre in November 1958. Back row from the left: David Hirst, Arthur Wilson, David Reekie, Steve Till, & Maurice Lapish. Centre row from left: Renee Burrow, Delia Broadley, Peter Powell, Anthea Topham, &Kathleen Webster. Front Row from left: Harry Burrow, Jack Wright & Bernard Atha.

more than its fair share of her handmaidens. It is only possible to name but a few, but the high kickers involved with the OMADS, the Top Town Team and the Operatic Society were second to none. They were even exported to less fortunate neighbouring societies. Carrying on a pre-war role was **Olga Brown**, who eventually handed the reins of responsibility to **Millicent Hirst** (Kitson). Millie was the architect of the troupe that set the standard for the amateur stage in Morley and beyond. It is a tribute to her success that young girls were eager to join the dancing team in the knowledge that it was the best, and that during their stay in her care, they would be well looked after.

The **Joyce & Dorothy Dancing School** took many aspiring dancers through their first faltering steps in Morley during the mid 20th century. **Joyce Rushforth** and **Dorothy Metcalfe** were dancers of exceptional talent and were responsible during the dark days of war for staging over 500 shows for charity as well as appearing with **The Revellers** in countless performances around Yorkshire entertaining the troops. **Jean Spruce** remembers the two with great affection and in recent times it had been hoped achieve a reunion of all concerned, but sadly both Joyce and Dorothy died before a date could be fixed.

In final memory comes the curtain call of all the entertainers very necessary for any operatic or church society to stage an amateur show, which does not pretend professionalism, but actually achieves it. It happened time and time again...IN MORLEY!

Early Entertainments

During the 19th Century the continuing industrialisation of the old towns in the West Riding of Yorkshire meant they were subject to massive social changes and expansion. Morley was not an exception. The construction of large woollen mills attracted a huge influx of workers and their families. In the 50 years from 1861 to 1911 the population of Morley Township swelled from 6,840 to 22,095, an increase of 223%. For the greater part of the 19th century the new mill working class were accommodated in small, overcrowded 'back to back' properties, without indoor toilets, proper bathing facilities or gardens. They were employed for long arduous hours in poor working conditions with inadequate financial remuneration.

In such austere times there was an eager demand for any inexpensive entertainment to ease and divert the mind from the drudgery of the day. So the scene was set for any form of diverting street entertainment. There were many visits to the town by an assortment of individual street performers, singers, musicians, barrel organs, tingalary men, and on one occasion, a dancing bear. These performers attracted groups of onlookers and were especially enjoyed by the children who followed them from street to street.

Wandering entertainers of a more organised kind also found their way to Morley; itinerant quacks, clowns, conjurors and strolling players offered amusement out-of-doors, in barns or in public houses. In later days the field belonging to the Nelson's Arms would become a venue for flower and agricultural shows, football and cricket matches, but in earlier times, after the enclosure of the commons, it had accommodated the tents and caravans of these early enterprising travellers. A rickety platform set in front of a caravan would be the stage on which to present clumsy conjuring tricks, clowning, fire-eating and various feats of agility. Gurning through a horse-collar by volunteers from the audience was a popular event. A clown introducing a lottery, or a lucky bag would often conclude the shows. There would be a number of prizes on offer, the principle one being something of considerable value, perhaps a silver watch. But the gullible public would only receive boxes of ointment and other quick quack remedies, never the valuable prize.

Another source of entertainment was the eagerly anticipated Morley feast, which in those days was held annually, for one week commencing on the third Monday in September. Before the construction of the Royal Hotel and adjacent shops in Morley Bottoms there was open land to enable the event to be held, but even so it spread over the site of the town quarry, down Low

Common (Station and Albert Road), up Middlethorpe (Queen Street), along Brunswick Street, and half-way up Chapel Hill. One of the principal attractions was **Sam Wild's 'Theatrical Booth'** where his troupe of artistes performed on a stage lit by a row of blazing grease pots depicting heroes, heroines, kings, queens, warriors and murderers. Children peeping through the chinks at the rear of the tent would be intrigued to see Hamlet patching his own coat or Lady Macbeth returning with a quart of ale from the old Malt Shovel, an inn situated on the site now occupied by the Morley Conservative Club.

'Old Templeton', another travelling theatrical, not only visited the town for its annual feast but also called at other times of the year to present popular plays, 'Jack Sheppard', 'Maria Marten, or The Murder in the Red Barn' and 'The Mirfield Murders'. On occasions Mr Templeton would engage the favourite Yorkshire tragedian Mr Henry Loraine to perform in works of Shakespeare. In the play 'The Lady of Lyons', Henry Loraine, as the character 'Claude Melnotte', was seen addressing with a dignified air, the character 'Pauline'. However on closer examination, 'Pauline'could be recognised as the lady who had earlier taken the admission pennies at the door, and later during the interval quickly passed amongst the audience selling oranges, apples and stale buns. Such diverse duties were necessary to keep the show on the road.

For many years, until early in the 20th century, Morley people greeted with enthusiasm the regular years round visits of their favourite travelling theatres. These migrant companies offered variety and music hall type of entertainment, with occasional primitive early silent film shows. Others presented dramatic productions staging their full repertoire with a different play being performed each evening.

The tented and alfresco theatres and their accompanying horse-drawn caravan homes for the artistes, would stay in the town for long seasons or short stays, setting up temporary establishments at the Scatcherd Lane Athletic Grounds, on spare land in Morley Bottoms or at the Feast ground opposite Morley'Oil, behind the old Dartmouth Arms.

The Princess Theatre was for many years a welcome visitor and always attracted good business from a populace ever eager for pleasant diversions. The type of entertainment offered, and the support it received can be gleaned from a contemporary report of the theatre's 1882 visit.

"Mr Clegg caters well for the public of Morley and continues to receive good patronage. The play 'Seven Sins' was produced and it was certainly one of the best dramas that have been given. A new popular play entitled 'Drink' was given; Mr C Hale was the life and soul of the act. On Saturday night nearly 2,000 people witnessed the 'Striking of the

Hour', an historical piece of Cromwell's times, full of interest and well sustained by the entire company. Mr Vollaire, the leading actor, is a good player, his articulation is bold and clear and the audiences show how they appreciate him. A variety of plays will be produced on this stage."

If the circumstances were accurately reported, there was a huge audience of nearly 2,000, demonstrating the capacity of such theatres with the bulk of the audience probably standing in the open air. It also shows the extent of the company's popularity in the district, and why it continued to visit Morley for many years. The size of the audience is also remarkable in relation to the town's population, which was only some 21,000 in 1882.

The members of travelling theatres must have endured an austere existence, especially during the winter season. This was demonstrated by the tragic events that overtook the **Princess Theatre** eleven years later, during the 1893 season in Morley. Mr Abraham Clegg established this theatre in 1858 and it operated principally in Yorkshire over a period of 36 years, visiting Morley on numerous occasions. When Mr Abraham and his wife died within a few days of each other, their daughter, Miss Marie Clegg, sold her permanent theatre in Heywood Lancashire, and with her brother, Mr Charles Clegg, took charge of the travelling **Princess Theatre.** Marie's husband, Mr Hodgson, was also a member of the theatre company but Marie was better known by her maiden name. Marie studied drama at an early age and at only seventeen played an entire repertoire of female Shakespearean roles such as 'Juliet', 'Lady Macbeth', 'Portia', 'Ophelia' and 'Desdemona'. She was a young lady with a lot of talent and could have had a bright career in the acting profession but she would not abandon her 'family theatre'. During its 1893 season in Morley, the theatre along with its attendant caravans was located in Morley Bottoms. There both Marie and her brother Charles were taken ill. Neither of them missed a performance, both struggling on until Miss Clegg had to take to her sick bed for one week. She recovered sufficiently to continue performing until Thursday March 30th when she had great difficulty completing her part in the play 'Routh's Wife', when once again she was found to be suffering from a lung infection. Meanwhile her brother Charles Clegg had been taken ill after having watched a cup-tie between Morley and Bruntcliffe, which lead to pleuro-pneumonia and his unfortunate death on the morning of Saturday April 1st. Marie already in her sick bed, was informed of her brother's death and the shock was so great she never spoke again but she was able to shake hands with her relatives, friends and members of her beloved theatre before passing away the following day. The brother and sister died within a few hours of each other, as had their parents before them. Marie's husband, Mr Hodgson, was also ill and was taken from his caravan to a bed offered in a local private house, where he eventually recovered. The funeral of Marie and Charles Clegg took place on Wednesday April 5th 1893, the service being conducted in the theatre by the Rev E James of St Peter's Church in the presence of about sixty relatives, friends and fellow actors. Several thousand people assembled in the area of Morley Bottoms and Station Road; the police under the supervision of Inspector Hobson, had some difficulty in holding back the crowd. The cortege of twelve carriages travelled to Heckmondwike cemetery and en route the members of another travelling company added to the long procession.

The Alhambra Theatre was another peripatetic theatre, which from 1904, visited Morley on a regular basis. It claimed to be the best company because it travelled with an efficient orchestra under the leadership of Mr Vincent Stanislaus Chapman. The proprietor, Mr Fred Blake and his company staged their entertainment at the feast ground during February 1907. A different play was presented each evening, with musical interludes by the **Morley Brass Band.**

It was reported during his visit in the spring of 1908 that Mr Blake offered the following productions before *"large and enthusiastic audiences even though the weather was most unfavourable"*. The programme demonstrated the versatility of the members the company and the hard work involved in producing the different plays on successive evenings.

The programme of events for the **Alhambra Theatre:**

'Mixed'. A screaming comedy
'The Parting of the Ways'
'The Little Outcasts'
'The Devils'Mine'. Interspersed with songs
'The Saughram or Conn why did you die?'An Irish drama
'The new Arrival'. Followed by singing and a sketch
'A Brother's Sacrifice'. A dramatised version of Ouida's 'Under Two Flags'.
'Our New M.P. A mysterious drama
'The Earthquake'. A new drama, first time in Morley, specially written for this theatre, with special effects designed by Fred Blake
Also singing by Messrs Attwood, Todd and Waller
'A Struggle to Live' and a funny sketch written by H. Plean 'On the Brain'
'Lesh, the forsaken Jewess'with Miss Alice Greenwood as 'Lesh'
'Lads in Red'or 'The Fighting Curate'

'East Lynne'The popular drama
'Rip van Winkle'or ' The Sleep of Twenty Years'and
song and dance by Misses Winnie & Bessie Blake
'Firematch the Trooper' followed by a concert and sketch
'The Earthquake' Reproduced at the request of many patrons
'The Power of a Mother's Love'
'Napoleon'a historical drama
'The Factory Lass'or 'All That Glitters is not Gold'
'The Ticket of Leave Man'
'Jealousies'A domestic drama.

During the holidays there will be a pantomime 'Babes in the Wood'.
No expense spared. Bright music. Pretty scenery.
Lovely dresses. Original jokes.

*A valuable acquisition has been made to the company in Mr Teddy
Sheeny.*

Mr Blake's Alhambra Theatre was a well-known and popular visitor
always giving value for money. In addition to the variety of plays
offered there were musical interludes at each performance, including
songs by Messrs Roy Walker, Bert Attwood, Will Blake, Fred Blake and
the sisters Blake; all the family participated. It was truly a Blake
enterprise.

At the Morley Borough Court in April 1909, Mr Blake was granted
permission for his ten year old daughter Laura to occasionally play a child's
part during the theatre's stay in the Borough. It was promised every care
would be taken of the child in the theatre, which closed at 10pm. It was
stated Laura was in regular attendance at a council school. The Bench
granted permission but stipulated that she could only appear on one
occasion each week. This condition was not offered to child performers at
the New Pavilion Theatre when it opened two years later; here the child
performers were required to work six nights a week!

In October 1908, when the Alhambra Theatre was working at Idle, Mrs
Fred Blake was taken seriously ill and had to remain there for some weeks
eventually rejoining her family who by then were performing at Elland.
The next venue was Milnsbridge and from there Mrs Blake was taken to
Leeds General Infirmary where she did not survive an operation.
Arrangements were made by Mr Blake to hold the funeral service at the
Morley Catholic Church, with Father Mitchell officiating. The whole of the
Theatre Company, friends and supporters from the towns in the area

attended. The interment took place at Morley cemetery. Mr Bert Attwood, a popular actor and entertainer, was a member of the company on each of the occasions it visited the town. This talented performer made numerous friends in Morley, who were sorry to learn of his death in 1911 at the Queen's Hospital in Birmingham. He had been taken ill on stage whilst touring with Mr Arthur White's Theatre Company, which he joined on leaving the Alhambra.

The Rhodes & Vinces Royal Entertainers offered a different type of entertainment at the Feast ground during the summer of 1907 when it was announced.

Commencing Whit-Saturday May 18th 1907 for the summer months
Change of programme and specialities each week
The most refined and original entertainers before the public
Small charge for seats, hat passed round those standing
Includes songs, duets, jokes and dances.

The Royal Magnets with Mr A Robertson as the licensee and manager, advertised its presence at the Scatcherd Lane Athletic Grounds from Monday July 20th 1908. Unfortunately because of the poor weather the performance of this 'out-of-doors' company had to be transferred to the Town Hall for the last two weeks of the season, commencing on Monday September 14th. Earlier in the year this company completed a tour in the south-west of England, having performed at Bournemouth, Plymouth, Sandown, Shanklin and Ventnor, before travelling direct to Morley. **The Royal Magnets Theatre** described itself as

The smart-set serenaders in an entirely new, bright, smart and up to date Alfresco entertainment under the direction of Mr Walter Gordon. Clever artistes. Smart costumes Everything to please. Nothing to offend the family entertainment of Morley Every evening 7.45 prompt. Doors open 7.15 Tuesday & Saturday afternoon 3.0. Doors open 2.30 Popular prices 2d, 4d, 6d, Children half price. Everybody goes to see the Royal Magnets. A first class stage lighted by gas.

The Excelsior Entertainers was another open-air theatre and its visit to Scatcherd Lane Cricket ground in 1909 coincided with the Alhambra Theatre's season at the Feast ground. The two organisations were not in direct competition for each offered a different type of stage show. They were in direct competition when they met in a charity cricket match at Scatcherd Lane on Wednesday May 26th 1909.

The Excelsior Entertainers offered

Grand opening night Monday May 3ʳᵈ 1909.

Something novel. Something new.

Smart costumes. Lightning programme. No waiting.

New songs, duets, trios, quartettes.

Interludes. Funny sketches. Concerted items by the following recognised artistes.

Deno and Drew

The great pantomime comedians will present during the season.

All their original musical comedy tit-bits, "Eh! That'll be nice".

Edward Stream

The light comedian and burlesque actor. Singer of the latest chorus songs.

J. P. McBride

Baritone & descriptive vocalist, late of the Royal Carl Rosa Opera Company.

The Excelsior Pictures

The latest and the best.

Lily Mould

Dainty soubrette.

Stuart Braide

Humorous entertainer.

Hilda de Grey

The Yorkshire favourite soprano, Tyrolean vocalist & burlesque actress.

Frank Deleno

Comedian, siffleur (whistling artiste) and expert dancer.

Engaged for a short season at enormous expense.

Change of programme twice nightly. Come in your thousands.

No expense is being spared in trying to make this the finest and most up to date Alfresco entertainment in the United Kingdom.

Great illuminations of electric light. Special scenery and novel effects.

Popular prices 9d 6d 3d Children under 12 6d 4d 2d.

Matinee every Tuesday & Saturday at 3.0.

Fresh air and entertainment combined. A marquee has been provided for wet nights.

Performance wet or shine.

Unfortunately there was almost continuous cold and rainy weather that badly affected the audiences during the three month visit. The General Manager of the company, Mr George Barry, eventually became the first manager of the New Pavilion in 1911.

The Copenhagen Theatre in 1908 was on a site in Commercial Street when Misses Mitford & Bond and their company performed the comedy 'Wanted a Wife'. On one occasion the performance was for the benefit of the Morley Tradesmen's Benevolent Association when a hearty vote of thanks was accorded to all on the motion of Mr R. Metcalfe (president of the Association) and seconded by Alderman W. H. Jowett (secretary).

The travelling theatre contributed much to the moral welfare of Morley, and inspired many an amateur to give entertainment a try in the atmosphere of the Victorian parlour and the music created by that era. The talents of the people spread into the churches and chapels as societies were formed to give amateur performers a platform. This emerging capability for self-entertainment together with the opening of the town's own New Pavilion Theatre, signalled the demise of the travelling theatre in Morley.

The tented big tops continued their tours, with such as **Lord Sanger's Circus** visiting Morley between the wars. This great impresario was also responsible for **Lord John Sanger's Circus and Variety**, which toured the country in 1946 & 1947 and although his tour did not include Morley, it did have a special significance for Morley's own E**rnie Wise** *'England's Mickey Rooney'* and **Eric Morecambe** in *'Strike a New Note for Comedy.'* The Big Top did not have a circus ring, neither could it boast exotic animals, but it did have a horse and a performing dog troupe, along with a clown and trapeze act. The 700 strong audience faced a stage with the emphasis upon variety acts. The show also included *'Our Lovelies... The Four Flashes...Dancing Feet.'* One of these lovelies was a **Doreen Blythe,** then 15 years old, who was destined to become the wife of **Ernie Wise** on 18th January 1953.

The Royal National Theatre toured Britain in 1998 with its 'Mobile Big Top'presenting Joan Littlewood's 'Oh what a Lovely War', and included a stop at Dewsbury. The ticket prices of £12 to £20 were somewhat higher than the 2d to 6d charges by the travelling theatres of 90 years earlier, and there was no facility to 'pass a hat round for those standing'.

The Temperance Hall.

Although no longer used for its original purpose, The Morley Temperance Hall is still situated in Fountain Street, erected in 1895 by the **Morley Temperance Society** at a total overall cost of £2,000. One of four foundation stones was laid by his Worship the Mayor **Charles Scarth J.P.**, on May 18th 1895. In that same year the Town Hall was built, which gives an indication of the emerging pride and confidence within the borough.

The Morley Temperance Society had been formed in 1832 at the instigation of **Joseph Dean**, a local blacksmith, echoing the formation of the national movement in that same year. **Dr. Swindon** presided over the meeting that was called to promote the idea.

The first floor hall was used for the occasional stage show as when the **Black Diamond Minstrel Troupe** performed there in October 1909. But it was also used as a cinema as early as 1911 when **Oliver Gomersal**, (described as a music hall proprietor), was served a summons by Morley Corporation, for non-payment of £27.13.0d to the Corporation for electricity supplied to him during his tenancy of the hall which he used for cinematograph shows.

The Yorkshire Animated Picture Company held a 'Grand Opening Night' on Monday April 10th 1911 when the hall was described as 'the

The Temperance Hall, Morley in the early 1900's. Most of the posters are advertising outings to London by the Great Northern Railway Company from the nearby Morley 'Top' station.

Interior shot of the 1ˢᵗ floor hall within the Temperance Hall.

house of realistic living pictures'. The opening programme included the films 'Her Adopted Parents', 'The Lover and the Count', 'Bronco Bill', 'How the Tenderfoot Made Good', 'Tontolin's Aeroplane' and 'The Curate's New Year Gift'. The admission prices were 2d, 4d and 6d.

By the following year **The Imperial Electric Picture Company** had taken over the tenancy, presenting films nightly, except Tuesdays, with matinees on Saturdays. The pictures were said to be 'pleasingly varied and very steady'. For a period from 1912, the hall was known as **'The Imperial Picture House'**.

The Temperance Hall was used as a cinema showing silent films well into the 1920's when **Mr 'Chiddy' Hardy** managed it. His one-man operation of the establishment became one of Morley's legends. After purchasing admission tickets from Mr Hardy at the Fountain Street entrance, his patrons were required to queue up the staircase until he eventually passed them on the stairs to unlock the hall door; he then collected the tickets he had just sold, before becoming the projectionist. The audiences were seated on long wooden forms. If the projector failed temporarily, or if any reels were inadvertently shown in the wrong order, there would be a loud chorus of catcalls and the thunderous din of children's feet stamping on the wooden floor.

The Morley Vocal Union rehearsed in the premises for many years, and gave occasional concerts in the hall. After the Second World War it continued as a church for quite a while until the owners decided to capitalise upon an undoubted asset. The premises became a base for a firm of Veterinary Surgeons until they too moved on. As we write (2002), the future use of this fine Victorian building is not known.

How much would it cost to buy the land and erect its like today?

The Victoria Music Hall.

Benjamin Hale Worrall was born in Morley in 1839 and on completion of his rudimentary education, he served an apprenticeship with **Mr. William Whitaker**, a master plumber of Chapel Hill. After some years in the plumbing business, Benjamin Worrall was able to purchase the Alliance Hotel situated in Queen Street. In 1880, after buying a plot of land in Hope Street, opposite his hotel, he opened Morley Market. He was also the owner of Morley's only baths that were situated in Zoar Street.

In 1882 the **Nelson Cricket Club** moved to a new ground in Scatcherd Lane and changed its name to **Morley Cricket Club**. Three years later Mr. Worrall bought the ground and a large plot of adjacent land which he named **Queen's Park.** The grounds covered the area between Fountain Street, Scatcherd Lane, the Great Northern Railway line and New Park Street. In addition to cricket matches the park was used for athletic meetings, brass band contests and horse trotting, a sport for which Mr. Worrall was an enthusiast. He owned a stable of horses.

Benjamin Worrall served in Morley's local government and he was in charge of the scheme to bring Morley its own water supply by the construction of Withens Clough reservoir and 21 miles of pipeline but he unfortunately died on 1st December 1892, at the age of 53, before the works were completed. At this time he was residing in Cragg Vale House in Hope Street and his last speculation was to buy shares in Blackpool Tower.

Mr. Worrall's background is a fascinating part of our local history but the real reason he is included in this book is because of his ownership of the **Alliance Hotel** where he established on the top floor the **Victoria Music Hall.** It was opened on the night of 6th September 1879 with the engagement of a ventriloquist by the name of Professor Ritching, a vocalist billed as Monsieur Ricardo and the Brothers Nash, negro comedians. Later the same year the name of the hotel was changed to the **Queen's Hotel.**

The Victoria Music Hall provided entertainment for some 17 years, until 1896, charging 2d, 4d and 6d for admission; the sales of the ale, which was brewed on the premises, often being higher than the ticket receipts. During its life the hall engaged every type of 'turn' available; trapeze artistes, comedians, vocalists of all kinds, dancers, animal acts, ventriloquists, acrobats, Punch & Judy, male impersonators, eccentric knock-abouts, tight rope walkers, dioramas, sketches, marionettes, jugglers, black & white minstrels, circus acts & sword swallowers.

The standard of the performers varied from the downright awful to that of excellence, with the better and more popular ones being offered return engagements. Fees varied from 10/- to £9, but most came away with around 30/- for the week. Artistes performing in the Leeds theatres would sometimes be engaged to do an 'extra turn'at the Victoria, with speedy transport provided by Mr. Worrall's own trap and trotting horses. An occasion remembered in the town for years was when a circus was hired, the animals were taken to the top floor without any problem until it was the turn of the young elephant, unfortunately it became stuck on the staircase and this resulted in an almighty struggle until the beast was eventually returned safely into Hope Street.

The Queen's Hotel in the 1880's. It had four floors with the Victoria Music Hall on the top floor. The board on the front of the building in Queen Street advertised the forthcoming attractions booked for the Music Hall. The cabinet on the gable end, in Hope Street, had a display of photographs taken by the Morley photographer J. Firth, his residence and studio in Queen Street being demolished to make way for the Town Hall.

In October 1882 it was reported *"Mr. Worrall spared no expense to cater efficiently for the amusement and comfort of his patrons by having the hall thoroughly cleaned and painted, giving it a very comfortable and attractive appearance. In addition to the new ceiling and wall decorations, the panels in the front and sides of the gallery were alternatively filled in with excellent oleographs and mirrors surrounded with gilt moulding".*

In addition to the **Victoria Music Hall** Mr.Worrall offered a variety of facilities to his patrons at the **Queen's Hotel** including:- Restaurant, Luncheon Bar, Dining and Coffee Rooms, Lavatories, Baths and Good stabling. He advertised Dinners from 1/- and Teas from 4d in the upstairs Commercial Dining Rooms and Dinners from 8d and Teas from 3d in the Working Men's Dining Rooms on the ground floor. Dinners and Teas could be sent to any part of the town with the promise orders would be promptly attended to.

In March 1897 the **Morley Town Council** accepted an offer from **Mrs. Worrall** for her to present an oil painting of her late husband to be placed in the Council Chamber. So should you visit our wonderful Town Hall and benefit from one of the available conducted tours, look up to **Benjamin Hale Worrall's** portrait and think upon this remarkable man. Later, if you have a mind to, take a walk along the street named after him, and look at the area he once owned. But perhaps his greatest legacy to the people of Morley was the part he played in bringing ample and fresh water to the town.

The hotel was reduced to its present two floors in 1939.

The Town Hall

Built at a cost of £41,227 the Town Hall was officially opened by the **Right Honourable H.H. Asquith Q.C.,M.P.** and **Mrs.Asquith**, on 16th October 1895. Within this magnificent building is the 'large hall', which for the opening ceremony, is said to have seated 1,200 people. After the 1902 Coronation of King Edward V11 and Queen Alexandra, the hall was renamed the **'Alexandra Hall'**. Over the years this hall has been a popular venue for many amateur and professional presentations, including concerts, plays, recitals, lectures, wrestling matches, variety and cinematograph shows. Examples of the professional theatre groups that have performed there are the **Black and White Minstrels**, which proved a great success in January 1909 and the Bert Grapho company. This group presented *"a new and original spectacle titled 'Village Nuts', a pantomime in miniature with never a dull moment",* for one week commencing Monday March 24th 1913.

An unusual occasion was on Monday April 17th 1911, and all the week, when Tom Diacoff presented the *"Greatest Sensational Cycling Act ever seen in Morley",* featuring Mrs. Diacoff, the *"World Champion Lady Cyclist",* in the 'Great Cycling Whiz'. It was claimed the act caused a sensation at the London Pavilion, in Continental Music Halls, and on a three-year tour of India. Also on the bill was Le Diablo, the *"World's Sensational Cyclist, who had caused a great sensation by looping the loop at the Leeds Coliseum".* The event was claimed to be the most expensive ever to appear at the Town Hall. The admission prices were 3d, 6d, 1/-. & 1/6. The programme included the projection of 10,000 feet of film. Mr. Tom Diacoff was, at that time, the general manager of the Alexandra Palace Theatre, situated only a few yards from the Town Hall, but there was insufficient space to stage this spectacular event at his own theatre. His loyalties must have been divided that week between the two venues.

In those early years of the 20th century the flickering and jerky silent films were a novelty that attracted enthusiastic audiences and the Town Hall was a popular venue for travelling cinematograph companies. The Excelsior Animated Picture Company arrived for a season in the September of 1908, after completing a successful 14-week run at the Irving Theatre, Seacombe, bringing with it, as acting manager, Mr. George Barry. This and subsequent visits to Morley resulted in him becoming a popular figure in the town and led to his appointment as the first manager of the New Pavilion when it opened three years later in 1911.

This company returned to the Town Hall in January 1909 when the film shows were supplemented with variety acts, including Mr. Barry in *"his latest American Song Scena"*, in which he gave an effective rendering of the illustrated song entitled 'If I Should Plant a Seed of Love'. This company was again presenting film shows at the Town Hall in October 1910 when, at the Morley Borough Court two employees of the company were charged with the theft of admission tickets. The case revealed that the name George Barry was a professional one, his real name being George Attack.

Another travelling film company was Henry Hibbert's High Class Animated Pictures that opened at the Town Hall on Monday January 6th 1909, for two weeks. The films shown included one of the Empire Day at Sydney *"with a marvellous drill display by 70,000 children"*. There was also the special engagement of a Miss Gertrude E. Crann. Also in 1909 there was a two-week visit, commencing on Monday October 4th, by the Orient Giant Electric Picture Company with a programme of both films and novelty entertainers.

Yet another mobile company, The Royal Animated Picture Company, arrived on Monday August 2nd 1912 and stayed into October offering programmes that included sequences taken of local subjects by the 'cinema camera'. One filmed report was of the funeral of Morley's third mayor, **County Alderman David Thackray J.P.** Another showed the funeral procession of General Booth, who had earlier visited Morley. The programme for the week commencing Monday October 7th 1912 included 'Hamlet' in which the famous Morley actor **Mr. Henry Ainley** figured prominently, but alas a silent 'Hamlet'.

The L & Y Exclusive Picture Company opened at the Town Hall on Monday April 7th 1913, for three weeks, and once again there appeared to be a division of interest between the Town Hall and The Alexandra Palace. On this occasion Mr. Ralph W. Sheard was the resident manager at the Alexandra Palace and also the general manager of the L & Y Exclusive Picture Company. During its stay the company claimed to be the sole owners of the exclusive rights to a film of 'Les Miserables'. Victor Hugo's masterpiece had been transformed to a film 12,500 feet long, in nine parts, giving a three hour continuous performance. Seats were bookable at **Birdsall Bros. (late Wallis), The Hatters & Hosiers, 85, Queen Street, Morley.** Further programmes included the films 'The Fighting Parson' and 'As in the Looking Glass' with Marion Leonard.

From those early days before the advent of silent films there have been, for well over 100 years, all kinds of events staged at the Town Hall for the benefit of the people of Morley. These events are so numerous it is impossible to record them here but let us hope this magnificent Morley building will be allowed to continue to offer entertainment throughout the 21st century.

Alexandra Palace Theatre.

The Morley Corps of the Salvation Army was founded in 1882 originally meeting in a room at Morley Market until 3rd February 1883 when "The Barracks" were opened in Albion Street. On Saturday 31st August 1907 Commissioner Hey, the Chief Secretary for Great Britain, opened a newly erected citadel, situated in Ackroyd Street, where it still is today. The transfer to the new stone built headquarters left vacant the previous barracks, a wooden structure situated behind the Manor House and alongside the Borough Arms, now the Slip Inn. When it housed the Salvation Army the building had been described as "not too comfortable or cheerful" and also as "a wooden shanty".

The old building was renovated and partly reconstructed and, on Monday 6th July 1908 it was opened as **The Empress Palace Theatre** with the aim of supplying "wholesome and amusing entertainments in the form of stage entertainment and animated pictures etc." The theatre was constructed of timber and must have been a fire hazard but prospective Morley patrons were assured that full consideration had been given to their safety. It was publicised every care had been taken against fire, the whole building being lit by electricity, special emergency doors provided and a fire proof iron room erected which isolated the auditorium from the projection equipment and this was claimed to be "one of the latest model bioscopes with every improvement and patent to meet the requirements of insurance companies". Application was made to the Morley Borough Court for a permanent music and dancing license and it was explained to the bench the aim was to provide variety turns and high-class cinematograph entertainment. It was stated the hall had a seating capacity for 573 persons and every precaution was taken against fire; there were fire buckets and fire extinguishers in different parts of the theatre, two large doors at the front of the building and a large emergency exit at the rear. The hall could be cleared in three minutes; there were no staircases. Inspector Vaughan reminded the Bench that the West Riding County Council had refused a stage license on the ground that the building was not in accordance with its regulations. Nevertheless the Chairman said the license would be granted on the condition there "should be no shouting in the street". By October 1909 the theatre had been re-named **The Alexandra Palace Theatre** and at that time the management emphasised the theatre was clean and comfortable and "thoroughly heated by the latest scientific principles".

During the evening performance on Saturday March 16th 1912 a film ignited but the premises were evacuated using both the ordinary and the emergency doors without panic or mishap. Fortunately two members of the Morley Fire Brigade were present and they quickly extinguished the flames before they could spread to the wooden walls and floors of the building. This incident caused sufficient damage to close the theatre for one week for redecorating and for new seating to be installed. That was the intention but as there was a national railway strike in progress it was not possible to transport the new seats to Morley and the reopening was delayed until April 2nd. Admission prices at that time were 2d., 4d. & 6d. There were a number of changes to the management over the years but they all seem to have been colourful characters and there were also all

Morley Town Hall in the Autumn of 1912 when it was the venue for the Royal Animated Picture Company from August to October.

types of variety acts engaged during the life of its stage. In the summer of 1912 there was a further name change to **The Alexandra Picture Palace** as by then the establishment was a cinema showing silent films with an occasional stage act.

It continued to exhibit films into 1915, the year it is thought to have closed.

The Alexandra Picture Palace in 1913 when it was a cinema showing silent films.

The New Pavilion Theatre

Mr. David James Collins the manager of the New Pavilion theatre in 1913 & 1914.

Asouthward walk along Morley's Queen Street brings into view the unexpected and handsome red brick and white tiles of the New Pavilion. Rising above the slope of South Queen Street and then soaring higher still at the rear, where the tower like structure originally housed the 'flies'over the stage, the building is today an incongruous sight, but it must have been even more so to the people of Morley in 1911 when they witnessed the appearance of its pristine and elegant façade in the midst of a then soot blackened all stone neighbourhood.

In recent years the building has been used as a nightclub and a bingo hall. Earlier, during both the silent and sound film eras, it was a cinema; it is, however, fondly remembered by many for its original function as a theatre, the heart of the town's amateur and professional entertainment. Over the years many varied events were presented at the New Pavilion including vaudeville, revues, variety shows, plays of all kinds, operas, ballet, musical shows, band concerts, jazz nights, musical evenings, organ concerts, political rallies, shows staged to provide funds for the victims of local disasters, for local and national charities or various war funds, and finally even religious meetings: all offered to the people of Morley from the stage of their own local theatre.

The year of 1911 was an unusually eventful and exciting time for Morley, marred only by the unfortunate death, at 61 years of age, of the Mayor of Morley Alderman **Joseph Haigh**, who died on 30th March whilst still in office. There were, however, joyful celebrations for the Coronation of King George Vand Queen Mary, which took place on 22 June. In April the Morley Borough attained its Silver Jubilee, 25 years with a Charter, a Mayor and a Corporation. On 5th July there was the opening of the tram route from the Leeds boundary at Churwell to Morley Town Hall, the line being extended to Tingley Mills on 21st October. Scatcherd Park, left to Morley by **Oliver Scatcherd,** was officially opened on 8th July and at the ceremony it was announced **Lord Dartmouth** had provided five acres of land for a further park, to be named Lewisham Park.

In addition to all these important events there was one in 1911 that would eventually give pleasure and enjoyment whilst entertaining generations of Morley people-the construction of the New Pavilion. In March 1911 it was announced there was to be, for the first time, a purpose built theatre in the town. The Coronation New Pavilion Co. Ltd. advertised for tenders in respect of the erection of the New Pavilion Theatre at the corner of South Queen Street and High Street. By May the theatre's first manager, **Mr. George Barry**, had been appointed and, on 27th May, the Mayor of Morley **Alderman S. Rhodes J. P.** performed the ceremony of the laying of the foundation stone. The construction continued at a rapid pace, the building being completed, including the interior fittings and decorations, ready for the opening on 11th November by the new Mayor of Morley **Alderman W. L. Ingle J.P.**

During its first eighteen months the theatre presented many variety bills, containing acts of amazing prowess. Drama was also offered, especially during the summer months when a stock company was hired. The theatre suffered a nasty fire on the morning of Saturday 1st March 1913, the stage area being destroyed but fortunately the auditorium was unaffected. The theatre reopened on 16th June 1913 with a new manager, **Mr. David James Collins**, and for the following year the theatre concentrated on dramatic productions. The years of 1915 and 1916 brought a mixed bill of variety, drama, musicals and opera. During the era 1911 to 1916 the variety bills usually included one or two silent films but it was decided to fit modern projection equipment and, on Monday 14th August 1916, the Pavilion became a full time cinema presenting silent films. The situation was now reversed and single variety acts were engaged to appear between films. This change was because of the shortage of acts caused by war work and also because of the ever-increasing popularity of cinemas. During the following years this policy remained unchanged until, commencing on 23rd September 1929, the Pavilion once again became a professional theatre presenting variety each week. Talkies had been invented and the audiences were no longer willing to pay to see silent films. Another policy change was made when talkie equipment was eventually installed and the Pavilion became a cinema again from 1st June 1931 although the popular stage show 'Sunshine Sally' was staged in 1933 and 1934. Back projection equipment was used for the films and the stage facilities were thankfully retained enabling the theatre to be used for amateur shows presented by local societies and organisations for the benefit of Morley audiences. The first society to book the Pavilion was the Old Morleians Amateur Dramatic Society on 19th February 1934, with the revue "Help". The Morley Technical Institute Amateur Operatic Society's first presentation at the theatre was 'The Desert Song' on 28th November 1938 and that organisation gave the last ever show staged there, 'Kismet', on 4th December 1967.

The New Pavilion closed as a cinema and became a Bingo Hall in July 1968.

It must be recorded that during two world wars the citizens of Morley, and the troops stationed in the town, needed entertainment to help them through those dark hard times and the New Pavilion did not let them down.

The Picture House

In June 1913 old cottages, in an area of Queen Street known as The Barracks, were demolished to make way for the town's only purpose built cinema. The Morley Picture House Ltd. had been formed with a capital of £5,500 with Mr. W. P. Schofield of Park Row, Leeds engaged as the architect. The object was to build a first class and well appointed picture-house with seating for 700 persons, together with the aim of offering a 'high class and refined entertainment.' The construction, decoration, equipment and furnishings were to be 'substantial and modern,' and an attractive tea lounge and a cafe were also to be included. Although primarily built as a cinema it was hoped it would also be used for meetings, dinners and various public functions.

During its construction there was an unfortunate accident when a workman fell to his death whilst engaged in asphalting the roof. The cinema eventually opened on Monday December 1st 1913 to begin a 46-year service to local cinemagoers, presenting film entertainment that provided pleasure through times that were often austere and difficult. The escapism it offered during two world wars was especially welcome. On Saturday evenings during and after the 39/45 war, the management operated two separate performances for which it was necessary to pre-book seats in order to ensure a place.

Initially there had been some reluctance on the part of the business people of Morley to purchase shares in the Morley Picture House Ltd. Fresh in their minds were the investments lost in the failed Morley Skating Rink venture. However the cinema was most successful and investors were well rewarded. Dividends eventually reached 40% and this rate was maintained for many years. The company eventually purchased the New Pavilion and operated it, under the same management, as a sister cinema to the Picture House.

In 1930 at a cost of over £2000, the British Thompson Houston Co. Ltd installed the latest 'talkie' equipment and on Monday May 19th 1930 the Picture House opened its doors to offer this new development in entertainment. The first talking picture presented was 'Sunny Side Up' which featured Janet Gaynor and Charles Farrell. Crowds flocked to see and hear it and there were full houses all the week.

The next major innovation was when the Picture House was closed temporarily for the installation of cinemascope equipment. The Mayor, **Alderman H. Malcom Smith** re-opened the cinema on Monday January 3rd 1956 when the first film to be shown with the new system was 'Seven

Brides for Seven Brothers' with Jane Powell and Howard Keel.

For some years there had been a demand for the Morley cinemas to be allowed to open on Sundays. Other towns and cities in the area enjoyed films on Sundays, some having had this facility for many years, but not Morley. Things came to a head when a public meeting was held in the Town Hall on Thursday December 13th 1957. The proposal that the Picture House and Pavilion be allowed to open on Sundays was supported by 88 of those present, but opposed by 89. Afterwards Mr. **Arthur Spencer**, manager of the two cinemas, described the event as a fiasco that developed into a religious meeting. On the following Monday afternoon the directors of Morley

An early photograph of the Picture House and the cinema's staff.

Picture House Ltd. presented a petition, supported by 250 signatures, to the Town Clerk and this was instrumental in the granting of a referendum. Only 2,000 of Morley's 28,000 electors visited the polling stations but the cinemas won the day by a convincing majority of 907. There were 1,409 votes cast in favour of Sunday opening and 502 against. The first film to be shown on a Sunday was at the Picture House on Easter Sunday April 6th 1958. It was a colour film entitled 'Hiawatha' with Vincent Edwardes.

Unfortunately the end was near. It was announced at the end of the following year that the Picture House was due to close having been sold for £15,000. Mr. Gerald Hylton, the managing director said *"I am sorry to see it go, my father built it before the First World War."* The final programme was on Saturday February 6th 1960, the last film shown being 'The Siege of Pinchgut' starring Aldo Ray and Heather Sears.

The building was re-opened as a Coopers supermarket but has since been divided into two retail outlets. The irony is that, for many years, one of these has been a video rental shop no doubt hiring out films that were originally exhibited in the same building when it was the Picture House. A further strange coincidence is that the granddaughter of **Mr. Spencer**, the long time manager of the Morley cinemas, was at one time employed at the video outlet. **Arthur Spencer** had been the manager since 1936 and had retired in July 1959.

The views of an Offcomed-un

You can blame the war for inflicting my amateur talents upon the eyes and ears of the Morley public. I arrived in the town in the spring of 1944 to serve King and Country as a very reluctant Bevin Boy. Having been ordered to obey the Ministry of Labour or go to prison, all was not well with my world

My discontent with life was total, for not only was the reality of being a coal miner an anathema to this manicured beanpole of a clerk from London, but my new surroundings were a complete culture shock. The impact of privvies, clogs and curlers against a background of woollen mills added disbelief to my disenchantment. In my ignorance I appeared for work nattily dressed according to the code demanded by my late employers The Amalgamated Press Ltd, a large publishing house, at Fleetway House just off Ludgate Circus, and in the shadow of St Paul's Cathedral. I mention this only to paint a comparative picture of my working environment prior to my blundering entry onto the Broad Acres.

It was no wonder that the good citizens of Morley reciprocated the disbelief with which I viewed my surroundings. I appeared to be every woman's 'love'. There was never any suggestion of passion, more an implied 'poor lad, he must be lost and missing his mother'. The men viewed my presence with suspicion, and were forthright. "*Ay up then lad, why isn't tha in't forces?*" Upon receiving my answer, the response more often than not was "*Well I've heard some tales in me time, but tha's a bigger liar than Henry Jenkins*". It took me thirty years to discover who Henry Jenkins was, and if you don't know who the fellow was, it gives me some crumb of comfort to leave you in the same state of ignorance that characterised my early days in the town. You'll understand that after fifty-seven years, I am as near a trueborn Yorkshireman as you can get, and I am proud of it.

Henry Jenkins? "*Tha can find out for thee'sen*".

I had never experienced industry in the sense of manufacturing something, but here at almost every turn, the sight, sound and smell of such activity bewildered me. The town seemed to have as many weaving sheds as it had churches and chapels. They made an interesting contrast of frenetic noise and calming peace, each demanding a lip service in order to maintain communion. There is a strange relationship between mill and chapel. Why else have the ensuing years seen the decline of both? Men and women 'of the cloth' have dwindled in numbers, and their houses have passed into other hands.

New smells invaded my nostrils. The musty, almost sour odour of unfinished cloth, particularly shoddy, gave purpose to the rag and bone man of childhood years. I now saw the result of his harvesting being put to good use in the triangle called the Heavy Woollen District. The rags I had once exchanged for a goldfish in a jam jar, were being turned into army blankets. I once ran the street with my windmill on a stick earned from the few bones and bottles I had recycled. Now I suffered the outcome of reclaimed bones and other abattoir cast-offs, as the bits found their way to Fatty Cake Row at Gildersome Cross Roads. Here the glue factory heated a pot and boiled its noxious brew. Those living or working in the area either cursed or blessed the wind according to its direction. Just over the road The King's Arms and The Spread Eagle offered hospitality, but when production was in the air in Fatty Cake Row, the licensees kept their windows firmly closed.

Those early days were hard. I was homesick and nurtured a dislike for this town built on seven hills. On top of it all I was bamboozled by the dialect, particularly in the workplace. When called to task for ignoring an order *"to sam it up"*, or suitably stung with *"what the hummer is tha laikin at, tha's mekking a reight mullock"*, there was no alternative other than to learn this foreign tongue. The process was to cause much hilarity. I had joined them, but I couldn't quite beat them. At least it helped to divert attention from my complete inadequacy as a coal miner. One old collier confided, *"doan't tha fret thee'sen Davy lad. Getting coil is summat tha hes ter be born to"*. Then after a long pause he added, *"Trouble is tha were stillborn"*.

In 1944 there were not many young men of my age around. The army had mostly moved south ready to swim the channel, leaving me to wave my shovel in a threatening manner in that direction where the real sacrifices were taking place. Most people were still in the forces or enduring long hours of work, sometimes having to travel to such places as Sherburn in Elmet, Thorpe Arch and Barnbow. It was a case of an early start and a late return home. In spite of all such difficulties the churches and chapels offered an array of entertainment. It was to be some two years or more before the pre-war amateur societies began to reform.

Morley was a large Borough that embraced Drighlington, Churwell, Gildersome, the Ardsleys, Tingley and Bruntcliffe. Putting those outlying districts to one side, how many places of worship were there in Morley during the 1940's? The Rehoboth, St Mary's Congregational, St Peter's Parish, The Bethel, The Friends' Adult School, Morley Baptist, Queen Street Methodists, The Zion, The Ebenezer, Cross Hall Methodists, Birks Chapel, St Paul's Church, The Mission. The list goes on. All would bravely put on musical evenings, plays, concert versions, and oratorios.

Each organisation relied upon singers from other choirs to augment their depleted numbers, but they did it all in good heart. I had never sung in a choir, and the world of oratorio was truly a daunting prospect. The people around me seemed steeped in the tradition of singing great works. The choristers were born and bred to this music. At the end of my first season of singing Messiah, I had just about learned not to blurt out 'hallelujah' in that deathly hush marked by a rest in the music. I couldn't read the dots and the squiggles, and I certainly didn't have perfect pitch. I borrowed the complete oratorio on 78rpm records. The work was contained in a purpose made carrying case and was extremely heavy. In learning the Messiah by rote, I must have got through a whole tin of gramophone needles, which were not easy to come by, so I had to resharpen them as I honed my musical knowledge of Handel. I certainly needled the neighbours.

"Who is he?" someone would ask in a disbelieving tone. *"Tak no gorm love"*, would come the reply, *"he's a Londoner and knows no better. He can sing a bit though"*. Bit by bit I was accepted, and little by little Morley grew on me. The Brunswick Chapel stands proud in my memory, for it was here that I was asked to be the bass soloist in Handel's Messiah for the first time.

There was always a supper or tea provided. How people managed during times of rationing is a mystery. My circle of friends grew, and it was ever the same story of open-heartedness. *"What's mine, is thine. Come in lad, you're very welcome. Seeing as how you're here, you'll give us a song"*. I came from an area where we occasionally spoke with our immediate neighbours, if we had to. Stepping beyond that mark was not the done thing. The blitz had seen a lowering of some barriers, but 'social attitudes' were very different to the ones I was discovering in Yorkshire. It was this new found relaxed attitude between the classes that was so refreshing. 'Them and us' rarely applied, particularly in the world of amateur entertainment. It mattered not a jot whether you were young or old, rich or poor, nondescript or titled. What did matter was the friendship and sharing of talent. At times the music, humour and drama was far from amateurish and reached peaks of excellence. This is borne out by the many who rose from the ranks of homespun entertainment to take up their craft in the professional world.

Each Saturday evening the Town Hall could boast of the best ballroom dancing, to the finest dance band one could wish to hear. **George Speight and his Orchestra** were local men doing untold good for morale, and doing it in a most professional manner. The Alexandra Hall would be packed with young people. The ladies were augmented by men home on leave, and a solitary Bevin Boy. This was long before The Twist and the practice of standing apart from your partner to exchange semaphore signals. Ballroom dancing was the practiced art of us all. The Waltz, Quickstep, Foxtrot and Latin American numbers reigned supreme. There

A musical quintet at the Bethel Chapel in 1927. Mr. Norman Hartley is at the piano. (also see page 208)

was the occasional Jive, Hokey-Cokey and Lambeth Walk, but my favourite was the Y Dance. Here, you took the girl in your arms and whispered into her ear, *"why dance?"*

I was rescued by the music. Once I had stopped feeling sorry for myself, I came to realise that virtually everywhere people were making music. I was hooked. Queen Street became a brighter place, the deafening clatter of the weaving sheds became the timpani, beating out a new and exciting rhythm.

The Pavilion Theatre provided Sunday evening concerts that not only brought good music and laughter to those drab war years, but also raised much money for local charities and the war effort. At that time I was an unknown amateur, but **Stella Hodgson** and **Charles Brearley** were honing my singing voice. The tremendous talent of Stella and many of her family provided untold hours of song and laughter around the piano at 174 Britannia Road. I was more or less adopted into the **Hodgson family** and hold warm memories and affection for them all. **Charles Brearley** was the organist and choirmaster at the Wesleyan Methodist Chapel in Queen Street. He was my first singing master and did much to iron out the creases and imperfections in a young bass voice. It was **Mr Brearley** (we were very formal in those days) who tried to lead me away from what he called 'the pot boilers'of Victorian ballads. Looking back, he was defeated by my lack of musicianship.

The return of peace had an uplifting effect in 1946 with the gradual return to civilian life of those men and women who longed to get back to the smell of the greasepaint. Two events in that year stand out in my memory; the first being the **Carroll Levis** talent competition sponsored by **Butterworth & Pilkington** and organised by **Eddie Butterworth**; followed shortly by the return of an OMADS revue. I hadn't a clue who or what the OMADS were, but I was soon to learn. The talent competition created a massive interest in the town. Scores of would be entertainers applied and we all had to attend auditions at the Co-op Hall, where the wheat was separated from the chaff. **Norman Hartley**, (my father-in-law to be, although I didn't know it at the time) was the official accompanist and derived much pleasure from the experience.

> *"I haven't got onny music, but can tha play 'Spake'?"*
> *"I am sorry, I don't know that one. How does it go?"*
> *"Spake, spake, spake to me Thora."*

Or

> *"Can you play 'Pipes'?"*
> *"Nay lass, I only play the piano."*
> *"I know that silly. What I mean is 'Pipes'. You must know it. 'Come follow, follow, follow, the merry, merry pipes of Pan'."*
> *"What key do you want it in?"*
> *"Ee I don't know. Does it have to be in a key?"*

There followed a grand final at the Pavilion Theatre, which had to stage a repeat performance to satisfy the demand. The Old Morleans asked me to take part in their first post war revue. 'What Now?' was a wonderful experience. I made so many new friends and the week was full of never to be forgotten incidents.

I acquired my first dinner suit, thanks to **George Wilson** the producer of the show. George was not long home from the war and lived with his wife at The Old Manor House Bruntcliffe. In peacetime he had been a rugby union player of some repute in the town, and carried the physique of a sportsman. Now the approach of middle age had bestowed upon him an imposing figure of authority. His presence and impressive speaking voice, led me to be a bit over-awed at first meeting, but our mutual interest in the stage soon changed all that. We discussed what I should wear for my main guest spot and he wrongly assumed that I would possess the appropriate eveningwear. This was a problem. To go out and buy any item of new clothing required clothing coupons, and choice was severely restricted. Everything carried a CC41 Utility label, which meant some government office strictly controlled the quality. As a coal miner I was entitled to a special allocation of clothing coupons, another piece of muddled ministerial thinking. Miners were not known for their sartorial elegance, and when working underground didn't wear a great deal anyway. Clothing coupons! I rarely used them.

Unwittingly I had accumulated a store of the paper tokens that were rich in bartering value. I went along to the Wilson's home to try on his pre-war dinner suit that no longer came up to the expectations of George's body. The sight of the wad of coupons I took along had **Mrs Wilson** reaching for her smelling salts, and we quickly struck a deal. The Wilson's were happy and I was the proud owner of a suit that was to withstand ten years of hard wear, before my growing sophistication found the large pointed lapels of the jacket to be no longer in fashion.

I clearly recall the day I bumped into a lady OMAD who was also involved with the show. I remember the exact location. We were walking at the junction of Bridge Street, High Street and South Queen Street. Pleasantries were exchanged during which my new acquaintance, who shall be nameless, made her memorable comment. Tapping me with an elegantly manicured finger, she mused *"how on earth does such a deep and rich voice come out of so puny a chest?"* I spent years thereafter pondering the merits of having an underdeveloped torso against the possession of a pleasing voice. The lady no doubt was trying to be complimentary, and at the same time attempting to be someone she was not. That is how phobias are born. I laugh now as I retell the incident, but this is with the benefit of years. Today the only person interested in my chest is my doctor, and the once pleasing voice has lapsed into retirement, like its owner.

The following year marked the first post-war productions for **The Tingley Sylvians** and **The Morley Technical Institute Amateur Operatic Society** (what a mouthful of a title that was to a greenhorn like me). I count myself fortunate to have been in both productions, but much is written elsewhere about these two societies. The demise of The Sylvians saddens me a great deal, but I can only rejoice at the resilience and survival of the **Morley Amateur Operatic Society.** The present day members deserve great credit.

Morley is a changed town in many ways. I come now only as a visitor and I am saddened to see the legacy of great buildings squandered to the commercial demands of today. I am as guilty as anyone else for allowing this to happen. **Paul Rollinson** is quite right in his comments (which appear later) when he says that the guardians of the operatic society's future back in the late 1960's, should have grasped the mettle and found a suitable local building to take into ownership. It is always hard at the time, but it gets progressively harder if nothing is done. Looking back on my twenty-six years as a citizen of Morley, my memory is awash with the sight and sound of a multitude of wonderful characters. Not all chose to 'get up on stage' and 'make fools of themselves' as they would put it, but their support for those of us that did, was wholehearted and unwavering. The Morley of those years I firmly believe was unique, both in its people and in its wealth of talent.

A World Premiere in Morley.

In January 1986 a letter was posted in the small university town of Tubingen about 20 miles south of Stuttgart then in West Germany. It had been written by Dr. Hans Schwarze, a member of staff in the English Philology Department at the University of Tubingen and was addressed to Morley Town Hall. After perusing its contents the Morley Area Administrator of the time **Mr. Bob Akeroyd** decided to forward it to my father **Mr. George W. Atkinson.**

It appears from the letter that during his studies and researches Dr. Schwarze had become an expert on the life and works of D. H. (David Herbert) Lawrence the early twentieth century Nottinghamshire born English novelist, poet and playwright. Perhaps his interest in the author stemmed from the fact that Lawrence had married in 1914 the divorced wife of a Nottingham professor, who was born Frieda von Richthofen. Originally she came from a German aristocratic family whose brother later gained a reputation as a World War 1 fighter ace known as the Red Baron. At the time he wrote the letter Dr. Schwarze had been asked by Cambridge University Press to prepare an edition of D. H. Lawrence's 'Plays' for publication by them.

D. H. Lawrence died in 1930 and presumably his wife inherited all his papers and manuscripts. Then either she disposed of them herself or they became dispersed after her death. Eventually much of Lawrence's correspondence and original manuscripts found a home on San Francisco Bay at Berkeley, site of the University of California. Some years previous to writing his letter to Morley Town Hall, Dr. Schwarze had been going through the Lawrence papers at Berkeley and had come across a cutting from the **Morley Observer** dated 24th March 1939. The cutting had the initials A.W. at the bottom of the report, indicating that **Arthur Wilkinson** had written it, at that time the editor of the Morley Observer. Besides giving a thorough review of the acting and production it was typical during this period to contribute background information to such reports. So from it we learn that the D. H. Lawrence play under review entitled 'ACollier's Friday Night'had been written in 1906 when Lawrence was only twenty-one; that it had remained in manuscript form until 1935 when Lawrence's widow Frieda had decided to have it published and that the performance by the Morley Adult School Players in March 1939 was the first time the play had been acted on the stage i.e. A world premiere.

Arthur Wilkinson in his review gives some indication as to why this should have occurred. He states that *"too much is not expected of a*

A scene from 'A Collier's Friday Night' presented by The Morley Adult School Players in March 1939. The actors from left to right:- Gilbert Atkinson, Gladys Holroyd (Atkinson), Ada Binks (Almond) and George W. Atkinson.

dramatist of that age (21), and the reputation eventually achieved by Lawrence is no reason for attributing to this very slight little piece qualities that it could not be expected to possess. One thing, however, may be expected and that is verisimilitude."

This is particularly true of the play's dialogue much of which is based on Lawrence's autobiographical experiences. **Mr. Wilkinson** bemoans the lack of action and drama in a three act play which simply records the events of one unremarkable Friday evening as they affect the different family members, father (the Collier), mother, two elder daughters, son of secondary school age wanting to be a teacher (perhaps based on Lawrence himself) and various members of the family. The play begins in Act 1 with father arriving home in his pit muck with the week's wages and after unfolding the events of the evening ends in Act 3 with the lighting of the candle to take upstairs at bed time.

Perhaps one reason for its selection by the **Morley Adult School Players** was that the play was being given as part of the British Drama League Festival for three act plays and an adventurous choice could perhaps gain extra credit. Many amateur dramatic societies at this time were members of the British Drama League competing in festivals to try and become better known outside their immediate local area. In March 1939 about forty different societies had entered the competition, each play being assessed and judged by a professional adjudicator. To show that the competition was really nationwide the adjudicator at Morley on Wednesday 22nd March was Frank Harwood of Tavistock Little Theatre. Other societies were mounting productions of works by Shakespeare, Sheridan, Ibsen and other traditional acknowledged playwrights plus those of modern women dramatists like Dodie Smith, Christa Winsloe and Clemence Dane and so a recently published play by D.H. Lawrence would blend perfectly with the other choices. The reward for obtaining one of the six highest marks in the festival was an invitation to travel to Buxton in April 1939 to stage the play there during a gala week of plays. Unfortunately the Morley group did not get to this stage of the competition but at the Saturday performance of the play the adjudicator's mainly complimentary report was read to the audience.

The producer of 'A Collier's Friday Night' was **Mr. John T. Kirk** one of the founder members of the **Morley Adult School Players** ten years earlier in 1929. Together with **Mr. George W. Atkinson**, another founder member, they produced two three-act plays per year between 1929 and 1939 building up a considerable reputation for the high quality of their performances, which included works by George Bernard Shaw, T. S. Eliot, D. H. Lawrence and, after the Second World War, by J. B. Priestley and Emlyn Williams.

During the war years the **Adult School Players** lost the use of their stage as the upstairs room of the 'chapel'building was requisitioned and used by a detachment of the R.A.S.C. a regiment which took over a variety of premises in Morley. Similar situations occurred at other chapels and churches. However, this gave an opportunity for actors from many different amateur dramatic societies to combine in staging the **1944 Co-operative Society Pageant**, specially written by the playwright L. du Garde Peach to celebrate a flourishing commercial enterprise during the last hundred years which had been initiated by the Rochdale Pioneers in 1844. The pageant was episodic in character and performed by innumerable Co-operative Societies throughout the country. In Morley it was performed on the stage of the Alexandra Hall in Morley Town Hall on August 1st, 2nd, 3rd, 4th and 5th. A photograph of the complete cast of approaching 150 was taken on the Town Hall steps and besides including many of **Morley Adult School Players** there were members of the Amateur Dramatic Societies at **St. Mary's in the Wood, the Rehoboth, Queen Street Wesleyans, Brunswick Primitive Methodists, Morley Baptist Tabernacle, St. Mary's Mission, St. Andrew's Church** and **St. Peter's Parish Church**. The pageant was financed by the **Morley and Drighlington Industrial Co-operative Societies** so no doubt there would be people from Drighlington in the cast too. People from choral societies and church choirs also took part and the ballet mistress was **Miss Millicent Kitson** who after the war was responsible for the dancing in many of the musical productions of the **Morley Technical Institute Amateur Operatic Society.**

After the war the **Adult School Players** obtained a much-improved stage, financed partly from the compensation received from the army. However, the Dramatic Society was not quite as flourishing as in pre-war days. Many of the players were considerably older, some had left the district, there was a shortage of young players and one of the original producers **Mr. John T. Kirk** decided to make the professional stage his career after being demobbed and went, among other places, to be with Sir Barry Jackson at Birmingham Repertory Company, ending his career as the under-manager at the Grand Theatre, Leeds.

Unfortunately no trace has yet been found of a book about D. H. Lawrence's plays by Dr. Hans Schwarze. In 1986 he asked to be put in contact with any surviving members of the cast who he says would be in their 60's or 70's. He gives a complete list of their names and two of them **Gilbert Atkinson and Ethel Brough** married in 1940 and celebrated their Diamond Wedding in the year 2000 (they are now living at Whitby) while in 2001 **Ada Binks** (later Ada Almond) and **Alice Kirk** (later Alice Hartley) both now widows, celebrated birthdays in their early nineties though sadly **Alice Hartley** died in early 2002.

Contributed by **David K Atkinson.**

Morley Adult School Players. The cast of 'Murder in the Cathedral' performing in St. Mary's Church, Morley on 30ʰ December 1939.

The Morley Vocal Union.

The Vocal Union more than any other singing group reflects the truly golden years of Morley's history. The success and ultimate demise of this choir almost parallels the establishment of a fine municipal borough and its eventual loss of independence.

The proud and pioneering spirit of the town fathers is mirrored within the choir's membership, for here shoulder to shoulder sang the civic leaders, shopkeepers, builders, mill managers and blue-collared workers who were the very sinew of the town. Here comradeship shone like a beacon, for the Vocal Union was a survivor of two world wars and the die-hards stayed together until age and a social revolution dictated otherwise. In the late 1960's, more and more people remained in their homes for entertainment and most young men of that era had little interest in male voice choral singing.

The disbandment of the Union occurred in July 1970 after a long and brave fight by the few remaining stalwarts under their then President **Horace Walsh** who is quoted at the time as saying, *"we are all getting old and there are no young ones to take over. Of the nine remaining members, two are pianists and one a conductor, all we need is singers."* Those nine good men were **Horace Walsh, Stanley Tempest, Norman Hartley, F Hartley, Roland Smith, Harold Walker, H Akroyd** and **Ralph Berry.**

In that same July **The West Riding Singers** (a mixed choir) issued its first LP record for public sale. Founded some years before in Morley by **Noel Anderson** of Gildersome using a large nucleus of local singers, the choir expanded its area of influence, before it too disbanded in later years. **The West Ardsley Male Voice Choir** were also appealing for new members on 12 June 1970, but to their credit they have survived and are still active in 2002.

Colin Crabtree has become over the years, a retainer of reference material of various sorts, and holds a keen appreciation of local history. He serves today as librarian of **Morley Music Society**, a similar task he found himself doing during his days with the Vocal Union. He recalls, *"there were two cupboards packed and jammed with four-part harmonies, and it was no small task trying to bring some semblance of order to the chaos. I have no idea where all those scores ended up, but one must assume another choir put them to some use."* Colin's elder brother Geoffrey was also a member at one time, and Colin recalls his brother's recollection of how he felt when he first stood in the ranks to sing, *"I felt overwhelmed by the 'organ-like' sound of the choir in full voice."*

The Morley Vocal Union on the platform at Morley's Great Northern Railway station before boarding the train en-route to Paris in May 1912.

The authors are indebted to the Crabtree family for much of the information provided about the Union.

Formed in 1895 the male voice choir was remarkable in many respects. Within three years of forming the first of many honours was gained in1898 with a First Prize at Pudsey; thereafter prizes were won every year until the outbreak of hostilities in 1914. In many years three, four and five prizes were gained, but in 1909 no less than seven awards were brought home from all over the West Riding and Lancashire. A certificate awarded for the Blackpool Musical Festival held between 14th & 17th October 1908, indicates the Vocal Union to be First Prize winners in the Class 44 Male Voice Choirs (Alto Lead) Open competition.

Morley's fame became international in May 1912, when the Vocal Union succeeded in winning the third prize of 1,000 francs (£40) in the group for male voices at the Paris International Musical Festival. Their performance was a splendid one, for they consisted of only forty-two voices, whereas some of the Continental choirs they faced were between a hundred and two hundred voices strong. In addition Morley gained first and second (divided) for the 'Sight Test' and also first prize for conducting.

The representatives of the Morley Vocal Union who made that memorable trip were, **Sam Smith** (conductor), **W. Chew, G.W. Littlewood,H. Nussey, Jesse Rogerson, J.W. Stakes, H. Stead, W. Thomas, H. Turner, J.R. Gledhill, E. Anderson, B. Corns, A.A. Foster, A. Lee, H. Sharp, W.H. Benson, F. Westmoreland, H. Crowther, J. Asquith, C. Charlesworth, B. Field, F. Hardy, R. Jarvis, J. Moss, S. Scholes, J.S. Smith, H. Tillotson,**

L. Bedford, Con. Carnes, J.W. Chapman, F. Clough, H. Hirst, J.W. Scott, J. Wade Smith, A. Stead, A. Wood, A. Broadhead, B. Fearnley, H. Lodge, A. Marshall, M. Moon, A. Sykes, H. Peace, W.A. Oakes and **E. Wilson**.

In 1914 the President **G E Baines Esq** (who features elsewhere in this book), was supported by **J W Stakes** Hon Secretary, and **Sam Smith** Conductor; the ensuing four years must have been a time of great difficulty, but the Union survived with flying colours.

The first wireless broadcasting studio in Leeds was designated 2LS by the BBC and established in 1925. One of the first broadcasts was made by the Morley Vocal Union conducted by **Willie Frudd** and accompanied by **Norman Hartley**. **Mark Moon** was the solo artist; his bass voice already winning a wide audience and a considerable reputation. **Mark** was known as the 'Yorkshire Basso' and had a considerable influence upon music in the area, not only through his own singing, but also through his son Cecil who died in March 1949. **Cecil Moon** was the leader of the renowned Harrogate Baths Quartet in the 1920's and for a short period was associated with **Tom Jenkins** (see his biography in 'Didn't They Do Well')

For some strange reason there was a sudden burst of interest in the Vocal Union in the local press during 1984, long after the demise of the choir. That stalwart reporter of local affairs for The Morley Advertiser **Phil Jackson**, or 'Pug' as he was known to his friends, seemed to be the instigator. The response received from the paper's readers was surprising. The first article appeared on 9th August of that year, and was the direct result of Phil Jackson receiving a photograph of a choir rehearsal from **Mrs Betty Houldin** the daughter of the then late **Tom Harrison**. Anyone who had dealings with Morley's Labour Exchange during the mid 20th Century would know Tom Harrison. Phil Jackson sought the services of **Ralph Berry** who was at one time the Hon. Secretary of the group and is described as a sprightly seventy-two year old in 1984.

Apart from some misleading information about the date of formation and a few other matters, this was an intriguing article and the picture brought back many happy memories for 'the off-comed-un' as I write these words in 2002. I well remember **Ralph Berry** and his family for they were near neighbours of my wife's parents. Ralph followed his father **Tom** into the choir, but only after a stringent audition. The fact that his father Tom was a member cut no ice, if you couldn't sing or hold a note, a refusal would be firm but polite. Ralph had the privilege of being interviewed by the above-mentioned great Yorkshire Basso-profundo **Mark Moon**. After singing a number of scales to order and running through a glee (which he had heard his father sing), Mark Moon commented, *"tha'll do lad."* Those three short words coming from such a man was like pinning a medal on young Ralph's chest. He was in the choir and remained so until the Union was no more.

Co-author David Reekie remembers his time with the Union was quite short, mainly because he was committed to so many other singing activities and in the early 1950's the responsibilities of a new young family were not to be taken lightly. "I was becoming a reasonable singer and actor, but fatherhood was a whole new experience, so certain activities had to be put to one side, and the Union was discarded. But I never lost the friendship of my fellows in the choir. Other than the Berry's (and 3ʳᵈ generation Ian who my son Chris and I got to know on the cricket field), there was Bill Crabtree and Harry Baker the optician. Bill was a charming man who had a quiet approach to all things, until he met a double fortissimo in a passage of music, for then his impressive bass voice took over the immediate vicinity. Harry Baker and his wife were friends to my family in so many ways; I shall never forget their support and the pleasure it gave them when I called to see them in their shop with my very young children. Being short-sighted, I was also a customer of Franks Opticians in Queen Street for many years, but I was far-sighted enough to recognize a truly lovely couple. The 'Baker Room' at Morley Public Library remembers them both today."

Here are more of Ralph Berry's thoughts made in 1984:

*"Fling wide the gates,
come out dauntless and true,
brothers of heart be stout
we are but few."*

So sang the Morley Vocal Union in the opening glee on a visit to Armley Jail, at which 500 prisoners and officials roared their approval amid tears of laughter.

"Horatio Stead of Gildersome possessed the nicest alto voice I have ever heard. It was like a bell, loud and clear. There was George Harrison, Cashier at Hield Brothers' mill; Tom Harrison for many years President of Morley Cricket Bowling & Athletic Club and manager at the local employment exchange; John Foster the blacksmith; Harry Wildman, Master Decorator for the Morley Co-operative Society and Alan Smith one of the finest crown green bowlers in Yorkshire."

Another interesting article and photograph appeared later that year in the **Morley Advertiser dated 15ᵗʰ November 1984.** The photograph showed some forty men in a set group surrounding the then Mayor of Morley **Councillor James Roberts**. The article posed the questions, 'why the Mayor and why a mill yard?' Again Phil Jackson wrote the article. Answers were quickly forthcoming from a number of sources including one from as far away as Morecambe, but the definitive replies came from **John Teale** (the then President of Gildersome Conservative Club) and whose father **Gilead Teale** was once President of the Vocal Union; **Mrs Crabtree** widow of **William (Bill) Crabtree**; **Mrs Joan Poole** whose father **Harry Culpan** was pianist for the group, and **Ralph Berry**. They were all unanimous that it was a Vocal Union event.

The Morley Vocal Union used many venues over the years for rehearsal purposes, but at this time the group were meeting in the Brunswick Hotel. But on invitation they were offered the free use of an upstairs room at the Conservative Club with the proviso that all the singers became members to comply with the law. The photograph may have marked this occasion in 1945, when many club members joined the singers as a welcoming gesture, but it is likely the event was the Union's 50th Jubilee dinner celebration that was held at the Conservative Club on 14th April 1945.

Among the group taken on Bank Street to the rear of the Conservative Club were:

Tom Harrison (President), **Fred Clough** (Conductor), **Harry Culpan** (Pianist), **Fred Scarth, Maurice Sykes, Jack Woodcock, Jesse Rogerson, Fred Field, Cyril Ingham, Willie Archer, John S Hartley, Gilead Teale, William (Bill) Crabtree, Charlie Rogerson, Tom Berry, Clifford Hill, Harry Wildman, Alan Wood, Wade Smith, Horatio Stead, Willie Ladley.**

Ever in search of an appropriate ending for this short review, we can do no better than pay tribute to four very special gentlemen:

In January 1948 a quartet from the Morley Vocal Union sang at the Mercantile Club. They were,

Horatio Stead
J W (Willie) Wilson
Tom Smith
Wade Smith

The foursome had a combined age of 298 years, the last named gentleman being just over ninety, (he had celebrated his birthday a few days earlier). Two of their numbers were survivors of the choir's successful Paris trip in 1912, and the quartet had first sung together in the early years of the 20th century in 1906.

They certainly knew how to sustain a note.

The West Riding Singers.

In 1964 **Mr. Donald Burrill**, the principal of the Joseph Priestley Institute of Further Education, arranged for a course on madrigal work to commence at the Institute's new centre at Bruntcliffe School, Morley. The first meeting took place on 29th April 1964 when The 'West Riding Singers' was formed as an affiliated course at the Joseph Priestley Institute of Further Education. It was decided the minimum age of members would be 17 years, there would be a limit of 24 voices and the declared intention was to specialise in glees, madrigals and church anthems with concerts to be given in various parts of the West Riding.

A special tribute must be paid to the founder members for having brought into being a group that was to develop and achieve considerable success over a life span of 31 years. The last engagement was on 9th September 1995. The founder members were:-

Elizabeth Sleight, soprano.
Martin Ingle, Tenor.
Richard Storr, Bass.
Noel Anderson, Conductor/Musical Director.
George Gomersal, Accompanist.

Of the original six members, three have unfortunately died. **Richard Storr** joined the Red Arrows and was regrettably killed in a flying accident. **Noel Anderson** resigned as conductor due to ill health, but remained as President until he resigned on 7th September 1976. Mr. Anderson died on 26th February 1977. **Mr. Harry Fearnley** was the first secretary and he held the post until he resigned on 5th October 1976, he died on 12th March 2000.

For a number of years 'The West Riding Singers' remained Morley based with a membership mostly comprising of local people. The majority of concerts and recitals took place within the Morley area until 12th May 1979 when a joint concert with the Black Dyke Mills Band, organised by the Morley Civic Society, was held in the Town Hall; this proved to be the last appearance of the Singers within the community that had witnessed their creation fifteen years earlier. As the choir developed a number of factors combined to dilute the association with Morley, these were:-

a :- To be able to complete on more equal terms in competitive Music Festivals it was decided a larger choir was necessary and auditions were held at the Leeds Y.M.C.A. and this recruited new members from outside the Morley area.

b :- Changes in the Further Education fee system meant that it became more economical to move the rehearsal venue from Bruntcliffe School to the newly established Leeds Music Centre in the Civic Theatre building and later to several Leeds schools, until finally settling at the Trinity and All Saints' Colleges at Horsforth.

c :- When **Noel Anderson** retired as the founder-conductor there was a gradual falling away of the choir's Morley associations when the new conductors developed into wider fields.

Over the 31 years of the life of the 'West Riding Singers'there were only three conductors :-

Noel J. Anderson 1964 – 1972.
Robert Crinall 1972 – 1973.
and
Paul Shepherd 1973 – 1995.

During that time the total number of concerts and recitals and other musical events was over 370, ranging from charity carol singing over a number of years in Leeds City station concourse, to memorable highlights such as recitals at Notre Dame in Paris and, nearer home, at York Minster and York Guildhall.

During its association with Morley, which ended with the Town Hall concert on 12th May 1979, there were 29 engagements in the Morley area:-
St. Peter's Church, Gildersome (1 in 1964), St. Paul's Church, Drighlington (4 in 1964, 1965, 1969, 1978), Central Methodist Church, Morley (2 in 1965, 1967), Bethel Methodist Church, Morley (2 in 1965, 1966), St. Peter's Church, Morley (6 in 1966, 1967, 1968, 1970, 1972 twice), Morley Town Hall (7 in 1966, 1967, 1969, 1971, 1974, 1976, 1979), St. Paul's Church, Morley (4 in 1967, 1968, 1969, 1970), Gildersome Baptist Church (1 in 1968), St. Andrew's Church, Bruntcliffe, (2 in 1969, 1971).

The total number of concerts and recitals given during this period was more than 180. This was also the period when all the competitive Musical Festival work was undertaken. The choir entered festivals, at some of the venues on a number of occasions, at Barnsley, Hull, Colne, Freckleton, Blackpool, Harrogate, Blackburn, Ilkley (Wharfedale), and in the Teeside International Industrial Eisteddfod in Middlesbrough.

Following is a selection of some of the choir's notable engagements :-

July 1966:	Teeside International Industrial Eisteddfod in Middlesbrough.
From 1968 onwards :	B.B.C. Radio Leeds recordings.
March 1969 :	'A Grand Evening of Music' at Morley Town Hall. A joint concert with the Leeds City Brass Band. Guest artiste Keith Swallow (piano).
May 1970 :	Leeds/Dortmund Exchange event at the Leeds Music Centre.
May 1971 :	'Spring Celebrity Concert' at Morley Town Hall. Guest artistes :-Keith Swallow (piano) and Paul Shepherd (violin).
May 1972 :	Leeds/Dortmund Exchange : visit to Dortmund.
July 1972 :	Recital in Lincoln Cathedral.
December 1972 :	Christmas music in Armley jail.
November 1973 :	Recital in Lincoln Cathedral.
June 1976 :	Yorkshire Arts Association 'tour' to Bedale, Penistone and Heptonstall.
May 1977 :	Recital in Ripon Cathedral.
June 1977 :	Yorkshire Arts Association 'tour' to three venues.
July 1977 :	Recital at St. Michael and All Angels, Hawkshead.
December 1977 :	Recital for Morpeth Music Society.
February 1978 :	Recital at Bradford Cathedral.
May 1978 :	Recital for Radio Leeds at Temple Newsam House.
December 1978 :	Recital at Thirsk Town Hall.
February 1979 :	Recital at Clothworkers Hall, Leeds University.
January 1980 :	'Let the People Sing' contest at the Royal Northern College Of Music, Manchester.
July 1980 :	Eisteddfod, Cleveland.
May 1981 :	Cotswold Tour: Pershore Abbey, Cheltenham and Chipping Campden.
May 1982 :	Recording of two cassettes.
May 1982 :	Cotswold Tour: Pershore Abbey, Burford and Chipping Campden.
December 1982 :	T.V. Channel 4: 'making the Most of........' (recording)
March 1983 :	B.B.C. Radio 4 : Live Morning Service.

May 1983 :	North Yorkshire Tour : Richmond, Masham and Hawes.
March 1984 :	Concert at Georgian theatre, Richmond.
July/August 1985 :	International Choral Competition, Neuchatel, Switzerland.
1988 :	Recording and production of 3rd cassette.
July/August 1988 :	French Tour : Notre Dame, Paris, Chartres Cathedral and Tours Cathedral.
November 1989 :	25th Anniversary Concert, Keighley.
May 1990 :	Spanish Tour : Seville, Granada and Marbella.
March 1992 :	Weekend services at Chichester Cathedral.

The 'West Riding Singers' was basically a small, mixed voice chamber choir, singing an ever-increasing repertoire of mainly 'a cappella' ie. unaccompanied music, covering many periods from the 14th century to the present day, both sacred and secular. As can be seen from the many different venues it was a travelling choir and not a fixed base choral society. It mostly relied on obtaining engagements and invitations from churches, cathedrals, music societies etc. There were, however, occasional concerts and recitals promoted by the choir itself and also a few events when larger and more extended works were performed, occasionally accompanied by organ or orchestra.

From the original four singing founder members and the group of about fourteen at the founding date of 29th April 1964, the membership gradually increased to its largest number of forty-five on the occasion of a joint band concert in Huddersfield Town Hall on 26th August 1972, but for most of the choir's life there were thirty to thirty-five members.

Rule 3 of the 'West Riding Singers' constitution was "*The aims of the Society shall be to encourage, promote and further the cause of Choral Music*". It was most certainly successful in this aim.

The authors wish to thank Mr. Colin Crabtree for allowing them unrestricted access to his detailed research work and archives in respect of 'The West Riding Singers'.

The Tingley Methodist Sylvians.
a.k.a.
The Tingley Sylvians Amateur Operatic Society.

In 1928 five young men, members of the Tingley Methodist Church, formed themselves into a quintet with the name **'The Five Rascals.'** The aim was to provide local entertainment and, at the same time, help to raise money for the Chapel's restoration fund. Their names were **Tom Gill, Jim Hill,Albert** and **Willie Jowett** and, on piano, **Clifford Barras**.

The group soon developed into a concert party and then went on to present three small operettas; 'Princess of Poppyland' in 1930, 'O'Hara San' in 1931 and in 1932, 'Pocahontas'.

The first secretary of the group was **Mr. L.G. Clay** and it was his mother who suggested the title **'Tingley Methodist Sylvians'**, a name that was retained until 1964. The primary object of the society was threefold; to keep together the young people of the Church, cultivate a taste for drama and light operatic music and to stage productions from which the proceeds would help the Chapel's restoration scheme.

In 1933 the society presented its first Gilbert and Sullivan opera, 'The Pirates of Penzance'. This was the start of annual productions, with two in 1934, up to and including 1940 when the war intervened. All were Gilbert and Sullivan operas with the exception of the 1939 production of 'The Rebel Maid' by F. Phillips and Gerald Dodson. During those difficult war years the society did, however, still continue to function giving small but very welcome concerts to appreciative audiences.

Full cast for the Tingley Sylvians production of 'Pirates of Penzance'1933.

The year 1947 saw a resumption of the Gilbert and Sullivan productions which were again continued annually until 1993, the only exception being the year 1991. In five of those years two productions were achieved. In those years the only exception was the 1951 presentation of 'Les Cloches de Corneville,' music by Robert Planquette.

By 1964 the society had outgrown the Chapel premises and it transferred to Woodkirk Secondary School for the production of 'The Yeomen of the Guard'. This coincided with the change of title to the **'Tingley Sylvians Amateur Operatic Society'**. Seven shows were presented during the six-year association with the school.

In 1970 the main productions were transferred to the then Morley Grammar School, commencing with 'The Pirates of Penzance', and this was the start of a 19 year continuous association with the school when 21 shows were performed there.

It was decided to stage the 1989 production of 'The Gondoliers' at the Theatre Royal and Opera House in Wakefield. This was the society's 60th Anniversary Year, its eighth production of 'The Gondoliers' and the centenary of the show itself; it being first performed in London on 9th December 1889. The society stayed at the Wakefield theatre for the production of 'Iolanthe' in 1990 and 'Yeoman of the Guard' in 1992; returning to Morley High School for the Tingley Sylvians Amateur Operatic Society's final production in 1993 of 'The Mikado'.

Over the years the society undertook many musical engagements besides the regular annual autumn shows. These included concert versions of 'Merrie England'; of Gilbert and Sullivan; choral works performed with well known-bands such as Yorkshire Imperial Metals; Gilbert and Sullivan concerts with professional groups such as 'Gilbert and Sullivan for All'; concerts for charities such as the Home Farm Trust and concerts in the style of the Old-Time Music Hall. A novel undertaking in 1987 was a Gilbert and Sullivan marathon with concert versions of all their 13 operas sung in about 17 hours.

A few members of the society formed the **West Ardsley Male Voice Choir** in 1964 and some members undertook other engagements throughout the area. Several also assisted other amateur societies and a few were members of 2 or 3 societies. There was a frequent interchange of principals, chorus members, scenery and costumes between the various Gilbert and Sullivan societies in the district.

*This history of the Tingley Sylvians could not have been written without information originally recorded by the late **Mr. Albert Jowett** who was one of the original founders of the society.*

***Mr. Peter Aldred's** invaluable assistance is also appreciated.*

An interlude of fiction, to give you a short rest from all this history, although we hope it reflects a little of Morley's social scene back in the 1940's

How we all started
or
'It was a dark and stormy night'

"T'was a dark and stormy night when me Nellie went away,
and I'll not forget it till me dying day."

That's Auntie Maude who is singing. She is trying to be tragic and heart-rending as befits her role in this Victorian melodrama. Maud has got one of those voices that is somewhere between soprano and coloratura. When she really lays on the vibrato, I am reminded of sitting in the dentist's waiting room, dreading the fact that 'I am next in', and having to listen as he 'fettles-out' some poor soul's back molar. The noise goes right through you, but for goodness sake, don't tell Aunt Maude I said so.

Poor woman hasn't had the best of luck, and I sometimes get the impression that she is desperately lonely. She was engaged to marry, but her fiancé was a sub-mariner in the Royal Navy, and the poor fellow went to an early grave in 1939 when the Thetis went down during trials off Liverpool. I remember them being together, and how happy they were in each other's company. Neither was in the first blush of youth, for Ken was a three-striper, and Maude was well into her thirties, when he asked if they could tie the knot. The few years since he was killed, what with the war and everything, have aged Aunt Maude beyond her years. She is painfully thin, which helps in giving her such a piercing voice. Dad reckons she'd make a good secret weapon if they could record her singing, and hang loud speakers out of the planes as they fly over Germany. He can say that and get away with it, because she's his sister.

We have had our usual Sunday tea about half-past five. In spite of the rationing, Mother always puts on a good spread when all the family are coming. Goodness knows where we put it all, because we had demolished a large lunch after Dad got home from the pub. He and Uncle Harry each had two rounds of Yorkshire pudding smothered in onion gravy, before digging in to a pot-roast with two veg. Mum had got a nice joint this week. It was beautifully tender, and there'll be enough left for Dad and me to take as sandwiches tomorrow, as well as the makings of a shepherd's pie. Dad knows it was horseflesh, but we daren't tell Uncle Harry because he is a bit finicky about food. There is a shop in Leeds between the Corn Exchange and the markets, where Mum can occasionally buy that meat which is deemed 'fit for human consumption.'

We all finished off with spotted dick and custard, which is my favourite, except for jam roly-poly. I always get a surprise with jam roly-poly. It's there on your plate, covered in lashings of custard, looking so innocent that you can't wait to put your spoon through it, and shovel that first portion into your mouth "Serves you right," chides Mother, "you ought to know by now that the raspberry jam is red hot. It's only just come out of the oven. Anyway you shouldn't bolt your food like that." Mum still talks to me as if I am a bit of a kid, which is strange seeing as how I am off into the army in a couple of weeks.

Mum and Dad, together with the ladies went to chapel after tea, and it was left to us lads to wash up and clear away ready for tonight's grand concert. Dad's cousin Cedric and his wife Celia were not expected, but they had turned up during tea. We had all heard the noise of Cedric's motorbike and sidecar, long before it had reached our back door, and Mum had resignedly left the table to set another two places. Uncle Harry is not all that keen on Celia, and likes to get a dig in when he can. He also reckons little to Cedric being able to get hold of enough petrol to run his combination, but he gets some sort of priority because of his work.

"What sort of bike are you running now Cedric?" he would say. And Cedric, ever the innocent abroad, would warm to his favourite subject.

"It's a 500cc Norton Harry, goes like a dream she does."

"Nay thou's wrong there Cedric surely. What with one C in the sidecar and another C in the saddle, that makes it a 502cc at least."

No one had laughed, but Harry enjoyed it, but I bet he wouldn't have said it had Celia been listening.

Hold on a minute, this is a really dramatic moment when the prodigal daughter returns home.

"Who's that knocking at my door?"

(sound effects provided off-stage by Uncle Harry)

"It's your little Nell, don't you know me any more?"

Little Nell is played by Celia, who is fourteen stone and unsuitably round for her height. Uncle Harry is quite right, about her fitting into that sidecar. I think Cedric must use a shoehorn.

"What happened to that actor guy who used to call you honey,
Did he leave you all alone, when you hadn't any money?"
"He was a smooth tongued guy and he could lie with ease,
and he had more money than a dog has fleas."

It is all of three weeks since we last performed this piece, and as I have not been given a part to play, I'm beginning to lose interest. I had better tell you a bit more about our Sunday get togethers before Uncle Harry gets up to sing. I'll have to keep quiet then or he will see me off into the yard, and I think it has just come on to rain. We are a regular little concert party really, and when friends and neighbours join in, it is as good as anything you hear on the radio.

Just now we are missing Florrie Smith, who lives next door, at least she does when she is at home. Poor Florrie is in hospital having all taken away. That's what Mum said the other day. I have no idea what she meant. I hope they don't take her piano away, because she's the best pianist round here. She is the official accompanist for the local Gilbert & Sullivan Society and really knows her stuff when it comes to the Mikado or Iolanthe. Dad sings the Nightmare Song from Iolanthe, and whilst I know the words, I can't quite keep up with him during the very fast bits. I don't know how he does it really, because he's got a loose fitting top set, and he is forever parting company with them at the most inconvenient moments. Not when he is singing though. When he gets to that bit about 'Sloane Square and Kensington Stations', they never budge.

Sorry, I have just been given a signal from Mum to put some more coal on the fire, and the scuttle's empty. This means a trip into the cellar. It's a job I dislike because there is only a one light at the top of the steps, and once you get into the coalhole, you're fumbling around in the dark. I can never find the shovel. Ah well, black hands or not, I shall be passing the 'keeping stone' and I shall sample some tasty morsel as I pass.

Oh lor! Look at me hands, I'll have to slip into the sink corner and wash. Mum keeps it curtained off when we have company. I can't be bothered to get the kettle off the hob, so it will have to be cold water, and I won't be able to get the soap to lather. This wouldn't have happened if the old folks didn't go down the yard so often, letting in draughts of cold air. The room would be warmer, and we'd use less coal. It's no wonder they have to stand with their backs to the fire when they get back. I wouldn't like to be that kettle; I bet it has seen some sorry sights in its time. I am sorry, I'll have to shut up, because Uncle Harry is about to sing, and he insists on absolute hush when he gets on his feet.

I am the Banderlero, the gallant Banderlero,
I rule the mountains, and I claim as contraband what comes my way

I can't imagine Uncle Harry ruling any mountains, or forcing anyone to give up their goods. He is only a little fellow and dumpy with it. The fact that he is nearly bald doesn't help either. I think that most of his audience are so taken aback by the basso-profundo voice coming out of such an unlikely body, that they sit in shocked silence until he's finished.

Roaming the mountains, an outlaw defiant

I wish I had the nerve to go and fetch some more coal.

The Grammar School & The OMADS.

Times change, and so of course do names. This proud educational body started life in 1906 as the Morley Secondary School before becoming a Grammar School, and again thanks to the political party of the day, we now call it something else. What is important is the tradition and history of the school, its staff and the host of pupils who have enjoyed a good education and gone on to make their mark in the world. Their roll of honour could fill a book.

Only four years after the school's founding, an Old Scholars Association was formed. That in itself is remarkable in that in a short space of time, the pupils of a new school wished to retain a link with what for many, is an unpleasant time and best forgotten. This body changed its title in 1912 to the Old Morleian Association, and as a result of much amateur entertainment activity, became better known as the **Old Morleians' Amateur Dramatic Society or OMADS.**

In 1960 a dinner attended by 250 guests celebrated the Jubilee of the Association, during which time twenty Presidents had held office; on this occasion fourteen out of the seventeen surviving holders were in attendance.

Over the years the OMADS (or entertaining arm of these old boys and girls) gave many plays and concerts, but their forte was the revues performed around the 1930's, 40's, 50's and 60's.

Here is a small selection of personal memories of those involved.

Paul Rollinson recalls :-

"I appeared in my first play at Morley Grammar School. In the fifth form, we were all expected to stage a play, probably the Shakespeare which was that year's GCE choice – in our case, Twelfth Night. I was chosen to play the old rascal Sir Toby Belch, and this was my first significant appearance in front of an audience. I also committed my first sin –by walking on stage without removing my glasses!

The next year we did a very different production, the modern comedy Sailor Beware. I played Henry Hornett, father of the bride. The following year we returned to Shakespeare for Romeo and Juliet, and I again played the father of the bride (Juliet's dad Capulet). So I was well into the habit of portraying an older character.

The school also staged an annual drama competition, in which teams from the four 'houses' competed. In later years, I remember Stella Scargill often

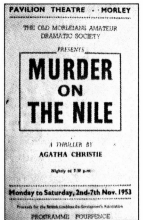

The OMADS revue 'Spring Fever' presented at the New Pavilion Theatre in 1948.

The revue 'High Time' was presented by the OMADS at the New Pavilion theatre in 1951.

The OMADS production of Agatha Christie's thriller 'Murder on the Nile' at the New Pavilion Theatre in 1953.

related to me how she had come to see this competition and, during the interval, as she sat towards the rear of the audience, she was noticed by the headmaster, **Mr F H Hulbert**, who, with a twinkle in his eye, asked her if she was talent spotting.

So maybe that was one way we novice amateurs found our way into the world of grown-up amateurs. Another way, after our schooldays were over, was to join the ex-scholars' dramatic society, well-known in the town by the acronym OMADS – alias Old Morleians' Amateur Dramatic Society. This was another group of highly regarded local players who each year (why only once a year?) presented a play, usually a comedy at the Pavilion.

More knowledgeable people later told me how talented these players were. In particular, it was said, **Grace Lindley** was a consummate actress who could certainly have made it as a professional. The same was said of her daughter **Anthea.**

But by the mid-Sixties the OMADS was not in a healthy position. Former pupils simply didn't seem to want to join, so in July 1965 the society decided to form a liaison with the senior pupils by staging an evening of one-act plays involving both OMADS and the school. They did one play, the school did another, and the third was cast from both sources.

I don't really think this had much long-term effect on the OMADS' future, and it gradually faded out. But it had introduced me to a collection of amateurs who were also members of the operatic society. Well we all have to start somewhere!"

The cast for 'Murder on the Nile' presented by the OMADS at the New Pavilion Theatre in November 1953. Included are Leo & Arthur Leathley, Norman Stevenson, Harold Brown, C. Norman Lee, Marie E. Rhodes, Michael Stead, Freda Corns, Cedric A. Sutcliffe, Elizabeth Johnson, Renee Burrow, Mary S. O'May & John T. Hawkins. The producer was Ladley Pearson.

Celia Hopkinson e-mailed from Nottinghamshire

"Does anyone these days remember the act of Wilson, Kepple, and Betty? **Leo Leathley**, **Cecil Fox** *(my father) and* **Hope Bryant** *worked out their own version of this, which used to bring the house down in the OMADS revues. The difference in the height between Leo and Cecil, and the slinky eastern charm of Hope was a winner. Amongst the sketches performed by Leo and Cecil was the golfing sketch. Old, familiar and guaranteed a chuckle. Then there were the monologues. The one that has stayed in my mind is 'The Parsons of Puddle'. Leo and Cecil dressed as vicars carrying open prayer books singing their amusing, slightly risqué story whilst executing a sedate dance during the chorus."*

Mrs Janet Wood wrote from Gildersome :-

"In 1938 I was a young **Janet Holmes** *when I entered the local talent competition at the Pavilion organized by the OMADS, as part of their revue 'Chuse 'Ow.' I went along with my friend and workmate Edith Gaunt who was an accordionist; we were employed at Greenwood & Walsh's mill. My mother made my dress for the occasion and accompanied me to the show,*

where I sang 'Sweetheart' from the musical 'Maytime,' which was made popular at the time by Nelson Eddy & Jeanette McDonald in a Hollywood film of that name.

Having to use a microphone made me feel nervous and strange, for at that time I had not been singing very long and had received no voice training. I wasn't even a runner-up, but was pleased to be presented with a large box of Black Magic chocolates

As a member of the Rehoboth Church Choir I sang many solos and eventually took singing lessons. Sadly the church is now demolished, but it once stood on Dawson Hill. At twenty-one years of age I passed my exams for ALCM and sang in many events at churches and chapels in the area. My husband and I are music lovers and still sing in choirs and with the Morley Music Society. Clifford also sings with the West Ardsley Male Voice Choir."

Mrs Olwyn Chew says :-

*"It is hard to believe that the late and famous **Ernie Wise** performed in front of Morley audiences on the stage of the New Pavilion theatre, but he did, although he was the twelve-year-old Ernest Wiseman at the time.*

During the week commencing Monday 14th March 1938 the Old Morleians Amateur Dramatic Society was presenting their revue entitled 'Chuse 'Ow" and this included a local talent contest. Ernie won his heat on the Tuesday night and then performed in the finals on the Saturday evening when he was declared the overall winner. I was a member of the OMADS and on this famous occasion I was not performing but was busy in the auditorium selling programmes and chocolates for the society. I well remember Ernie's performance, he came on stage playing the part of a cheeky lad and he was very popular with the audiences. Dressed in short trousers and flat cap, he was full of confidence as he tap danced and told jokes, one of which was,

When I awake in the morning I toss a coin,
If it comes down heads I go out to play,
If it comes down tails I go to the pictures,
If it comes down on its edge I go to school.

This incident has become part of Morley's theatrical folklore, but of course, it was not realised at the time how famous the performer was to become."

Ronnie Barraclough comments:-

*"**Mrs Chew** has mentioned that **Ernie Wise** was an entrant in the OMADS local talent competition that was held at the Pavilion Theatre each night of the week commencing Monday 14th March 1938, with the winners going forward to the Saturday night finals. The competitors were cleverly*

introduced to the audience by raising the curtain on a broadcasting studio, each performer chatting with the announcer in the style of the "In Town Tonight" radio broadcasts, which were popular at the time.

*To assist my research into the history of the Pavilion theatre I corresponded with **Mr Wise** in 1998, and although ill, he was kind and patient enough to give me his personal reminiscences of the occasion. He well remembered taking part and winning the contest but, at the time, he wished he had not won because his father kept the prize money of £3. 3s. 0d, no doubt to assist the family budget, whereas the other entrants were presented with a box of chocolates which Ernie would have preferred because he could have kept them. He also recollected that during the Saturday evening one of his clogs went missing and he finished the finale with a clog on one foot and an ordinary shoe on the other. It is interesting that **Janet Wood** confirms the award of a box of chocolates to the non-winners in her letter. It was only one year later that **Ernie Wise** was performing at the Leeds Empire theatre whilst on tour with Jack Payne in 'Band Wagon'."*

'What Now?' '**the offcomed-un**' reminisces

*"The highlights of that week in 1946 were many. How could the show fail to entertain with the talents of **Harold 'Leo' Leathley, H Cecil Fox, Hope Bryant, Arthur Wilson and Tommy Marshall** on parade. The latter two gentlemen performed a comedy duo, with their own brilliant brand of inebriated innuendo. Anyone following them on stage had great difficulty in maintaining the 'quick-fire' continuity insisted upon by the producer **George Wilson**.*

*The rehearsed cue for the ensuing act rarely worked, and it was not unknown for **Tommy Marshall** to depart completely from the expected. At times it was total mayhem. At one point the duo's exit down right was a cue for music to mark the entrance downstage left of The Singing Bevin Boy (me) rendering a very serious version of 'Way Down Upon The Swanee River'. The singer fell into the water of his own imagery for two nights running, and had to make a hurried exit, leaving the Musical Director none too pleased as he quickly silenced the orchestra, ready for a second go. When it was decided to keep this particular contretemps in the show, with a scenario of loud shouts coming from the orchestra pit, the terrible pair of **Wilson and Marshall** reverted to the script without prior reference, and wreathed in satisfaction, stood in the wings enjoying the sight of a bewildered singer and nonplussed **John Wilson**, the MD. They truly 'didn't give a damn', for I was a very raw 21 year old and they were all mill-owners, but we were all letting our hair down after six years of war.*

*Here marked the return of The Sand Dance a lá Wilson, Betty and Keppel, as executed by Messrs **Fox, Bryant & Leathley**. All who saw the*

146

performance remember it, for the uproarious, side-aching laughter that gripped the audience. They were far superior to the professional act they parodied. And talking in professional terms, there was a superb troupe of dancing girls who really added glamour to the show.

One untoward incident occurred during the week. There was a male visitor backstage who had nothing to do with the revue, but who seemed to be known to some of the cast. During the interval, the heavy front of house curtains were drawn, when suddenly, this chap appeared upon the apron of the stage and began to harangue the

Morley's famous sand dancers. Cecil Fox (on the right), Hope Bryant & Leo Leathley.

audience with accusations. Everyone was his oppressor, and the diatribe was far from complimentary. His shrieks and shouts had an immediate disturbing effect. All persuasion to get him to leave the stage failed, until male members of the cast and stage crew had to forcibly remove him. The poor chap put up a desperate fight lashing out with kicks and punches. He was finally sedated by a doctor, and eventually taken away. The incident was never discussed and never reported. Most strange."

An interesting report was found in the 23rd November 1951 issue of **The Morley Observer:-**

On Tuesday afternoon last, The Grammar School held its Annual Speech Day. The young music master **Donald F. Webster** arranged the programme, and the standard of singing (especially by the soloists) was high.

Occupying a seat in the balcony was **Mr C. W. Towlson**, musical director of the Morley Music Society. The Chairman County Alderman **Harry Hardy**, remarked that Mr Towlson would be listening keenly for any recruits to the Music Society's ranks.

The soloists were **Maureen Spurr, June Rhodes** and **Moira Riley**, with **John Barstow*** providing piano accompaniment with distinction beyond his years.

*Now Professor of Pianoforte at The Royal College of Music, London.

The Morley Technical Institute Amateur Operatic Society.

Later known as

The Morley Amateur Operatic Society

Founded in 1927

And still functioning in the early 21st century

Authors'note: When we embarked upon gathering information for this book, by far the greatest response came in the name of this society. We received contributions from all over the United Kingdom and overseas from ex-members, yet strangely, little input from the present membership. There were notable exceptions in the shape of three very young ladies who went to a great deal of trouble because of their enthusiasm for the amateur stage.

Society Officials (as at the close of 2001).

Past Presidents
  1927 - 1928 J H Willis, Director of Education
  1929 – 1931 Charles F Thetford
  1932 – 1935 Councillor Alex Wilson JP
  1936 – 1965 County Alderman Sir Harry Hardy
  1966 – 1977 Donald Burrill, Director of Further Education
  1978 – 1979 Harry Burrow
  1979 – 1980 Renee Burrow
  1980 – 1981 Christine Barras
  1981 –1982 Graham Inman JP
  1982 – 1984 J W Preston
  1985 – 1986 A F Bramley
  1986 – 1987 Leslie A Curless
  1987 – 1989 Barbara Holliday
  1989 – 1991 Hazel Noble
  1991 – 1993 Reginald Taylor
  1993 – 1996 Geoff Snowden
  1996 – 1998 Josephine Marshall
  1998 – 2000 Steven Holt
  2001 - Susan Geary

Life Members
  Jan Dawson * Janet Middlebrook * David W Hunt * Maureen Jones
  Renee Burrow * Steven Holt * Barbara Holliday * Jeffrey Holt * George
  Longden

Holder of NODA Diamond Bar
  Renee Burrow

Holder of NODA Medal for 50 years service
  Hazel Noble

Holders of NODA Medal for 25 years service
  D A Reekie * D E Hirst * J McCracken * P Powell * B Holliday * C Firth
  J Middlebrook * G Snowden * J C Snowden * M Jones * G Brooke
  M Eames * C E Collinson * J Marshall * S Geary * G Taylor * J Holt *
  S Holt * S Marshall * M Scargill * E Pashley * K Barron.

Officials of the Society in 2001:-
  Chairman - Glennis Taylor
  Secretary - Melanie Holt
  Treasurer - Joyce Benn
  Business Manager - Barbara Holliday
  Wardrobe - Jean Carter
  Patrons - Joan Snowden
  Tickets - Ann Lockwood
  Musical Director - David Hann
  Accompanist - Sarah de Tute
  Stage Manager - Peter Benn
  Deputy - David Ingham
  Sound - Robert Brett

The Young Generation.

The **Barracloughs** were surprised to receive a visit at home from cousins
Victoria, Jennifer and Clare Callery offering their contribution to the
book being prepared about amateur entertainment in the town. Their stories
are reproduced exactly as they wrote them. They surely are the beacons
upon which the Society and the Morley public must focus and navigate
toward achieving a venue 'for the town – within the town'. The need is for
a small theatre capable of properly staging the productions for which this
Society is justly proud. Local audiences are not prepared to travel to the
Leeds city centre after dark and risk the hazards that are all too abundant.

Morley appears to have lost its sense of identity during the last quarter of the 20th Century and too much is dictated by the remote City Fathers down in the valley of the Aire. Why should our operatic friends have to stage their productions in Leeds? Why should faceless bureaucrats continue to destroy the heritage of a great town? Is there a reawakening of a civic identity in Morley? Possibly so, but let those responsible provide the means and support that the amateur stage needs to survive, for it is the barometer of a community's well-being. There is sufficient wealth in the old borough; Morley has become the heart of an artery of motorways leading to all points of the compass. Were civic leadership to engage with commercial sponsorship, who can say what might not be achieved.

Victoria Callery (writing in October 2001)

Performing Arts

"From a very young age Performing Arts (Dancing, Singing, Acting, etc) became a very strong hobby of mine. By the age of three I joined a Dancing School called Victoria Stansfield. I really enjoyed Dance lessons and within one year of joining I was chosen to play the part of a goblin in the public Pantomime called Cinderella. My dance tutor chose me and as it was my first time I was extremely excited, to make it even more professional it was held at Wakefield Opera House, which was a huge honour as I was only four (one of the youngest in the cast).

The Pantomime went really well I mostly sang with other children in a small group and did quite a lot of dancing supporting the main characters or dancing in a trio. The costumes were stunning and each and every one of us had one specially made, our hair and makeup, it was all done to perfection, so the show went just as planned and I couldn't wait to join in my next pantomime.

After my first pantomime I was a lot more confident and decided to participate in competitions. I mainly did solos but sometimes for a change did either duets or trios. These events normally took place on Saturdays dotted all over the country; sometimes I came home with medals or trophies. But at the age of six I decided to leave the Dance Class and try and look for one nearer home but I couldn't find any that suited me. Since then I have never been back to another Dancing School.

Four years later.

Then when I was ten I heard from my friends Holly Beck and Victoria Caldow that there was going to be a Morley Pantomime. They had seen it advertised in a Morley newspaper and it was going to be called 'Jack and the Beanstalk'. When they told me I jumped at the chance, as it was another chance for me to perform again. On the following Monday after finding out I went to the dance shop to buy Jazz and Tap shoes for the audition, I was

150

so excited but nervous at the same time.

Finally the audition day came and we all gathered into one room where the director and chorographer told us all to sit down and be quiet. They then split us up into groups and asked us to sing, dance and then perform solo. We could do anything we wanted that reminded us of the music.

After the long day I was picked for the pantomime and so were both my friends. We would go every Tuesday for practice and near Christmas when there wasn't much time left we would go every evening.

The practices became a lot harder as I had to remember all the songs and dances I was in (as I was in quite a lot). Then a week before we did the show our costumes came and we were able to practice performances in the Town Hall where the show was to be held.

All in all we would be doing five shows with two of them held on the same day as it was a matinee. That was the toughest, as it was very tiring. The shows finished about ten to ten thirty so I didn't get home until eleven thirty and when the matinee was on the next day we had to be back at the Town Hall for one o'clock to get all our makeup on ready for the show that afternoon.

The following week the pantomime had a very good write up in the Morley newspapers so the show was obviously a big hit. My friends and I were really pleased and couldn't wait to participate in another Morley pantomime.

After the Morley pantomime I have now taken up a new different hobby Irish dancing. I go every Monday and thoroughly enjoy it and because most of my family is Irish they all encourage me every step of the way."

Jennifer Callery aged 10 (her letter is also dated October 2001)

"I have been in three plays, one was a Christmas play and the two others were the 'Wizard of Oz' and 'Rats'.

In the Christmas play I had to read in front of a live audience, however the problem was I had a very bad cough and cold so when I was reading was all croaky and I felt like screaming, but I got a good cheer.

In the 'Wizard of Oz' I was in the choir, except this time my brother James was in it and my cousin Clare. James was a soldier and he had to wear this suit, which made him look fat and everybody started laughing. Clare was a munchkin and a jitterbug so she was mainly singing and dancing on the stage.

In 'Rats' I was the main part because I was a rat. We had to wear these tatted clothes, which looked like a tiger had been ripping them. We also had to wear a hat sideways and some sunglasses (personally I think I looked cool). 'Rats' was mainly a musical.

I really enjoyed doing all these plays and I hope I will get picked for another play in the near future."

Clare Callery aged 12 (October 2001)

"I have been in many school plays, but my favourite was one that I did in Year Six at Churwell Primary School. It was called the 'Wizard of Oz' and is a very well known musical. In this play, I was one of the natives of Munchkin land, which is where the play was set. I had to do a solo in front of the audience, which was very embarrassing. Then I had to be a bad guy called a jitterbug, which is a strange animal which dances people to death. At the end when all the cast sang a song together, people commented that I smiled all the way through.

I am no longer at Churwell primary school, but at Batley Grammar School. Last year I did a Christmas Concert 2000. This was a choir and a school band service in which the band played songs and the choir sang songs. In a few of the songs, the audience could join in. It was a great success and I enjoyed it."

Thank you Victoria, Jennifer and Clare. Your contributions were not sought, but arrived bursting with your enthusiasm for live amateur theatre in the town. You may well have given others the lead that heralds a reawakening of such interest in the town.

Four Generations 1927 - 2000
Back in 1927 **Kathleen Lodge** performed in the "Mikado" at Morley Town Hall little knowing that she was setting a trend that her great-grand-daughter would follow nearly three quarters of a century later. Kathleen married **Jimmy Fawcett** in 1933 and their daughter **Pamela** was a dancer with the Society for many years, and a member of the successful Top Town Team. Pam became **Mrs Alderson**, and it is her granddaughter **Katie Alderson** who carries the family flag today.

Kathleen Fawcett was a great stalwart of the Operatic Society, and was still helping in various ways in the post-war productions. She was one of the founding celebrants during the golden jubilee of the society in 1977.

Almost 75 years after her great grandmother's appearance in the Mikado, **Katie Alderson** made her first appearance for the Society in the pantomime "Robinson Crusoe". Katie began dancing at the age of three at **The Rachael Swann School of Dancing** and passed her audition for the Society with flying colours. Grandma Pam reported, "she loved every minute of the

The New Pavilion theatre enters the new millennium as the 'After Dark' night club.

pantomime, and shed tears when it was all over."

But what of the person who is the missing 3rd generation in the above story? Pam's son **Mark Alderson** took no part in amateur theatricals, preferring football and cricket. He now plays golf. Congratulations on your talented daughter Mark; this story could not have been written without you.

The Pavilion Years.
An introduction by David Hirst

David Hirst in 1960 when he played 'The Heavenly Friend' in the MTIAOS's presentation of 'Carousel' at the New Pavilion Theatre.

"The Morley Amateur Operatic Society was founded in 1927, and until the outbreak of the Second World War in 1939, had a successful existence performing a mixture of Gilbert & Sullivan operettas and musical comedies.

The Pavilion Theatre became available as a regular venue for the Society's major annual show during the years immediately following the War, and this building was a major contributory factor to the prosperity enjoyed during the golden years of 1947 to 1967. It was originally built with facilities for theatrical performances, and this made it almost perfect for the Society's principal activity, the production of musical comedies.

The building was at that time in regular use as a

cinema, which meant comfortable seats for an audience of some 800. A splendid balcony complemented the sloping floor of the auditorium, and it was here in the front row of the Dress Circle where the town's dignitaries were seated during the Friday evening performance. With such logistics, everyone was ensured of a good view of the stage.

The Society at that time was officially known as the Morley Technical Institute Amateur Operatic Society, and was in fact an evening class under the aegis of the then West Riding County Council. The standard of singing and dancing was extremely high, for in addition to the annual Pavilion show, concert versions of grand opera were performed, including such major works as Aida and Carmen. Some idea of the popularity of the classes can be gauged from the society's 1960 performance of Carousel, which had a cast of over 70.

These years followed the long period of wartime austerity, and preceded the meteoric rise of television in the home. There were less demands on people's leisure time than today, and amateur clubs and societies of all types flourished within the walls of church and chapel premises. Cinemas and theatres too were well attended. This then was a golden age when large audiences were attracted to the Pavilion for the Society's shows staged in the November or December of each year. It was quite common, for queues to form at the box office, particularly on the first day that the booking office opened.

Much will no doubt be written elsewhere about the many talented people who appeared in the shows over the years, as there was always an abundance of gifted singers, dancers and actors. It is to another kind of talent and skill that a great amount of credit should be given. I mentioned earlier that the Pavilion was an almost perfect venue for the Society's shows, but there were drawbacks.

The principal problems centred round the size and shape of the stage area. While the audience saw a wide proscenium arch, the area behind that arch narrowed considerably, with little room to left and right to enable an easy flow of people. The back of the stage tapered to form a not very large triangle with hardly enough room for the stagehands and electricians and the large amounts of scenery and properties. In these circumstances where a large group of chorus members was waiting in the wings to make a grand entrance and meet the unwavering discipline of the Musical Director's baton, any person trying to leave the stage, could be hard pressed to find a bolthole. So the fact that cast members were often packed in close proximity to one another, could account for at least six couples who met and married during shows at this time.

So it is then, that a tribute has to be paid to the many people never seen by the audiences, the back-stage staff. All dedicated volunteers who

154

overcame the many problems that staging a large musical at the Pavilion threw at them. The Stage Manager was always a key figure in this area, as once a production starts, he is the man in control. In this respect the Morley Society was always fortunate in having a series of highly competent men occupying this post. When one looks in more detail at the enormity of the problems that they faced in preparing the theatre for a production, it will be seen that, time and again, their patience and skill were tested to the full.

Being in regular use as a cinema, The Pavilion was not available to the Society until after the last film performance on the Saturday night. With a dress rehearsal scheduled to take place during the afternoon of the next day, a tremendous amount of work had to be completed. A time consuming operation was the removal of the cinema screen and speakers, and by the time this was completed, lorries were waiting in South Queen Street, loaded with scenery and properties, all of which had to be manhandled into the theatre.

Then began the process of hanging backcloths, curtains and lighting battens. With a fly-platform some 35 feet above the stage, this was an arduous and to some extent, dangerous operation.

Stage lighting too presented its problems particularly in the early days when makeshift equipment was often used (made up by the stage staff), and included the use of biscuit tins as reflectors. The electrical power supply to the cinema was tested to its limits during shows that required complicated lighting. On one such occasion, the extra demand caused a complete blackout during a performance, leaving the cast and the audience very much in the dark. It eventually became necessary to increase the capacity of the power supply by the installation of new mains cabling.

The work of setting up the stage went on through the night and during Sunday morning, each scene being set up in turn and then taken down to be stored in such a way as to be easily and quickly located during the show. This was a complicated business, particularly where a show had many scene changes involving a need for speed and dexterity, in absolute silence (not always achieved).

Another problem with the Pavilion was the acute shortage of dressing room accommodation. 70 members of cast could not be accommodated in the cramped and rather dingy area under the stage. The ladies of the chorus together with make-up and costume staff used this area. Gentlemen of the chorus had to make their way across the yard at the back of the theatre into St Paul's Sunday School to make their costume changes. This was done come rain or snow. During one show the Sunday School was not available, and the men were obliged to change in the vestry of the church, which involved running backwards and forward across the main road in assorted costumes, braving the traffic and the catcalls of local youths. Fortunately *the traffic was not heavy in those days, which is more than can be said of the comments."*

Curtain Up.

Ronnie Barraclough & 'The Offcomed-un.'

The OMADS made a success of using The Pavilion during the 1930's for various productions, and this must have prompted the Operatic Society to spread its wings and move to the theatre in 1938. 'The Desert Song'was an immediate success.

On 11th November 1938, **The Morley Observer** led with the headline

A 4.0 am Queue in Morley:Amazing Rush for "Desert Song" Seats.

The popularity of the MTIAOS's choice of the Desert Song as their annual presentation has been demonstrated in amazing fashion this week.

On Monday morning the booking office in South Queen Street was besieged as early as 4 o'clock in the morning by members queuing up for seats and when the booking was opened five hours later there was an enormous queue waiting. Throughout the day those engaged on the booking were kept busy, and there was still a queue in the evening and the booking office did not close until long after the usual closing hour. Some people had to stand in a queue for several hours, and even then had to leave to go to their work and were still without tickets when the day was over.

"It was an astonishing and delightful start", Mr A. E. Turner, Hon. Secretary of the society, told the Observer reporter. "The public has shown that they are pleased with the choice we have made and are keenly looking forward to the show. There have never been bookings approaching such weight on the first day, he said, since the society produced 'Merrie England'eight years ago."

Saturday Cleared Out

After the first days booking there were no seats left for the Saturday evening performance at the theatre. Bookings for other nights are satisfactory, but the officials of the society are anxious to point that there are still a very large number of seats available to the public. There are particularly a large number of low-priced seats available.

This is the first time the Society has decided to present their annual production at the Pavilion.

Morley Observer 25th November 1938

Booking heavy but still plenty of low priced seats available for the middle of the week.

Morley Observer 2nd December 1938

No more than a handful of seats vacant on any night of the week.

The intervention of the Second World War was to mean many fallow years for the society. Members became scattered all over the globe on various wartime duties, and for those who remained at home, spare time was at a premium. Any show that required a large cast and extended rehearsals became impossible to stage. The interruption was to last eight years, so it is no small wonder that both the enthusiastic amateur and the paying public rejoiced to see the rebirth of live musical comedy. Yet this was in marked contrast to those earlier generations of amateurs who found their activities cut off by the impact of the First World War, for there was a Morley Operatic Society during the early years of the 20th Century. A reference to this appears elsewhere, for the authors accept that the present Society was founded in 1927 having no continuity with the earlier operatic group, such was the impact of that 'war to end all wars.'

The return of the Morley Technical Institute Amateur Operatic Society with their first post-war production of 'The Vagabond King'was only their second experience of using The New Pavilion Theatre. It was a remarkable show for many reasons.

Many of the cast had no experience of playing in such a large production, and those having to administer and stage-manage a musical comedy of such complexity, had not done so for eight years. The stagecraft of the old hands was not in question, but for newcomers, it was another matter. Everyone had experienced a huge gap in continuity and not all had anticipated the difficulties and lack of facilities to be found backstage at the New Pavilion.

A strict discipline was needed to move a large chorus on and off the stage into almost non-existent wings. Any hesitation after stepping from the stage meant that the next person behind began a shunting motion causing those attempting to leave the stage to come to a juddering halt. The smooth flow of people had to be carried out in complete silence, which was not easy, particularly when obstacles along the way had to be negotiated.

There were metal stays supporting the scenery, numerous cables, and stored scenery. Performers in costume passing in opposite directions within that confined space often became welded in embarrassment. Hooks become enmeshed with lace, or buttons on a sleeve would snag in the most unlikely locations. Funny? Yes, but hilarity had to be curbed backstage in the ever strict pursuit of silence.

Having left the stage the gentlemen of the chorus were often faced with a change of costume, and it was necessary to leave the theatre for some remote dressing room. For them access was via the 'stage door'that opened directly onto South Queen Street from the rear of the stage. The door was the type seen in most places of entertainment and emblazoned with the words **'Emergency Exit. Push bar to open'**. As the act of 'pushing the bar' made a lot of noise which the audience could hear, and the fact that if the door was closed, those on the outside couldn't get in, mayhem could prevail.

But versatility being the watchword, one could leave the stage as a liveried servant and next appear as a rabble-rouser serving the cause of Francois Villon, **Clifford Barrass**

"onward, onward, swords against the foe,
onward, onward, the lily banners go.
Sons of toil and danger, will you serve a stranger?
And to hell with Burgundy."

So who cared about the small matter of a door?

The conditions both on stage and behind the scenes played havoc with the vocal chords of most singers. The atmosphere was dusty and dry, and for anyone having a demanding role to sing, the fear of 'drying up' mid-piece was very real.

So various performers would arrive each evening well stocked with their favourite antidote to ensure constant lubrication of the mouth and throat. All remedies were considered medicinal, including the wonderful elixir of equal parts of port and brandy. This potent mixture could only be taken in moderation, but it did wonders for the voice and was efficacious for stage fright, and an upset tummy. There was a period when potash tablets served a useful purpose. These tiny lozenges could be slipped under the tongue during solo work etc., but those who had not signed the pledge, usually preferred getting into the spirit of things with the afore mentioned gargle.

The difficulties of performing at The Pavilion were nothing compared to the problems faced by the stage crew, particularly with a demanding show such as 'The Vagabond King'. Again the people involved were comparatively new to that venue, and the physical limitations of storing and handling complicated sets were enormous. To their great credit they coped, but only just. Certainly after 1947, a greater emphasis had to be placed upon the Society's ability to stage any show under consideration.

During that Monday evening 3rd November 1947, the many and varied scene changes, wrought havoc. The final curtain came down around 11.15pm, with many members of the audience having left to catch the last buses. To the great credit of everyone (excluding the Producer) faults were quickly put right. Certain set changes were eliminated, and some scenes played before drawn curtains, enabling the following scene to be set up behind. The players upped the tempo. The stage crew worked like demons and sped through the changes. The improvement prompted some wag to remark, *"if we're not careful we shall be disappearing up our own overture"*.

For all its faults The Vagabond King was a success on the strength of the cast and its ability to create 'make belief', while those behind the scenes battled with reality. The joy of the audience at seeing a live musical spectacular again was most evident. The music was stirring, as was the singing of the principals and chorus. It was to set a standard for years to come.

Both on and off stage there are many incidents that make a particular show memorable. The Vagabond King was no exception. The scene was the court of King Louis during the siege of Paris by the Burgundians, with the whole cast on stage, to witness the arrival of a Burgundian herald, played by the late **Harry Burrow**. The herald had come to court to deliver an ultimatum to King Louis, on behalf of the besieging army. The speech was a diatribe of all the terrible consequences that would befall the citizens of Paris should Louis not surrender the city.

Pillage, rape, murder and plunder were each in turn heavily scored, leaving the court stunned and silent. That is, except for one citizen standing behind the royal throne in the shape of Edward Booth, (an original member from 1927), and a man of swarthy complexion and large proportions, guaranteeing his 'stage presence.'In real life Teddy was a hospital porter at Leeds General Infirmary, and was well used to human suffering. During the silence following the Burgundian Herald's speech, Teddy leant forward and quietly whispered to the King, *"you're in the shit now your majesty."* But was it a stage whisper? We all hoped it was!

Stage Whispers.

Of the Operatic Society I have memories of many small happenings over the years, which are probably of no interest to anyone else, but for me, hold many cherished recollections of my father Cecil Fox. So wrote **Mrs Hopkinson (Celia Fox)** *from her home in Nottinghamshire.*

"My earliest memory is of 'The Vagabond King,' the first show after the war. I was eleven years old when I went to the dress rehearsal and was amazed that such chaos could produce such a good performance. I was confidently informed that a bad dress rehearsal was always a good sign.

I remember **Clifford Barras,** *such a changed character on stage from that in real life. His voice and everything about him was different as he absorbed the role of Francois Villon. The music was stirring, and each year brought the magic of a new musical. I heard them so many times that I almost knew them by heart.*

After the Saturday night finale came the presentation of flowers and speeches from the Pavilion Stage. **Harry Hardy** *(later to become Sir Harry) always calling my father "Cicil", much to our amusement.*

On my first visit backstage I wondered how do they manage with hardly any wings to move into, and that narrow little staircase down to those pokey dressing rooms?

*I remember my father's (**Cecil Fox's**) decision to retire once he'd achieved his ambition to play Hardboiled Herman in 'Rose Marie'. He kept his word and was able to relax and enjoy other performances in the years to come until his death.*

*Several more memories are tucked away in my mind and although I no longer see the shows I still keep in touch with **Jocelyn Simons (McGough)** and **Renee Burrow**. They were two of the original principals from the first days when I was introduced to the Operatic Society at the New Pavilion Theatre Morley."*

Sheelagh Senior (nee Woodcock) writing from Liversedge

"I was talking to Betty Shelly (Briggs) last night at the Music Society, about Ronnie Barraclough's book on the history of the New Pavilion, when Janet Wood, who sits next to me, said "I'm in that book. I was on with Ernie Wise in a talent show back in 1938". She was then Janet Holmes aged 16. It's a small world."

*I have memories of the M.T.I.A.O.S. in the 1950's. During a dress rehearsal at the Pavilion, the producer **Ted Gilbertson** addressed the cast saying that there was to be no knitting in the wings; me in my innocence (all 20 years of it) exploded and said there wouldn't be room for needles and wool in such a cramped space. I didn't know that he meant 'no kissing or cuddling'.*

*When we did 'Showboat', I was one of the darkies, and the make-up was extremely difficult to remove. It seemed to ingrain itself into the skin. I felt as if I had the dirtiest ears in Churwell School.....and me a teacher! One of my happiest memories was doing a dance in 'Showboat' with **Peter Newton, Peter Powell** and **Anne Saynor**. We weren't in the official dance troupe, but we gave it our all and enjoyed every moment."*

Margaret Nowell (now Meg Bunney) writes as follows :-

*"It was the tradition in our family that each year we went to see the production by Morley Technical Institute Amateur Operatic Society. Imagine my delight when the time came for me to actually take part. I felt immediately at home upon joining the Society, as I already knew so many of the people involved. The ballet mistress, **Millicent Hirst**, was my first dancing teacher; **Mary Bentham** was a near neighbour; **Peggy Haigh** worked opposite to where I lived, and **Clifford Barras** was a business acquaintance of my father. All were long serving members of the Society.*

The first production in which I appeared was 'White Horse Inn' in 1959 and the Society asked me to gain the permission of both my mother and my school, as I was then only sixteen years of age. I can still remember the

'Babes in the Wood' presented at the Ebenezer Methodist Church with Willie Roberts & Reg Taylor as the robbers, Harold Schofield the policeman, Margaret Nowell (Bunney) & Barbara Kellet the babes and Hilda Buttery as the dame.

lyrics of some of the songs, and the great fun we had trying to coordinate the dance in which we exchanged slaps on the thighs and faces with our partners, called a 'shuhplattler.'

The other production I appeared in before going off to college was 'Carousel' in 1960. Looking back, I must have been brimful of confidence, as I auditioned for the part of Carrie Pipperidge, but was asked to join the dancing troupe, and take the part of the acrobatic dancer in the dream sequence. I had never danced on stage with a male partner before and realised this role was to be a real challenge. I remember when the rehearsals began in earnest, and we worked very hard perfecting the demanding duet with my excellent partner Bernard, since of course, **Councillor Bernard Atha OBE**, and a Lord Mayor of Leeds.

Eventually the week of the show arrived and the tension and excitement were mounting. I seem to recall that the dress rehearsal did not run smoothly, but when it came to our big moment on the first night, I made my entrance on stage, standing proudly on Bernard's rock steady shoulders. The rest of our pas de deux followed, with some spectacular movements that made the audience gasp, and each night this happened with great success, repaying us for all our hard work in rehearsals.

During the final performance, some of the cast were enjoying celebration drinks, but I was told quite firmly that I was not allowed to join them until after the acrobatic dance with Bernard. Only then did they say "alright, you

can now have a shandy, well you are only seventeen". Happy days."

"*My only appearance with the Morley Amateurs*" by **Shirley Downes (nee Grimes):-**

"My grandparents originated in London, and arrived in Morley before the 1st World War when grandfather was appointed, manager of Morley's Pavilion Theatre by the Coronation New Pavilion Co Ltd. **David James Collins**, prior to his residence in Morley, had been an actor. Grandmother, along with her three sisters was also on the stage as, indeed, was my great-grandmother.

In view of this family history I think it was most appropriate that the tradition continued, albeit in a small way, when many years later, three of **David James Collins's** granddaughters trod the boards as amateurs at the Pavilion Theatre. My sister Margaret entertained there during the war playing her accordion in the **'Hot Spots'** concert party to help raise funds for the British Legion. My cousin, also called Margaret, was an accomplished dancer in musical productions staged by the Amateur Operatic Society, and I was able to make my one and only appearance at the Pavilion as a member of that society.

It was Easter 1955 and I had just left school as a 15 year old when I decided to join along with my neighbour and lifelong friend **Keith Spruce**. As a girl I had been in the audience at a number of the musical shows and it always seemed like magic to me. The orchestra playing the introduction, the lights slowly going down and then the raising of the curtain to reveal a colourful scene with the cast singing and dancing dressed in beautiful costumes.

Perhaps I fancied myself on the stage among all the action, so along I went with Keith to join the society where his uncle, **Peter Powell**, introduced us to some of his fellow members. Peter was, of course in many productions usually playing the leading comedy role. I was apprehensive, at first as I was shy and unsure of myself, but I became more confident as the rehearsals progressed.

The production that year was 'Quaker Girl,' and I was to be one of the

This photograph from the November 1955 production of 'Quaker Girl' shows a Quaker Girl, top left, Nancy Woodcock (now Stephenson), and four Villagers. Front centre is Lilian Westmoreland and front right is Shirley Grimes (now Downes).

singing villagers. I went along to the dining hall at Morley Grammar School each Tuesday and Thursday where the rehearsals got more intense as the year progressed and the date of the show crept nearer and nearer. The principals, the dancers and the singers rehearsed separately until the exciting time when everyone was brought together and the show rehearsed straight through.

When the costumes arrived it was hilarious trying them on and laughing at each other when they were too big or too small. Then the Sunday arrived, the day before the opening of the show, when most of the day was spent at the Pavilion in full dress rehearsal with the orchestra, and not going home until the producer was fully satisfied with everyone's performance.

After obtaining permission to leave my employment early each night of the week so that I would be in time for 'curtain up,' I had a week of sheer enjoyment and excitement being on the theatre's stage instead of out front in the audience. What a wonderful week it was, perhaps grandfather was looking down in approval.

All the months of hard work had been well worth while, the show was a success and I remember rounding off that marvellous week with a party for all the cast at the Grammar School on the Saturday before going down to the Pavilion for the final performance.

Unfortunately this was my one and only appearance on the Pavilion's stage because of the changes in my employment, meeting new friends, including my husband to be and joining him to sing in his skiffle group. Perhaps if I had stayed with the 'amateurs,' who knows, maybe I could have become one of the principals whom I so admired and gazed upon with awe when they were performing. Ah well, Que Sera!"

Lorna Tipling, writing from Penn, Wolverhampton :-

*"I have many memories of the Operatic Society. I was a dancer and we used to rehearse in Morley Grammar School, Tuesdays and Thursday nights. There were about twelve of us, and our teacher, **Millie Hirst** (nee Kitson) really worked us hard. We did spend some time in the musical rehearsals, as there were numbers to learn. Then the dreaded day would come when scores had to be put away and we had to sing everything by heart.*

In the spring we used to perform a concert version of an opera, and I used to enjoy working on the quite difficult scores of such works as "Carmen" and 'Il Trovatore'.

Occasionally we would take a trip to see another company perform the same show as we were putting on. We once went to Barnard Castle. Little social groups sprang up within the company, one of them being a rambling club. We would meet usually on a Bank Holiday Monday and we would catch a train to somewhere like Skipton, and we would do quite a long hike.

Brian Robertshaw and **Trevor Carr** were usually the leaders. I am still in touch with Trevor Carr and his wife. We had a couple of trips to Blackpool where we used to stay at a large hotel at the North end. We would go out on a Friday night and come back on Sunday. A trip to the Pleasure Beach was always great fun, but it was usually cold as we went very early or very late in the year. One year the coach broke down on the way back (by a pub would you believe) so the landlord stoked up the fire, kept the bar open, and there we waited for a replacement coach to come out from Morley – not too much of a hardship.

There was always great excitement when the costumes came. Also when we finally rehearsed on the Pavilion stage and the producer came over from Blackpool. Of course we dancers were always having the occasional panic during performances when a button or press-stud would pop off, or a headdress would slip, but it was all part of the fun. We all got on very well with each other, although as teenagers, we were always a bit in awe of the principals."

Trevor & Jean Carr writing from Bushey, Herts:-

"I doubt if you will remember me as I was a member of the operatic society for only a short time. At the age of 15 I had formed a Concert Party and produced several revues at **St Mary's Congregational Church**, where my father, the **Rev Frederick H.Carr** was Minister. I was then called-up for National Service, and my service in the Army extended to 2 years because of the Korean War.

After a year at Ingle's Leather Mill in Churwell, I went to college in Chelsea, so I was away from Morley for much of my young adult years. Returning as a teacher at Peel Street Boys School, I joined the Operatic Society where some of my 'old' concert party now performed - **Lorna Tipling, Margaret Peel, Jean Fawcett, John Batty** and **Geoff Stockdale.**

We were all in 'The Quaker Girl' (1955). It was during the rehearsals of 'Quaker Girl' that I got to know Jean, and we became good friends, furthered by the time we spent together with a group of operatic friends at a memorable Blackpool weekend. The following year we were married and moved to Hertfordshire.

My short time in the Operatic Society was not only very happy and enjoyable, but it was there I met and fell in love with Jean, my wife to be. Jean and I are still singing with a local concert group, averaging some 50 performances a year, and raising money for charity."

164

The Pavilion Cat.
(I've got a 'feline' your fooling)

We will call her 'Puss in Boots', for not only was she a stage struck feline, but also had an addiction to footwear. Fortunately for the Society her appearances on stage during a live performance were few, but one occasion is still remembered.

In the middle of a scene she made a grand entrance down stage right, moving with the grace and assuredness of her kind. After all this was her domain and she had every right to see what all the fuss and palaver was about. To the delight of the audience dear Puss decided to stop and view the proceeding from a sitting position carefully chosen so that she might enjoy the warmth of the footlights without singeing her tail. She was also most careful not to get too near 'her in prompt corner.' The actors carried on as if nothing had happened. So did the cat, for she became bored with it all and left the stage with an air of assured condescension.

For the most part Puss reserved her undoubted talents to backstage activity and demonstrated her largesse by sharing her expertise with those whom she considered worthy of her attention. Two such lucky individuals were **David Hirst** and **Hazel Noble**.

David was quite unsuspecting of this animal's generosity when he found his particular present in his footwear at the close of a performance. Most people will know that Mr Hirst is not renowned for 'putting his foot in it,' but in that instance, he clearly didn't have a leg to stand on.

With the attitude of Annie Oakley as she sang, *"anything you can do, I can do better",* we can do no better than to let Hazel tell of her experience in her own words.

"When I performed in The Merry Widow at the Pavilion Theatre the dressing rooms were in the cellar where the walls were decorated with brown paper. I was playing 'Praskovia' and had a lovely green velvet dress with train. The theatre cat had her kittens on the train, but she was removed, kittens and all, into a box. There was no mess or anything on the train and I wore it on stage as if nothing had happened."

This is the only piece of 'litter-acy' in the whole book

The Power of Advertising.

One of the 'legends' in the history of Morley's amateur operatic society relates to the 1938 production of The Desert Song. Such was its popularity when first presented, that the demand for tickets was quite incredible. Within just one day the show was a sell-out. In truth, this was not quite the case. Queues started outside the booking office at 4 o'clock in the morning and on at least one night, the 'sold-out' notices went up. What would today's society give for audiences like that?

By the mid-sixties, attracting audiences had already become a battle, and several clever tactics were dreamed up.

For *Annie Get Your Gun* in 1965, with **Stella Scargill** in the title role, the society tried a novel tack: to publicise the show on beer mats, which were handed round the town's pubs. It was a clever idea. Most landlords were always grateful for such things, and the customers were soon lifting their glasses to read the intriguing slogan: **They're doing Annie**

The same show also benefited from press publicity organised by the society's first Press Officer, **Derek Hudson**, who later became chief reporter at the Yorkshire Post, travelling the world and in particular covering the early trouble in Ulster at the start of the Seventies, and later reporting from the conflict in the Falklands in 1982. Back in 1965, he managed to get several *Annie* items into various newspapers, including a small item in the mass circulation Sunday People, reporting that people backstage would be able to hear what was happening on stage through an internal radio link.

Another original idea for publicity came from **Stan Townend**, who ran a silkscreen printing business in Pudsey, and for many years designed and printed the covers of the society's programmes.

When little known 'Pickwick' was being rehearsed in 1972, Stan came up with the idea of plastering the town with 'The Pickwick Paper', a newspaper about the show. Quickly the 'paper' was prepared, 'splashing' the show's story about spinster Rachel Wardle eloping with the Dickensian con-man Alfred Jingle, and using photos from the programme. As for getting the newspaper distributed around the town, members donned costumes and took on the demanding task of visiting pubs and working men's clubs to spread the word.

We also called on the help of Harry Secombe, who was so closely associated with the show. It happened that during the build-up to the Morley show, he made a week long appearance at the Wakefield Theatre Club. He was renowned as one of the kindest men in show business, and he readily agreed to write a programme note carrying his best wishes. This fact also appeared in local newspapers, bringing a little more publicity.

Yet another publicity scheme was employed at this time. On the Saturday morning immediately before opening night, several members dressed themselves in appropriate costumes and mingled with the crowds of shoppers in Queen Street, while others rode on a lorry supplied by **Jim Collinson** – a publicity ruse that was repeated for several more years.

For the 1961 production of 'The Merry Widow' a great furore broke out over the Society's pre-show advertising. Whether the gimmick was in bad taste or not is open to conjecture, but as they say *"no publicity is bad publicity"*. A look at the following full page six-inch article in The Yorkshire Post, (which was complete with photographs) tells its own story.

Merry Hell Over Merry Widow's Smiling Mourn.
By David Bruce

Merry hell has broken over the head of 'The Merry Widow' of Morley. For a gimmick aimed at promoting Morley Technical Institute Amateur Operatic Society's presentation of 'The Merry Widow' has been labelled *"morbid, distasteful and offensive"*.

Publicity material printed on Victorian style funeral cards is at the heart of the trouble.

'In Memoriam' is printed on the face of the funeral cards. Inside they read, "Madam Anna Glavari wishes to announce the sad death of her husband. But she is quite happy about it. See The Merry Widow at Morley Town Hall, Monday to Saturday, November 23-28 1970."

Madam Glavari – 'The Merry Widow' – is played by **Delia Broadley** of Wheatfield Court, Pudsey. A hundred of the cards were printed for distribution round clubs and pubs. But they met with a hostile reception.

The Mayor of Morley, **Ald. George Rogerson**, commented *"although the cards are within the context of 'The Merry Widow' I do not think they are in good taste"*.

The Mayoress, **Mrs Margaret Rogerson**, said *"I think they are distasteful"*.

The **Rev G. Eric Forman**, Superintendent Minister of Morley Methodist Circuit, said *"It is a clever idea, but I can see the funeral cards causing distress"*.

Mrs Joyce Lacy, landlady of The Needless public house in Scotchman Lane, Morley, added *"They are morbid. They do not amuse me a bit. They are offensive"*.

Mrs Barbara Holliday, publicity secretary of the Morley Operatic Society, said she hoped the cards would not upset anyone. She added *"we have now stopped distributing them because of the adverse comments. These days people are not coming to shows like they used to do. This was an attempt to make them sit up and take interest"*.

There are no prizes for stating how many times 'The Merry Widow' was mentioned, and it is of interest to note that all of those local personalities called upon to make comment, were staunch supporters of the operatic society. It makes you think!

Barbara Holliday's comment about falling public support only three years after the loss of the Pavilion as a venue, certainly reflects the dire circumstances with which many local societies were faced in the closing quarter of the 20th century.

The society's second production of 'Oklahoma' in 1976 used a clever and picturesque method of advertising. Children in eye-catching costume toured the town on a gaily decorated float or should we say a brewer's dray? Certainly a well thought out gimmick, for the famous Tetley shire horses were used to draw the ensemble. What better way to grab the attention of the public!

More Stage Whispers

David Hirst writing from his home in Morley :-

"There are many stories of mishaps with the Society and various properties during performances. One leading lady had her big solo number somewhat abruptly curtailed when a large piece of scenery fell on her. Needless to say she soon recovered and carried on in true theatrical tradition.

During a fight scene in 'The New Moon' real swords were used, and as a result of over enthusiasm, one gentleman of the chorus was carted off to hospital with a bad cut needing several stitches. This was **Harold Gilbertson**, *brother of Ted. Both had a keen sense of humour as others will surely relate.*

In the same show Harold missed his scheduled exit from the stage, and found himself stranded high above the main deck of the good ship whatever it was, in a false section of scenery representing the poop deck. This was merely a walkway with no exit into the wings, clad in painted canvas to give an impression of railings; the audience could only see him from the waist up. Unfortunately for Harold, his ruse of play-acting 'the look-out' became less and less appropriate as the time approached for a poignant love song to be performed below him. It was time for Harold's ingenuity to take over; he adopted that age–old comic trick of walking down an imaginary set of stairs, legs ever bending lower until the body disappears from view. For the rest of the scene Harold lay flat on his stomach and waited until he could make his escape.

Then there was the final dramatic scene in 'Show Boat' when the jetty on which several of the principals were standing, collapsed leaving them standing up to the waist in a large box section. Luckily no one was seriously hurt in any of the shows."

Letter received from **Delia Batty (Broadley)** at her home in Bakewell, Derbys :-

*"I had a very nostalgic afternoon going through old scrap books and thinking about the 'Morley Years'. Of course I have many wonderful memories of the days at the Pavilion Theatre. I think my main one is my 'one night stand' in 'Waltz Without End' and being on stage in a 'real theatre' for the first time. How we all got through that night I shall never know, although I do believe it was mainly due to **Harry Burrow**."*

(Editor's note: This was the occasion when Delia, then unknown to Morley audiences, understudied the principal role because Jean Lloyd had a throat infection. Delia had previously performed the part for Trinity Methodists in Pudsey. She took over a difficult and demanding role at the 11th hour, and stepped onto a large stage, unrehearsed with other principals or orchestra. Her appearance was to be the forerunner of many stunning performances over the years. This story was featured in the Morley Observer on 7th December 1957).

'Waltz Without End.' At only a few hours notice and without rehearsal a member of Pudsey Amateurs, Delia Broadley, had to step into the leading role of Wanda for the M.T.I.A.O.S's annual production, which this year is 'Waltz Without End.' It was not until 5 minutes before the curtain rose on the first night that the Pudsey girl met her leading man Harry Burrow. The part of Wanda, the spoiled daughter of a Polish nobleman should have been played by Jean Beilby, who however had suffered from a cold for about two weeks and felt at Sunday's dress rehearsal that she could not do justice to the part. Miss Broadley was called in and asked to stand by. Before the show opened on Monday Mrs. Beilby tried several of the musical numbers but decided to stand down and so, without rehearsal, without meeting many members of the cast, and without knowing the stage, Miss Broadley played the part. Happily she knew it well, for it was only two weeks ago that she played the same role with Pudsey A.O.S. To play the same role at only a few hours notice must have been quite an ordeal. It was, however, an ordeal, which she overcame to give a sparkling vivacious performance and some delightful singing. Harry Burrow had rather a difficult first night. He had to appear opposite someone with whom he had never rehearsed and until he settled down at about the middle of act 2 this difficulty was apparent. But Mr. Burrow has a voice, which is capable of thrilling the least musical ear and in act 3 his singing of the lively 'Fools Follow a Rainbow' set a standard of which any professional could be proud.

(Delia continues)

*"I remember the night when the electric power failed and the whole theatre was plunged into darkness. **David Reekie** went on stage with a torch and together with his father-in-law **Norman Hartley** at the piano in the orchestra pit, kept the audience entertained for a long period of time. I was down in the dungeons (sorry dressing rooms under the stage) with **Stella Scargill** when the lights went out and we held hands and felt our way out. Surprisingly I don't remember being scared, but I would be now. Norman was my uncle and David married Mavis, a first cousin.*

*One romance I do remember happened during 'Brigadoon'. **Fred Stokes** was an import from Garforth and playing a principal role. There was a close link being built with the Garforth Operatic Society, largely due to **John Green** the Producer. Many Morley members assisted at Garforth, it was a happy arrangement. Fred Stokes came into the show and met **Eileen Farmer**, and love blossomed. I recall Eileen being in tears at the after show party sobbing, "I'll never see him again". However, she did, and they ultimately married and had two sons."*

Jocelyn Simons (McGough) writing from Aylesbury:-

*"I appeared in the first show after the war 'The Vagabond King.' I was 17 years old when I took an audition for the part of Katherine, never thinking that I would get it, but I did. I had sung many times as a soloist with **The Cosmos Concert Party** (almost all under the age of 18) who entertained soldiers in hospitals, such as Pinderfields and Menston. There were many 'do's' in Morley and its environs, but I had never taken on such a responsibility.*

*The producer was a very old man, and I have to say, wasn't much help. I had to rely on **Cecil Fox** and **Clifford Barrass** to pass on their stagecraft and guide me through. I remember with great pleasure receiving seventeen bouquets at the Saturday night performance, and I reckon everyone in the cast had gifts handed over the footlights. The first night must have been the longest show in memory. Scene changes slowed everything down and the audience was not best pleased. Lovely experience though.*

*I always remember **Ted Gilbertson**. In the 'Vagabond King' he played King Louis, and during the court scene, because of the large cast, he was unable to get down from his throne for me to address him – except for the final night. I turned to speak to him sat on his seat of power, and he was nowhere to be seen. Suddenly a voice whispered in my ear "I'm here you fool, I'm here!"*

*The following year in 'New Moon', I was supposed to be dragged on stage by two sailors, but they were not anywhere to be seen. They finally arrived and all was well, except that poor **Cecil Fox** was on stage alone, waiting* for our appearance. I think he was sitting on a log with only a hat as a prop. The things he managed to do with that hat were incredible, and the audience was laughing their heads off. What a trouper and fine performer Cecil was.

In 'Lilac Domino' I was supposed to be sobbing my heart out on my father's shoulder, yes it was **Ted Gilbertson** again, and he was saying in my ear, "There's consternation at the convent, Mother Superior has found the seat up." So I was really laughing, not crying.

I was a member of the **St.Mary's Players** and we were able to put on many straight plays. I attended the church and remember the **Rev Fred Carr** and his family. **Trevor Carr** is I know mentioned elsewhere in these remembrances. Trevor had an elder brother Rex, and a younger sister Marie.

Morley had many thriving choirs, with perhaps **The Morley Musical Society** being top of the tree. Each church and chapel boasted a choir, and there was much integration of effort when the oratorio season came round.

Leo Leathley's Concert Party travelled far and wide, and was always fun to perform with. We were always well received by the public. Happy, happy days. There were so many fine singers in the Borough of Morley. **Jean Scott, Emily Fletcher**, and **David Reekie** come readily to mind, but there were many others."

Christine Brook (Smith) writing from her home in Morley

Christine Smith (Brook) when she performed in the 1960 presentation of 'Carousel'.

"Morley had the most wonderful talent of any small town that I know of. I met my late husband **Leslie Brook** because of our membership of the Operatic Society. We were friends at first and just singing members, when **Dorothy & Sydney Ladley**, and **Joyce & Alf Holliday**, would invite us out on trips.

We went to the Scarborough Open Air Theatre, concerts, meals at each other's homes and so on; best of all was our musical soirees around the jolly old piano singing all the songs of the shows. Super days.

Leslie and I got engaged during 'The Desert Song.' We married in 1964 only four months after starting our courtship, and these were the best and most wonderful years of my life. Music was our common interest and we were in various choirs after the operatic society.

Leslie passed away at Christmas 1977 leaving a legacy of treasured memories."

Mary Scargill writing from her home in Morley:-

"Steven Holt has all the programmes from the first show in 1927 to the present day. I have in my possession the 'fan' hair decorations used for the first show, 'The Mikado.'

During the show 'Pickwick' at the Town Hall there was a courtroom scene when we sat on benches, the front one collapsed and we fell backwards on to the back row. We managed to stay upright until the end of the scene only by leaning on those behind us, but it was very painful for those at the back as the wooden plank was resting on their legs along with the weight of five people. The show went on and the audience didn't notice it.

A scene in 'Orpheus in the Underworld' presented in 1987, called for a hot air balloon for which I borrowed a wicker mill basket. On arrival at the next rehearsal I was horrified to see the producer had cut the basket in half to enable it to fit on the stage. Luckily when I returned it, the mill owner accepted my apology and said it did not matter.

On one occasion I had had an accident and appeared on stage with a plaster cast on my leg, which was covered by the long dresses used in the show. Later I was wearing a calliper but had to remove it for a scene at the seaside in 'No No Nanette' 1982, when we were wearing old fashioned bathing suits.

I was performing on one occasion in a pantomime being presented at Bruntcliffe School, when the cast had to struggle through snow to get there. It turned out there were more people on the stage than in the audience, but the show went on.

I think we were the only society to present 'Charlie' awards for things going wrong. Silly mistakes by performers or stage crew would qualify for one. The presentations caused a lot of hilarity at the party given after the show.

During the run of 'South Pacific' in 1992 at the Town Hall the ceiling collapsed, luckily during the night, or it could have been a real tragedy had it occurred during the show. The show had to be abandoned except for one night when it was performed in the Morleian Room for the families of the cast. To do this everyone had to work very hard to create scenery from rolls of wallpaper and anything they could lay their hands on.

*There was of course the tragedy of our much-loved **Tony Roberts** who collapsed and died at rehearsal. He is still missed by all who knew him.*

*An interesting item is that **Steven Holt** has never missed a show since he joined the society, and his mother Betty helped front of house and as a tea-lady. She was very ill in hospital during the run of 'Hello Dolly' in 1999 at the Civic Theatre, Leeds but she was allowed out of hospital specially to see the show, but unfortunately, she died shortly afterwards.*

A person who had been a member of the Ebenezer Methodist Chapel told me that after one show a letter was received complaining that it was disgusting a church group should show their legs. I wonder what they would think of some of today's shows?"

Pam Fawcett writing from her home in Morley:-

*"I joined MTIAOS in the dancing chorus along with my cousin **Pauline Taylor** (nee Beveridge) for the 1951 production of 'Magyar Melody'. Our dancing mistress was **Olga Brown** at that time; later on **Millicent Hirst** (nee Kitson) took over.*

The ladies of the chorus and the dancing girls had dressing rooms under the stage of the New Pavilion. Our room had been the 'coal-hole' or so I was led to believe. They did clean and paint it out for us. The gentlemen of the chorus were outside the Pavilion in a room that I think was part of the Working Mens'Club.

I have long and happy memories with the Society from 1951 to my last production of 'Oklahoma' in 1958. In 'Showboat' (1956) we had to black-up. In this day and age I don't think it would be deemed politically correct, but who knows?"

Reg Taylor remembers Holy Smoke & Legionnaires with lustre :-

"Two incidents with the MTIAOS at the Pavilion; in 'Carousel'during the Heaven sequence, someone opened the stage door, and all the smoke effects were blown into the auditorium. They could see us, but we couldn't see them.

In 'Desert Song' during some wintry weather, the soldiers appeared on stage (after their dash from St Paul's school) with snow glistening in their hair and on their boots."

Extracts from a letter received from **Peter Powell** from his home in Churwell. The remainder of his story appears elsewhere.

"I was conscripted into the Royal Navy in 1942 until 1946, and on demobilisation, being at a loose end, joined Morley Amateur Operatic Society in 1947. My first appearance in a full musical, 'The New Moon' was in 1948 at the Pavilion Theatre (now a night club). From 1948 to 1964 I appeared in every annual show playing comedy roles in several of these productions.

I remember the dressing room arrangements for the men at the Pavilion. If you were a principal you got to dress in the old projection box backstage, a cramped and cold place it was too – heating was an old antiquated gas ring, not at all satisfactory.

The men's chorus and 'small parts'used the schoolroom at the rear of the Pavilion, and gained access by crossing the schoolyard and climbing up an arrangement of boxes into the fire escape door some six feet above the ground. Not an easy task if your costume consisted of silk stockings, knee breeches and frock coats, not to mention the powdered wigs, particularly if it was "chucking" it down.

I shall never forget the year we did 'Rose Marie'. The men couldn't use the schoolroom and were ensconced in the St Paul's Church vestry on the other side of South Queen Street. The looks on the faces of the public as Mounties, Red Indians, lumberjacks etc emerged from the church and crossed the road, were a sight to behold. One night in particular was quite hilarious, it was snowing rather heavily, and all the male chorus in body stockings with little aprons back and front, and feathers stuck in our wigs, paraded across the road, just as a crowded bus pulled up at the bus stop. It is a wonder that that double-decker didn't topple over as all on board rushed to one side to get a better view. Never before, and certainly not since, have a line of Mohican Indians been seen crossing the wintry wastes of Morley so near the Fountain Corner.

Those were the days; it was never the same after the Pavilion "chucked us out". The Society did find alternative venues to stage their shows. The Town Hall was acceptable I suppose, but it did not have the atmosphere of a theatre."

A few recollections of life as a member of the MTIAOS, **Paul Rollinson** writes from his home in Brighouse:-

"Where do they come from, amateur entertainers? How do they get started? Where do they learn their craft? Are they born with a complete set of ready-honed talents? Is it a bit like buying a freezer meal from Sainsbury's – open it up and it's ready to be enjoyed?

When we go to see an amateur show, we usually find a real mixture of abilities. Some amateurs would be better suited to selling tickets or sweeping the stage. Others improve each year. And some are quite simply totally competent; given the right opportunities, they'd be more than able to earn their living as professional entertainers.

*In my own early experience of local amateur shows in Morley, it was quite clear to me, as an impressionable teenager, that two of these nearly-professionals were **David Reekie and Stella Scargill**. But where had they come from? Where had they acquired their ability? God (or nature) had given them wonderful singing voices, plus a natural ability to walk* confidently on stage and over the years acquire total stagecraft.

A very different case was **'Big Jim' Collinson**, *who joined the society in the late sixties with his pal* **Geoff Brook**. *They weren't asked to audition – the society welcomed any new male member with open arms (though they'd have to be very long arms to stretch around Jim!) – so it must have astonished everyone in the society when they first heard Jim's magnificent bass voice. He was completely without musical training, but I remember* **David Hirst** *remarking that if Jim had started out earlier, with the right training, he could have ended up playing leading roles with the world's top opera companies.*

Jim must have been in his Forties when he made his first efforts on the amateur stage. He was a successful businessman with a large family and a big house down Scotchman Lane, and because of his business experience, he was inevitably asked to take on some of the society's business matters.

In some ways he regretted this, because his whole reason for joining the society was to give him a break from his day-to-day work. However I suspect that he was really pleased to play a useful part for the society in this off-stage role, as he never seemed at ease in front of an audience and eventually stopped altogether.

Everybody has to start somewhere. My own abilities (acting, definitely not singing) started with the childhood habit of doing funny voices and accents, and then impersonations of entertainers seen on TV.

One of the 'legends' in the history of Morley's amateur operatic society relates to the 1938 production of The Desert Song. Such was its popularity when first presented, that the demand for tickets was quite incredible, within just one day the show was a sell-out. In truth, this was not quite the case. Queues started outside the booking office at 4 o'clock in the morning and on at least one night, the 'sold-out' notices went up. What would today's society give for audiences like that?"

Curtain Down.

We are indebted to **Paul Rollinson** for the following contribution.

"KISMET means 'fate', and it did prove a somewhat fateful show for the society: it was the last one to be presented at the Pavilion cinema, which had for many years been 'our theatre', but not for much longer. In 1968, its owners decided to close it as a cinema and use it as a bingo hall – a sad end to a theatre, which had housed so many memorable productions over the years.

Getting a show on stage – that is, physically on stage with all the necessary scenery, furniture and props – is the responsibility of the 'stage

175

staff' who are usually taken for granted by both audiences and cast alike.

The 'stage staff' are really not staff at all. They are office workers, shopkeepers, estate agents, teachers, in fact all breeds of ordinary civilians. Unlike the cast who has had weeks to rehearse and prepare, they come together for only one week each year and immediately form a cohesive team. They toil diligently, silently and usually without much thanks, to make sure everything's in order for us selfish people who show off on stage.

As one scene follows another, there is the hard work of gathering all that's needed for the next scene. Collected from whichever nook and cranny it is being stored, then silently lifting it on to the stage and placing in exactly the correct place for the next scene. All achieved in the half light of backstage - well it is a task never given the recognition it deserves.

To most cast members, the Stage Manager is an ogre whom they encounter only once a year (in show week) when he fiercely rules that dark labyrinth known as Backstage.

This ogre doesn't speak often, except perhaps to growl 'Shift'or 'Hey up' to those people who don't realise that ultimately it's his responsibility to make sure that "It's Alright On The Night." The scenes must be set correctly, as if by magic, with not only the right bits of furniture, but also with the props that performers need left ready and waiting. All done within the right timetable which ensures that the curtain not only goes up, but does so on time.

The role of this ogre was taken during the 1960s and early 70s by the late **Eric Pashley**, whose own dour, taciturn persona was ideally suited to the role. Those who took the trouble to get to know him discovered that he was really a kind, gentle giant who enjoyed a laugh as much as anyone else. He later surprised everyone in the late sixties when he teamed up with the equally large **Peter Broadley** to appear on stage and make people laugh. Do you remember him as an oversize woman dancer performing Joyce Grenfell's song 'Old Time Dancing?'

Eric took his role as Stage Manager with an unyielding diligence. Like many of us, he believed the term 'amateur' simply meant unpaid, which didn't prevent him from approaching his craft in a professional manner. And so, when the committee selected the show Kismet as the production for 1967, he had serious reservations. He felt that this Arabian Nights fantasy presented huge difficulties for his department.

In the event the show, which used the music of Borodin as the basis for songs including 'And This Is My Beloved'and 'Stranger In Paradise', was a spectacular success – a very respectable production to mark the society's final show at the Pavilion Theatre.

The only bad moment for Eric came one night when he and his crew made their usual trip across the road to the Fountain pub for a quick and well-

deserved drink in the interval. Actually, they went before the interval, because that was the most sensible time: they'd already set their last scene for Act One, and now had the chance to take a break before they returned for Act Two. While the cast and audience were still spending the interval in their own ways, and the stage curtains were still closed, Eric & Co would return to the stage, 'strike'(i.e. remove) the existing scenery, and replace it with whatever was needed for the start of Act Two. This they did – well more or less.

That particular evening, they rushed back from the pub to the theatre in the December drizzle, and hurried through the stage door to do their stuff. Within a few minutes, everything on stage was 'struck'. The only trouble was that in their eagerness, they had removed the opening scenery for Act Two, which the few non-drinkers of the stage crew had already put up in readiness for Curtain Up!

Its change of role provoked a period of uncertainty for the operatic society. It seemed that, without much warning, the imminent closure of the Pavilion was ripping the heart of the society. Nothing would be the same again, we feared. We know of course that the society survived, thrived, and moved on to further successes. But at the time, we felt that we were simply 'going through the motions', uncertain of a long-term future.

This sea change was also reflected, no doubt unintentionally, in the society's choice of their next show – Rodgers & Hammersteins' Flower Drum Song, very different from their blockbusters, like Oklahoma and South Pacific. The storyline, about how Chinese people lived in America, involved characters of a very different style, and the show's whole nature was very different. It was, in truth, also less popular and, frankly less appealing. Further it contained fewer hit songs, and though the music was undoubtedly a major part of the show, the production style needed to be more realistic and the performers needed to have more of an acting background. The eventual cast was a major change from the very popular team that had become familiar to regular audiences.

The fundamental differences combined with the need to find another theatre. This pressing matter occupied much of the society's time, though little-known and oft-forgotten possibility was also considered; if there was no obvious venue for us, what about buying our own premises, or even building them?

*This was clearly a brave dream, but **Morley Rugby Union Club** had recently made a similar move. Their base in Scatcherd Lane had been a rather basic grandstand with, underneath the tiers of seats, a rather basic clubroom with the fundamental bar in a large room. This served as an after-match gathering place for supporters and also the venue for the club's monthly 'dances'. It had to be admitted that it hardly represented the finest* *in club facilities.*

In the mid-sixties, the brave and ambitious leaders of the club had decided to 'bite the bullet'and build brand new club premises from scratch. In time, this impressive new social club took shape at the rear and side of the grandstand, and very quickly became a major factor in the club's growing feeling of pride and purpose, as well as bringing in useful finance through the bar takings. They now produce a sell-out annual pantomime in this building.

With this as an example, a few members of the operatic society wondered if the loss of the Pavilion would prove the catalyst to a similar renewed sense of purpose. Whilst it seemed unlikely that finances would allow us to build our own premises, it might be possible to rent or lease a suitable building. Maybe no such appropriate building existed, and as the more imminent need to produce the next show took priority, the idea of establishing our own theatre club faded.

As for the next show, the final outcome was that Flower Drum Song was presented in 1968 on the stage at Morley Grammar School, where a brand new school hall had been built in recent years. Despite the modern stage and two large purpose-built dressing rooms (normally occupied in school time by young rugby and hockey players), it was by no means an ideal choice. It's out of town position was no help in attracting audiences.

So it was all change again for the next show in early 1970 – the society hired Morley Town Hall, the very place where the society had begun in 1927. In a similar back-to-our-roots mood, it was thought safer to produce a tried and tested crowd puller, the well-established and popular Merry Widow.

The hiatus of being forced out of the Pavilion was now passing, and the Town Hall continued as the venue later that year for the production of another old favourite, The Desert Song.

*For 1971 we turned again to the more recent creation of Rodgers & Hammerstein, producing The King and I. Richard Garnett of Guiseley was asked to play the King, while **Beth Pashley** was excellent as Anna Leonowens.*

With another success under our belt, the Society's confidence continued to grow, but the annual dilemma arose again: What show to choose for 1972. The eventual choice came about in a more democratic way than usual. Out of nowhere, there came a growing clamour to stage the recent West End Show Pickwick, based on Dickens's Pickwick Papers.

The show had been inspired largely by Harry Secombe, who was ideal for the title role of a tubby, warm-hearted, well heeled but innocent Victorian gentleman who, with his three fellow members of the Pickwick Club, travelled around England getting into all manner of scrapes. Apart from its very popular hit tune 'If I Ruled The World,' the show was not well known, and various carloads of members travelled to Ashton-under-Lyne to see the Dukinfield amateurs present what was a regional amateur premiere of the show. All who saw it were immediately convinced that it would prove an ideal society show, with lots of involvement for the chorus and a large collection of ancillary Dickensian 'characters,' such as the unprincipled solicitors Dodson and Fogg, and the prosecuting counsel in the courtroom scene, Sergeant Buzfuz.

*And so it turned out that Morley's Operatic society was to produce the Yorkshire amateur premiere of Pickwick. The title role went to **Tony Roberts**, a society stalwart and recognised as one of the kindest, warm-hearted and generous people in the society. He also had a roly-poly figure, which made him the obvious choice for Samuel Pickwick.*

However, because the show was so new to the realm of amateur theatre, no organisation had a set of scenery to hire out. Until this time, scenery was something that the cast gave little thought to. That wasn't surprising because it usually appeared, as if by magic, only on the day before dress rehearsal, when there was no time to stand and gaze at scenery.

The scenery was usually very impressive. It was, after all, hired from a specialist company. The society had determinedly refused to go down the road, which other societies had followed, building and painting their own scenery. The invariable result of this do-it-yourself policy was a very unprofessional appearance.

As we had already been forced out of the Pavilion, thus losing the ready-made aura of a real theatre, we were keen to make the auditorium of the Town Hall as much like a proper theatre as possible – and that included using professional scenery.

For Pickwick , however, this was not possible. It simply did not exist. We had little choice other than to build our own scenery – a mammoth task for the stage team. Eventually it proved a great investment, and as Pickwick grew in popularity other societies decided to hire our scenery.

The choice for 1973 was the better-known Hello Dolly! And for 1974 the society, with growing confidence, chose the less-obvious Orpheus in the Underworld, which despite its title, was just a light-hearted pastiche taken from classical literature. Good fun, but not really an audience puller.

In 1974, we chose The White Horse Inn. For this, the society again decided to provide its own scenery, but engaged the services of a couple of students at a local art college to design and paint the backcloth. The Friday evening before the Saturday dress rehearsal, the scenery arrived. The excited anticipation of a handful of members who were at the Town Hall that evening quickly turned to disappointment. The main backcloth, which should have represented the setting of the White Horse Inn, in the real-life lakeside village of St Wolfgang in picture postcard Austria, was presented

From the left: Delia Broadley, David Reekie, Harry & Renee Burrow in 'Oklahoma' at the New Pavilion theatre November 1958.

as a vast, very plain sheet without charm. The cloth was painted in the simplistic, even crude style, of a toddler's colouring book. A large oval of mid-blue (the lake), was surrounded by an area of lavatory-door green (the meadow), under a bright blue sky. And that was it.

Disaster loomed. What could be done at this late stage? Well, as we all know, it is precisely at times like this that people rally round and pull out all the stops. The party of deflated members took their leave of the Town Hall and repaired to the Cricket Club in Scatcherd Lane to drown their sorrows, where they began to relate their news to other members who were still unaware of the scenery situation.

Gradually, the mood of despair began to turn to a more positive attitude. Something had to be done. One member, **Paul Rollinson**, who had a little ability at art, was talked into trying to do something with the useless backcloth. Something? What? Overnight, the solution was found on the record sleeve of an LP of the show: a full-colour picture of the town square in St Wolfgang in Austria, the setting for the real-life White Horse Inn. It would create the ideal backcloth for the show.

So first thing Saturday morning, with the help of a couple of pots of paint and some brushes, the original artistic disaster was transformed, inch-by-inch, into the village square in St Wolfgang. By Saturday lunchtime other members turned up, and added the finishing touches – real brushes in pots, arranged around the stage to create an even more effective picture.

Once again, the show proved to be a great success."

The chorus in 'Oklahoma' November 1958.

The Revellers.

The Revellers was a Morley concert party extraordinaire. Its founder, principal comedian and unique driving force was **Harold (Leo) Leathley**. In 1930, he and a Morley dentist, **D.R.Brash-Grant**, were asked to produce a show at Morley Town Hall in aid of Morley medical charities and this became the forerunner of an organisation that gained prominence as **The Old Morleians Amateur Dramatic Society,** fondly known as the OMADS. The show was staged on Tuesday 28th October 1930 and included **George A. Liley, Sam Barron, Tom Burniston, S.B. Brook, Ladley Pearson, Robert (Bob) Stead, E.D. Fox, R.W. Smith, Vernon Westmoreland** and **Harold (Leo) Leathley**.

Two years later in 1932, **Leo Leathley** produced a revue at the Town Hall on behalf of the Morley cricket club in aid of the club's bazaar. Both the show and Leo Leathley were overnight hits, which gained him local fame as a producer as well as a comedian and so **The Revellers Concert party** was born. On this occasion the cast included **Fanny Robertson** (contralto), **Mrs. T.L. Watson** (violinist), **H. Cecil Fox** (baritone), **W. Lockwood** (pianist) and the comedian **George A. Liley**. With several members of the OMADS on board the group commenced a long series of voluntary efforts in aid of local charities.

At the outbreak of war in 1939 The Revellers immediately burst into action to provide top class entertainment for the forces, soon becoming the premier concert party under the direction of Northern Command as part of **Voluntary Entertainment Services** or 'VES', for short. At first they operated from the YMCA in Albion Street, Leeds, but moved to Greek Street with the YMCA very early in the war. Members wore an attractive silver and white enamelled lapel badge depicting the White Rose of Yorkshire with the inscription 'VES,' each letter took up one outer petal at the top of the rose, and 'Northern Command' occupied the lower two petals. This continued to be a badge of pride and was worn for many years after the war. As I write the one belonging to **Norman Hartley** lies on my desk.

The British Legion (West Riding County-Northern Area) placed an advert in The Yorkshire Evening Post calling for volunteers, and the first meeting of local artists was held on Friday 29th September 1939. By the November of that year *'a voluntary organisation for the provision of entertainment to the Forces stationed in Leeds and surrounding districts'* was up and running. The Revellers entertained an Anti-Aircraft Battery at Wellington Hill on Tuesday 7th November 1939, an RASC unit in Middleton on the following Friday of that week, and units of the 11ᵗʰ Armoured Division at Fenton Street Barracks on Thursday 16ᵗʰ November. What a 'hell for leather' start for those performers.

A year later after dozens and dozens of engagements, the party was at Harewood House Convalescent Hospital for Officers. This establishment appears to have been under the same command as Menston Hospital, for there is correspondence on file from the Colonel Commandant concerning visits.

Early letters from various military commands pays little heed to security and clearly indicates the whereabouts of army units, including the Royal Norfolk's and many AA posts.

Most weekends its members would leave Morley en-route to 'somewhere in Yorkshire' to entertain the soldiers and airmen at camps and RAF stations throughout the county. The artistes willingly suffered long tiresome journeys in black out conditions and in fog, rain and snow, all at their own expense and in their own 'free' time. On return to Morley, usually in the early hours, the weary entertainers could only snatch a few hours sleep before returning to their normal every day places of work. It was a magnificent voluntary contribution to the war effort by the Morley artists, their efforts certainly being appreciated by the entertainment starved troops. The only concession received was the issue of petrol coupons for those fortunate enough to still have a car on the road.

During the first year of the war **The Revellers** entertained over 20,000 soldiers and airmen and at the time **Mr. Leathley** said *"We've entertained in unfinished camps, in wooden huts without electric lighting or stage but also in fully equipped garrison theatres. After shows we have been entertained in sergeants' messes, with doorstep sandwiches served on tin plates, and by officers with food comparable to that in a first class hotel".*

In early 1941 The Revellers presented their hundredth show since the outbreak of hostilities. By this time half a million men and women on active service had been entertained and some 5,000 miles travelled.

There was a short break from the arduous travelling when The Revellers gave their 150ᵗʰ wartime performance locally, at the Pavilion Theatre in Morley on Sunday 18ᵗʰ January 1942, so notching up an average of six shows in every calendar month in just over two years. **Vincent Mulchrone** reported on the show from the wings, in his official capacity as news reporter for the Morley Observer, just before joining the RAF, *"A stranger in Sunday night's audience might have known there was something 'special' about the show he was enjoying. He would have been perfectly right, for the Morley Revellers were putting everything they knew into their 150ᵗʰ war-time production, and the packed-to-capacity house was eating it up and yelling for more".* The ticket receipts for that evening were donated to the

British Legion to provide a treat for children of serving men and war orphans in the district.

During their travels the Revellers experienced many unusual, funny and unforgettable moments. Here are just a few that were recorded at the time.

As a rule the show was non-stop but one night at a gun station there were seven enforced intervals. Seven times the alarm bells rang and each time the hall was cleared.

At a small isolated post some 70 miles from Morley, the leading soprano, Emily Fletcher, opened the programme by singing 'Whence Came You to this Lonely Place'.

On one occasion an air-raid alert on the journey home forced the party to take shelter in a thick wood and, to the tune of 'I Was Watching a Man Paint a Fence', the group sang 'We Were Stuck in a Bus in a Wood'.

When attempting to leave an aerodrome it was found that Ann Sanderson, the Revellers' crooner, had mislaid her identity card. This moment was immediately seized upon by the sergeant -of-the-guard to suggest she spend the night in what he described as "a very comfortable guard room".

During performances there were often interruptions by the air-raid sirens but usually the shows carried on regardless. However when the alarm was sounded at one RAF station the show had to cease temporarily to enable an officer to order the Lewis gunners to man their posts.

At a large camp the appearance on the stage of the Revellers' chorus girls prompted one private to leap to his feet and shout "Take their names, sergeant, take their names".

When Leo Leathley made his first appearance on the stage at a Garrison theatre many miles from home an unmistakably Morley voice from the audience shouted "How Do Harold".

After travelling through fog for two hours they arrived at a camp where the officer asked where in the room did they want the boxing ring. The mistake was quickly rectified, a stage erected and the show went on. Fortunately the boxers never arrived.

The Revellers arrived unexpectedly at a camp. An officer ordered the bugler to call the men on parade and when 'fell-in' they were delighted to find, they were to be given an evening of entertainment instead of some sudden duty.

The shows were often given in difficult conditions. At one venue a stage was specially erected, and what a stage! Tabletops were nailed across beer and packing cases, with good old army blankets (probably made in Morley) as curtains.

Just as the concert was about to start at a small army unit with few facilities, when a deserter was brought in to face his commanding officer.

He was already ensconced in a prime position in the front row of the audience. Not wanting his evening interrupted, the Major ordered the soldier to remove his trousers. 'B'aht breeks' the offender was seated at the back of the hall, while the officer carefully folded the man's trews and sat on them until the final curtain.

Here are some of the reviews earned by those remarkable artistes.

Harold 'Leo' Leathley.

"Past master of all types of comedy, he has refused many professional offers."

"The group is led by that inimitable amateur comedian and founder member."

"The audience immediately take him to its heart."

"Several sketches and cameos were enlivened by his antics, and his sure comic touch was seen at its best when he appeared before the curtain in confidental mood. His nods, winks, pursing of the lips, shakings of the head, and meaningful silences spoke more than volumes in this all too brief excursion into the back gardens of local life.

'I've got eight children, he said, seven living and one in Churwell'."

Emily Fletcher.

"Well-known local soprano who has been a member of the Technical School Operatic Society and has also appeared in an OMADS revue."

Anna Watson.

"The Revellers' violinist has had experience of similar work in the last war (1914/18), and this has proved invaluable to the party."

"Anna Watson demonstrating a remarkable technique on the violin."

Ann Sanderson.

"BBC crooner and has broadcast only this week with Michael Frome's band and is billed by the Revellers as "The Queen of Swing".

Hope Bryant.

"In burlesque she is hard to beat. She won fame in Morley by her performance when the celebrated Eastern dance was performed."

"That mistress of burlesque, her stonewall expression is the perfect counterpart of Leo's mobile countenance and plenty of fun is promised when the pair appear on the stage together."

Joyce & Dorothy.

"These girls are the cleverest dance team that Morley has seen."

"Only one dancer might be performing so neatly do they time their routines."

Verna Haigh.

"The Morley pantomime star who lends a professional air to the show."

Harry Burrow.
"The popular local baritone who took the part of the Red Shadow in the Operatic Society's 1938 production of 'The Desert Song'."
Jack Bottomley.
"Very popular with the troops as a leader of community singing is this 17 year old with his accordion."
Jack Popplewell.
"The Churwell song writer of "If I Should Fall in Love Again", introducing his song successes, with Emily Fletcher as vocalist."
Jimmy Firth.
"The 19 year old who has taken the place of Arthur Leathley (now in the forces) as stooge to Leo."
Norman Hartley.
"The whole show, of course revolves round this celebrated local pianist."
"Five hundred soldiers were laughing at Norman's quiet antics on his revolving piano stool, when two of the buffet legs splintered and down went Norman! Back went the heads of five hundred soldiers. Norman found that audiences are appreciative of tricks done the hard way."
The Revel Girls.
"An attractive chorus."
"The chorus have proved a very big and important addition. They comprise Betty Bryant, Barbara Barron, Amy Sanderson, Rene Sanderson, Margaret Stead, Mary Taylor, Margaret Smith, Dorothy Carr and Margaret Toulson. Miss Stead is proving an admirable understudy to Ann Sanderson."
George Speight & Norman Hartley at two pianos,with Dick Platt at the drums.
Or George & Stan Speight on two pianos, with Dick Platt.
"The trios are practically indispensable to the party."
Walter Leathley.
"Behind the scenes is stage manager Walter Leathley, brother of Leo, a great asset to the productions."
The Revellers continued their voluntary contribution to the war effort until the cessation of hostilities but that was not the final curtain by any means, for the concert party carried on through the 1950's and 60's raising money for charitable causes and entertaining those detained at Her Majesty's pleasure. Regular prison visits were made to every prison in the West and North Ridings of Yorkshire. A typical example is the one made to Northallerton Jail on Sunday 22nd September 1957. *"The show was excellent by any standards and the audience was full of appreciation. **Leo Leathley** held them in laughter as compere and mimic. **Norman Hartley** accompanied the show and had a solo spot with 'Autumn Concerto' and*

snatches from 'No No Nanette'. **Nancy Sykes** *sang, among other numbers, 'Love Could I Only Tell Thee', selections from 'Showboat' and 'Something Wonderful'.*

David Reekie *sang Negro spirituals, 'The Sergeant Major's on Parade', 'The Hippopotamus Song' and selections from 'Oklahoma', and* **Dennis and Stella Scargill** *obliged with 'Happy Days and Lonely Nights', 'Glad Rag Doll', 'Ain't She Sweet' and were inundated with requests for more. They obliged, to the rhythmic hand clapping of the prisoners, with 'Singing the Blues'. The* **Tolson Brothers** *entertained with their harmonicas. It was a great show and one of the prisoners said it was the best he'd ever seen. Another proposed thanks by saying that the party had not only given them excellent entertainment but also made them feel they were not forgotten men altogether".*

At that time the Northallerton Prison was categorised as a 'preventative detention' establishment and housed men under long sentences for reoffending.

1965 and still going strong

Twenty years after the close of hostilities, a reception was held in the Mayor's Rooms at Morley Town Hall to mark a special occasion for Morley's leading pianist and accompanist. In an evening of unashamed nostalgia, all surviving Revellers who could, gathered to pay tribute to **Norman Hartley** and to present him with a gold wristwatch. A book was treated during the evening containing the signatures of all those present.

His opening page states,

To Norman Hartley
Reception in Morley Town Hall
9ᵗʰ April 1965
to celebrate his 70ᵗʰ Birthday
Congratulations & all good wishes
From
The Revellers & their guests

A message from Morley's leading citizen simply read,
With our best wishes to an old and valued friend
Harry Brewster Mayor
Jean Brewster Mayoress

There followed the signatures of the Brewster's two children
Anne Brewster & John Brewster
Among the one hundred and eight signatories were family and friends representing every walk of life in the town and its societies. Reading

186

peoples signatures almost 40 years later is not easy, but the authors will try.

The family.
Norman & his wife Linda, daughters Muriel & Mavis and their respective husbands Eddie Walker and David Reekie, (son Donald lived in Calgary Alberta unable to attend). Grandchildren Julia & Christopher Reekie, brother Percy Hartley and niece Delia Broadley.

The Guests in alphabetical order.
W & F Akeroyd, Harry & V Baker, Bob & Nancy Barron, Joyce Beckett *(of Joyce & Dorothy)*, Harry & Jean Brewster *(Mayor & Mayoress)*, Anne Brewster, John Brewster, Peter Broadley, Les & Christine Brook, Harry & Rene Burrow, Dick & May Clark, Mr & Mrs C A Cookson, Bill & A D Crabtree, S & H Crumpton, G F & W Drake, James & Kath Fawcett, J W & M Firth, George A & E Firth *(Town Hall Supt),* Albert & Emily Fletcher, John H Foster, Cecil H Fox, Phyllis Green, Amy Hardy, B Hargreaves, G W Harrison, Arthur & Marion Hartley, Fred & Hannah Hartley, David E & Millicent Hirst, Cyril & B LIngham, Noel & B Jelly, David Johnson, Verna Killerby *(Haigh)*, Arthur Leathley, Harold & Sue Leathley, Christopher Leathley, Jimmy Leathley, Walter & Mary Leathley, George & Lena Liley, Phillip & Lisbeth Lockwood, Clive & Molly Mitchell, Gloria Munday, Marjorie Myers, Mabel Needham, Margaret Nowell, Eric & Beth Pashley, Tony & Clarissa Roberts, H & H Robertshaw, Dennis & Stella Scargill, Martin Scargill, Fred & Mary Scarth, Jean Scott, Roland & Wendy Smith, George & Rene Speight, Dorothy Spivey *(of Joyce & Dorothy)*, Nancy Sykes, Vernon Sykes, G & E Teale, Stanley & Gladys Tempest, C R & H Virr, C & H Walker, Brian Whalley, Harold Whitehead, GW & C Wilson, H A & A Wilson.
We shall never again see the likes of The Revellers!

The Show that Hitler Cancelled.

Tom Gomersall and **Ronnie Barraclough** were recently reminiscing about their happy boyhood days as members of the 7th **Morley (Grammar School) Boy Scout Troop.** There was talk of pleasant and exciting times at camps under canvas, cooking in the open air and evening singsongs around the campfire with mugs of cocoa in hand.

The conversation turned to less happy times. It was 1939 and the arrangements had been made for all Morley's scout troops to combine in the staging of a Ralph Reader type 'Gang Show' at Morley's own theatre, The New Pavilion.

There was so much enthusiasm, youthful zest and hard work involved in the many rehearsals that the show would surely be a success.

Unfortunately all the preliminary work was in vain, Mr. Hitler intervened, war was declared on Sunday 3rd September and the show had to be cancelled.

Amazingly, after such a long passage of time, Tom remembered the words of the theme song which was specially written for the show and which contains the motto on the Morley Borough Coat of Arms, 'Industria Omnia Vincit', (Work Conquers All).

INDUSTRIA OMNIA VINCIT.

> All around the earth, in every land,
> You will find us guides and scouts—a happy band,
> With a friendly smile and willing hand,
> To help the helpless through.
>
> While there are good deeds waiting to be done,
> Without a thought of glory to be won,
> We'll be prepared to carry on,
> As we have been taught to do.
> We may be tall or short or lean or stout,
> We may be guides or scouts there is no doubt,
> That we'll smile and whistle, chests thrown out,
> As we travel along the scouting trail.

With our staff in hand, and our kit in a pack,
We face ever onward, never looking back,
Be the way ne'er so rough or so heavy the load,
We can win to the end with these rules of the road,
INDUSTRIA OMNIA VINCIT AND
OUR SCOUT LAW, BE PREPARED!

The official programme for the Carrol Levis
'Search for the Stars'. (see page 190).

A young Harold 'Leo'Leathley, top class
comedian, producer and for many years the
unique driving force behind much of Morley's
theatrical entertainment. (see pages 181 to 187).

How Carroll Levis Discovered Morley's Talent.

Carroll Levis (1910-1968), born in Toronto, Canada, became famous for his shows, introduced by the tune "Stardust", which he presented both on the radio and in the theatre. The shows consisted of his "discoveries" for which he claimed to have auditioned a quarter of a million different turns.

Carroll Levis' "Search for the Stars" came to the New Pavilion on Sunday 10th March 1946 billed as "First Time in Morley: Morley Area Final" it was sponsored by the Morley Advertiser in aid of the Soldiers', Sailors' and Airmen's Families Association (President H.M. Queen Mary). The Morley Mayor and Mayoress, **Alderman and Mrs. T. Redick,** attended.

The name **Carroll Levis** was extremely popular at that time and the opportunity to attend one of his shows, although he was not personally in attendance, and support the best of Morley's talent, was so irresistible that, on the day the bookings opened at Midgley's shop on South Queen Street, a queue had formed at 6.30 am. The bookings opened at 9.0 am and by 10.10 am the theatre was fully booked. Hasty arrangements were made for a repeat of the concert to be staged on Sunday 31st March but on this occasion there would be no judges. A booking plan was rushed to Midgeley's and all the seats for this "unofficial" show were sold by 5.0 pm that same day. The admission prices were 2/6, 2/- and 1/6.

The panel of judges, who had to select two winners to go forward to the Leeds Area Finals, was **Miss Olga Wakefield, Miss Margaret Smith, Mr. A.S. Oakes, Mr. A.H. Jowett and Mr. G.W. Atkinson.**

The two winners were:-
Bill Woollin, (23), Tenor or Crooner, Railway Fireman, 2, Thorpe Ave., Thorpe, and
David A. Reekie, (20), Bass, Bevin Boy, 57, Howdenclough Road, Bruntcliffe.

The next four in order of merit were:-
Ada Raimond, Vocalist, Factory Worker, Bradley Place, Morley.
Margaret Parker, (14), Musical Comedy, Shop Assistant, "Cyrelldon", Scotchman Lane, Morley.
Brian Jarvis, (19), Cornet Solo, Apprentice Draughtsman, 33, Ingle Avenue, Morley.
Peggy Haigh, Vocalist, Heald Knitter, 52, Watson Street, Morley.

The following also took part:-

Marjorie, Will & The Two Dots, Variety, Dressmaker & Engineer, 10, Commercial St., Morley.
Cliff Bywater, Trumpet, Glassblower, 4, Birch Street, Morley.
Clifford Drake, Monologue, Engineer, 4, Brunswick Place, Morley.
Mavis Walsh, (17), Soprano, Weaver, Glen Mill Cottages, Morley.
George Stonehouse, Crooner, Engineer, 42, Foster Street, Morley.
Mary Wilcock, (17), Vocalist, Tailoress, 9, Syke Lane, West Ardsley.
June E. Melton, (14), Song & Dance, Schoolgirl, 3, Askey Avenue, Morley.
Margaret Collins, (18), Whistler, Waitress, 111, Bridge Street, Morley.
Lily Maude, Vocalist, Housewife, 5, Bowling Row, Cockersdale, Drighlington.
Thomas R. (Taffy) Williams, Baritone, Lorry Driver, 25, Peel Street, Morley.
Brian Hawkins, (14), Soprano, Schoolboy, 51, Dartmouth Avenue, Morley.
John Maskell, Tenor, Miner, 15, Kitson Street, Tingley.

The guest artistes were:-
Norman & George on Two Pianos.
Maharg, Magician, from his recent Garrison Theatre successes.
Leeds Sylvians.
Alan Broadhead, Popular Schoolboy Soprano.
Jean Loyd, Schoolgirl Vocalist.
The Four Martinis. (They may only have performed on March 31st)

Compere:- **Mr. Fred Balchin.**
Accompanists:- **Mr. Norman Hartley & Mr. George Speight.**
Stage Manager:- **Mr. H.B. Arnold.**
Producer:- **Mr. E.S. Butterworth.**
Stage Lighting etc.:- **Mr. Donald Hardy.**

The repeat performance on Sunday March 31st 1946 was again sponsored by the Morley Advertiser, in aid of S.S.A.F.A., and both concerts were exceedingly well received by the audiences, all the artistes being generously applauded on each occasion.

The stars from these concerts were included in a further concert arranged for Sunday September 15th 1946 in aid of the British Legion.

Morley Top Town Team.

The programme cover for the Morley Vs Ossett Top Town Contest at Morley Town Hall on 18th February 1958.

The Morley News & Observer announced its intention to organise a 1958 Heavy Woollen District Top Town Competition with each team having a maximum time of 75 minutes, with no restriction on the number of acts to be fitted into the available time. Morley quickly formed a committee consisting of the Mayor of Morley, **(Alderman Frank Sykes,) Councillor H. Leathley, Millicent Hirst, Norman Stevenson, Clifford Barras, Norman Hartley, Dennis Scargill and Malcolm Haigh.** Auditions were arranged and a Morley team was selected which, in due course, proved unbeatable.

On 11th February 1958 the Morley team travelled to Ossett Town Hall to compete against the Ossett team. The judges for that round of the competition were Mr. Duel Luscombe, producer of the Court Players at the Prince's Theatre, Bradford; Mr. G. Hemingway of the Yorkshire Evening News and Mr. Tom Moss, retired star comedian and T.V. talent scout. They voted two to one in favour of Morley. This was the only occasion when Morley did not gain a unanimous verdict.

The home leg against Ossett was at Morley Town Hall one week later, on 18th February. The judges were Mr. Tony Iveson of Granada Television, Miss Pat Jackson of the Yorkshire Evening Post and Mr. Clifford Johnson of the Dewsbury Pioneer Amateur Operatic Society. All three judges voted for Morley. After the show the youngest members of the team, **Brenda and Barry**, made a presentation, on behalf of the Morley team, to **Gloria Mundy and Blanche Walton** who were both celebrating their 21st birthdays.

When Morley met Batley at Morley Town Hall on 3rd June 1958 the judges were Mrs. Bertha Keighley of the Leeds Art Group, Mr. Peter Bernard, manager of the Huddersfield Theatre Royal and Mr. Frank Crosland an associate of Mr. Barney Colehan. The Morley team won once again with a vote of three to nil.

Two days later, on 5th June, the Morley team had another unanimous verdict when it met Batley on its home ground, Batley Town Hall. On this occasion the judges were Miss Eunice Woodfield of Doncaster, Dr. Clifford Towlson and Mr. Harry Cook of the Northern Opera & Drama Society.

All the shows were fully booked, with many people being turned away, whilst all the proceeds were donated to charities.

Morley's presentation was described as "a slick and colourful production brimming over with originality". There were songs, dances, humour and drama all on the same bill and the audiences loved it.

The producers for the Morley team were **Leo Leathley** and **Norman Stevenson** and the choreography was by **Millicent Hirst**.

The Commeres, Anthea Topham and Pat Ross, announced all the acts for Morley's Top Town team performances.

Below are details of the Morley artistes along with reviews written at the time, which record the variety and high quality of their acts: -

1 'High Stepping' **The Debutantes** gave the show a good start with 'Mama'. It was an act with dancing of the highest calibre and they were particularly well received.

2 **Vernon Sykes's** act was one of sly humour, ringing a bell with every line.

3 **Brenda & Barry Collins** a brother and sister act, performed with slickness and polish in their crisp tap dance routine.

4 'Mime & Mirth' **Fred Dale**, dressed in a sack, had the audiences roaring with laughter whilst miming to a record of 'The Lost Chord'. His act gained loud applause.

5 **Blanche Walton** a soprano with a wonderful personality was impressive with her rendering of 'Getting to Know You' from the 'King & I' and the waltz song from 'Tom Jones'.

6 **Stella & Dennis Scargill** piano and banjo were as polished as anything on the London stage

7 **Leo Leathley**, What a comic! What style! From his entrance to his exit the audience howled. It was non-stop down to earth humour put over in a brilliant style. He went further on the way to establishing himself as Yorkshire's Al Read.

8 'Waltz Time', **'The Debutantes'**, in white be-jewelled dresses with golden crowns, brought Morley's star crooner **Brian Scott** into the lime light with 'When You Are in Love'. **Susan Firth and Elaine Currie**

The Teenage Ramblers Skiffle Group. From left to right:- Tony Rooley (guitar), David Cromack (banjo), Jimmy Bywater (guitar), Billy Purser (bass), and Kevin Smithson (guitar) with Steve Bullock (washboard) at the front. Mr. Rooley and Mr. Bywater are featured in the 'Didn't They Do Well' section of this book.

delighted the audience with their solo dances.

9 The Morley Five Skiffle Group (Ossett contest) and later **The Teenage Ramblers Skiffle Group** (Batley contest) played well-known rock numbers with a faultless demonstration of music in the modern manner and were great favourites of the audience. They then provided a perfect backing for the clever miming of **Alan Rhodes and Ron Whittam** with their comedy calypso number mimed to Stan Freburg's hit number 'The Banana Boat Song'.

10 Fishy Business, (Steve and Son) were actually **Norman Stevenson & Freddy Pickstone** and their act was described as comedy of the 'deadpan' variety with a dash of real Goon-type humour.

11 Four Hands in Harmony **Norman Hartley and George Speight** have their own style of playing and a very effective one it is. Four perfect piano hands in harmony. The fact that these two accompanied the show gave added zest to every musical number.

12 'Oklahoma' **David Reekie and The Debutantes**. The most colourful scene of all. David Reekie, who has a splendid baritone voice, looked the real thing with neckerchief, boots, check shirt and belt. The Debutantes were dressed as 'cow-girls' in red shirts, white shorts, white hats, white boleros and cuffs with red frills, together with white boots with bells attached David Reekie's selections from 'Oklahoma' in his rich voice,

The Debutantes in their Oklahoma costume. " A dancing act of the highest calibre."

together with the dancing of The Debutantes, made the most colourful and tuneful ensemble in the whole three hours of entertainment.

13 'St. Joan' This was a real contrast with a highly dramatic rendering of a St. Joan speech given by **Gloria Mundy** who was dressed in black and had just a single spotlight playing on her.

14 'Old Tyme' The Old Time Musical Hall sketch, complete with the famous Can Can by **The Debutantes**, brought Morley's performance to a rousing finale.

'Ave Maria' **Nancy Sykes** and the **Boy Choristers**, (Batley contest only), a well-staged production with Nancy Sykes singing the contralto solo part supported by six boy choristers from local churches. How fortunate Morley is in having such a fine singer as Miss Sykes in their ranks.

The Commeres, Morley's stagecraft was revealed in a number of ways but none was more effective than the announcing of the acts by the two shapely commeres **Anthea Topham and Pat Ross.**

The Producers. It was written that the highest possible tribute must be given to **Leo Leathley and Norman Stevenson** for extracting such a wealth of talent from the auditions. They were complemented on producing such a colourful and slick show, with a smooth organisation and presentation.

Norman Hartley & George Speight were particularly praised for the use of the pianos in the Morley show. Norman Hartley also wrote the music for

Blanche Walton with the two Commeres and four of the Debutantes.

Morley's own signature tune 'Top Town'with lyrics by **Grace M. Lindley & Stella Scargill**.

The Debutantes were **Susan Firth, Margaret Nowell, Elaine Fawcett, Joyce Buttrey, Pam Fawcett, Elaine Currie, Pat Copsey and Lorna Batty.** A judge congratulated **Millicent Hirst** on her training of The Debutantes whose dancing he said was up to professional standard.

The Teenage Ramblers Skiffle Group: The members of the group were

The Top Town Trophy being presented to the Mayor of Morley, Alderman Frank Sykes, by Derrick Boothroyd the editor of the Morley News & Observer.

Tony Rooley (guitar), **David Cromack** (banjo), **Jimmy Bywater** (guitar), **Billy Purser** (bass), **Kevin Smithson** (guitar) and **Steve Bullock** (washboard). Five of the boys were pupils at Morley Grammar School and one at Batley Grammar School. The group was very popular and attracted many bookings including Saturday morning performances, between films, on the Star Cinema circuit. They reached the finals of the 'Six Five Special'competition but because of their school commitments it was not possible to take up an offer to play the pantomime season at the Huddersfield Theatre Royal.

Norman Stevenson was a comedy actor, entertainer and co-producer of the Morley Top Town team.

Tony Rooley is now **Anthony Rooley** expert lutenist and leading authority on medieval music. **Jimmy Bywater** became a children's television presenter and actor.

The Boy Choristers were **Robert M. Hall, James F.C. Leathley, Jimmy S. Pinder, Christopher C. Rogerson, Howard Rogerson and David A. Woodhead.**

Choreography: **Millicent Hirst.**
Stage Manager: **Arthur Leathley.**
Wardrobe Mistress: **Marjorie & Margaret Firth.**
Programme Sales: **Margaret M. Pickersgill.**
House Manager: **Jack Brumfitt.**
Publicity Manager: **G. Frederick Pickstone.**
Décor: **Grace M. Lindley & Laura Fant.**
Sound Effects: **J. Hargreaves.**
Make Up: **David Smart & Ann Cardwell.**

The Top Town Trophy was presented to the Mayor of Morley, Alderman Frank Sykes by Derrick Boothroyd the editor of the Morley News & Observer.

Grateful thanks are due to Major Norman Stevenson of Croft House for the enthusiastic interest he showed in this project, and for his kindness in allowing the authors the loan of his programmes, photographs and the actual Top Town Trophy. Unfortunately this kind gentleman passed away on 29th May 2002.

Pantomimes, Pews & Revues.

Most of us hold treasured memories of our youth, and none the more so than our association with others within the Christian community. The experiences of wartime were particularly poignant and we are grateful to **Jackie Batten** (sister of **Marjorie Trowsdale**) for her recollections all the way from Queensland Australia, recalling her days with the **St Paul's Youth Group.**

"I have a copy of an old photograph of the entire cast of a pantomime presented in either 1940 or 1941. I am the fairy on the right in the back row. There were many other such seasonal shows and I always seemed to end up being the fairy. The shows I remember most vividly were the Youth Group concerts, staged by a dozen or so enthusiastic teenagers who wrote the sketches, painted the scenery and performed on stage. I even wrote sketch called 'The Wooing of Ooswung Lou', based on an oriental theme; it made the audience laugh, but would never have won any prizes. The performance, which drew the most laughter and applause, was that of Jack Tullett in 'The Colonel Takes a Bath'. Jack was a tall gangly youth, all knees and elbows, but he was very funny on stage. He joined the Royal Navy shortly after our final performance.

We had no electronic sound system, and Margaret Saunders provided piano accompaniment for the entire show and on one occasion the piano was placed in a position where she could not see the stage. My main job was to train the chorus line for these revues and for some pantomimes. I also did a few solo dance spots. Among the Youth Group dancers were four brave lads called 'The Four Sweethearts' who did a mock ballet in football boots and tutus. The act brought the house down and they had to respond to numerous encores. The St Paul's Youth Group did its best to help the war effort by providing an evening of fun and laughter; and despite the blackout, we played to packed houses.

My dancing days and association with the Youth Group ended in 1943 when I started nursing training. For quite a while I missed the companionship of my friends. They were

A photograph taken on the occasion of the 1959 annual dinner of the Morley Branch of The Yorkshire Bookmen. Peter Dews on the left, with George W. Atkinson and Margaret Saunders

The entire cast of a pantomime presented by St. Paul's Youth Group 1940/41.

worrying times, for we kept hearing of young men whom we knew being posted 'Missing', 'Taken prisoner of war', or 'Killed in action'."

Margaret Saunders former Head of **Cross Hall Primary School** and an ex-member of the Operatic Society contacted us from her retirement home in Thirsk, North Yorkshire. Margaret is in good health and most comfortable living near brother **Derek and his wife Mayla.**

The children's' school pantomime one year was 'Sleeping Beauty'. The girl who was acting the part of the princess had lovely long hair. Whilst she was asleep, the prince entered with his large entourage, (he had to be accompanied so that parts could be provided for as many pupils as possible). The group gathered around the sleeping princess and when the moment arrived for her to awaken and sit up there was no reaction, she just lay there motionless. The prompts asking her to sit up were getting louder and louder, but she remained unmoved until the command to *"sit up"* was loud and clear. This at last brought a response from the princess when she called out in disgust *"I can't, he's standing on my hair".*

In 1976 Yorkshire Television had the excellent idea of presenting a good class children's orchestra on its Christmas show to be broadcast throughout the country. The **Cross Hall Junior School Orchestra** was the one chosen. The fifteen members aged 8 and 9 years who could sing as well as play at least two musical instruments, were to take part along with the popular singer of the day Gilbert O'Sullivan.

On Tuesday 23rd November the well-known singer was welcomed to **Cross Hall School** where he rehearsed with the children. On the following day they met together at the Leeds studios where they made a television recording before a live audience. The Morley children sang with Gilbert

O'Sullivan on the two songs, 'We Will' and 'Get Down' and accompanied him with their musical instruments for 'Ooh-Wakka-Doo-Wakka-Day', the music for which had been arranged by their music teacher **Mrs J Atkinson.**

The talented children were: **David Tench, Helen Richardson, Justine Dickinson, Paul Langley, Elaine Rowling, Amanda Price, Emma Smithson, Sophia Drake, Jane Hunt, Helen Evans, Vicki Jones, Nicola Woodward, Julian Marsden, Josephine Langsdale** and **Nichol Walsh.**

From early childhood I'd been aware of a vague ambition to appear on stage, writes **Paul Rollinson.** Each year I was taken to see the pantomime produced by the amateurs at **St Peter's Parish Church.** Though the parish hall would seat only about 180 people, even using the window ledges down each side, this was live theatre and held a special excitement.

In the era (mid-Fifties to mid Sixties) the Dame was always played by **Ernest Cooper**, who apparently was my father's cousin, though I didn't know him then (he died about 1988).

Joyce Niven who was the headmistress at St Peter's Infants School often wrote the scripts, production was by **Dorothy or Sydney Ladley**, who were also members of the Morley Operatic Society, and other names prominent at that time included the sisters **Gloria and Pauline Mundy.**

I'm not sure exactly how, in around 1962, I was asked to join the **St Peter's group** to fill a very minor role in a play, which I cannot remember.

My only connection with amateur entertainment, other than MTIAOS, writes **Reg Taylor**, has been at **Ebenezer Methodist Church** in Fountain St. In the late 1930's a **Young Peoples Society** was formed that produced a pantomime in the autumn. I can remember **Edgar and Willie Roberts and Harold Schofield** took the comedy roles. A surviving principal girl is **Kathleen Sykes (nee Slater)**. During the war when casting became difficult, a revue type of entertainment was given. In the 1950's pantos and plays were resumed for a few years. The photo (see page 161) is of **Margaret Nowell** and **Barbara Kellet** as the Babes in the Wood with **Willie Roberts** and myself as the robbers, **Harold Schofield** as the Policeman and **Hilda Buttery**, the Dame. All the usual things went wrong from time to time; the house curtains sticking halfway or only one curtain moving and the harassed stage crew seen trying to rectify the problem; lights fusing; people falling off the stage; actors missing cues; prompters heard by every one except the actor.

Pantos have been a good source of income at several churches, **Bethel, Cross Hall, St Paul's, St Peter's**, and **St Andrew's**. The last two still present their annual panto. There may be others.

The Rehoboth Congregational Church was tucked away off the beaten track on Dawson Hill, and unless one was a member or had occasion to visit, its very existence tended to pass unnoticed. This was not the case in the mid 19th century when many of Morley's large musical gatherings were centred upon the Rehoboth, and a reputation was born for high-class musical entertainment. Its existence was the end result of a difference of opinion within the congregation of St Mary's in the Wood (the Old Chapel), when a breakaway group formed the "New Old Chapel", at the top of Chapel Hill. After some years of fund raising this new band of Congregationalists left behind a burial ground that is there to this day, and built the Rehoboth high on Dawson Hill. Sadly this newer chapel was forced to close in the years following the Second World War, and the worshippers returned to the mother church. A literal case of burying their differences.

This era of high status for the chapel seemed to stem from the talents of **George Hirst**, son of Morley's celebrated violinist **David Hirst**. Young George was the organist at St Peter's Parish Church, having started playing at the age of eleven. It is reputed that he could play from memory Bach's 48 preludes and fugues, and became one of the most celebrated organists in the North of England. **George Hirst's** fame attracted to the town the talents of Mrs Sunderland (Yorkshire's Queen of Song) to give a recital at the chapel in 1862. This was followed a few months later by an organ recital by Dr William Spark, the Leeds City organist and friend of Samuel Sebastian Wesley.

We are grateful to **Clifford Wood** of Gildersome for providing programmes and newspaper cuttings covering a very successful period for the church's drama group immediately after the 39-45 War.

If the name of the drama society was like a changing feast, so was the menu of top class drama on offer twice a year. The Players, known as **'Rehoboth Young People's Society** in 1947, became the **'Young People's Drama Society'** and finally just plain **'Dramatic Society'** in the space of nine years. Was it that the members were all getting older, or did it also reflect the onset of a social change that was to alter the face of Morley?

Many well-known names from the ranks of amateur entertainment in Morley were involved with the Rehoboth plays, and many people who ran local businesses too. This was an influential church staging quality productions. Entrance to see their 1951 offering of 'Sit Down A Minute Adrian' a three-act comedy by Jevan Brandon-Thomas cost two shillings (old money of course).

Their first post war show stands proud for one fact alone; it was reviewed and reported upon for The Morley Observer by that late and great **Vincent J Mulchrone** (read about him in the chapter 'Didn't They Do Well'). The society had chosen a most difficult play, and this is reflected in VJM's critique. The report is dated March 1948.

The Rehoboth Young People's Society's 1948 production of the play 'Passing of the Third Floor Back'.

Rehoboth Players Brought Old Jerome Play To Life.

"Pat on the back this week for the Rehoboth Young People's Society who last weekend gave us a very creditable, if not credible, 'Passing of the Third Floor Back'.

The incredibility was with the script rather than the players. The conversion of Jerome K. Jerome's odd characters in a matter of minutes from every sort of nastiness to Christian charity and brotherly love would strain the gullibility of a babe.

Those people tolerably human in the first act inhabit an antimacassared boarding house in Bloomsbury. There's a toping major with a crabbing wife, a neurotic spinster, a retired bookmaker inexplicably desiring the major's daughter, an elderly lady 'come down in the world', and that familiar character, a young painter prostituting his art (sorry Art) because as he says, 'people don't want ART'.

Then there's the landlady, her young 'slavey' who is also an ex-jailbird, and two gentlemen who have so far escaped that distinction, Mr Samuels, who promotes phoney silver mines, and Mr Larcom, described with a touch of unabashed "melerdrammer", as Mr Samuels' 'jackal'.

Upon those thoroughly nasty characters descends as the new lodger in the third floor back room, a gentleman whom the audience know immediately for an emissary from the deity, if not Jesus Christ himself. Possibly by thought transmission, the lodgers catch on to this, too, and during the

In November 1950 the Rehoboth Young People's Society staged 'The Fourth Wall'.

second act make a number of convenient entrances and exits so as to learn, mark, and inwardly digest some cleverly administered Christian teaching.

This, if I may digress, is the cleverest part of the play. The stranger obviously knows his creatures and loves them. He is subtle in his appraisal of their grudge against life, and his method of straightening them out."

High-powered conversion

*"But the lodgers are converted at a rate that would put a high-powered revivalist meeting in the shade, and their converted selves are just too good to be true. The more credit then to the **Rehoboth Players** who pulled this situation out of the mire like seasoned troupers."*

Mulcrone then goes on to cover each individual performance, both on and off the stage. To say the least, here was one reporter who enjoyed his writing, and took the trouble to actually sit through the whole performance.

Rehoboth Productions of the time.

Bardell v Pickwick	None So Blind	Third Floor Back
Pantomime Rehearsal	Laburnum Grove	Bird In Hand
Are You A Mason?	The Late Christopher	The Fourth Wall
The Prize Pigeon	Bean Farley Goes Out	Sit Down A Minute
Plenty of Time	I'll Leave It To You	Adrian
The Black Dog	The Passing of the	A Play For Ronnie

'Sit Down a Minute Adrian' was the Rehoboth play in October 1951.

A very elderly lady sent us her memories of the **Morley Adult School Players** or MASP for short, which sounds like a nest of crossbred moths and wasps. **Alice Hartley** set down her story in beautiful copperplate handwriting, and whilst she too covered the world premiere performance described by David Atkinson in a chapter devoted to 'A Collier's Friday Night', the rest of her offering is presented here just as she set it down. We are saddened by her recent death and hope that her shared experiences will form a worthy epitaph to this lovely lady.

*"My maiden name was **Alice Kirk** and I was the sister of **John T. Kirk LGSM LRAM**, whom I know you are writing about as a special tribute. This pleases me very much, for we were all proud of his achievements. John kept a logbook and cuttings from the press for every show we gave, but to my great sadness there is not now anything left of all this work."*

"In 'Hobson's Choice', which as you may know, takes place at Hobson's Shoe Shop that he runs with his three daughters, his employee worked underneath the shop, and my brother had a hole cut in the floor of the platform and the two male characters had to crawl under the stage and make a grand entrance, as if from the cellar. I played the bossy daughter who set her cap at her father's employee and forced him to marry me. I remember the scene of our wedding night and entering dressed in a nightgown holding a candle, to demand that he come to bed. The laughter in the Adult School had to be heard to be believed and we played to packed audiences every night for a week; always a sell-out, but there was no

television to distract."

"After the war we had an extension made to our small stage and at least ten men and sometimes some of us young ladies would help to pull it in position, but it took some effort.

The Rehoboth Chapel, Dawson Hill.

When we gave 'Murder in the Cathedral', by T S Eliot, I cut out all the ladies dresses from new curtain material and others helped with the sewing. We also made whimples for the nuns' head covering. The mens' costumes had to be borrowed. People of all ages took part in that show, and at one of the final rehearsals John was disappointed with the cast, but one old lady of some seventy years said 'nay John wait till we get wer girdles on'. She meant when we were all dressed up in our costumes. There-after the password for a dress rehearsal was 'wer girdles'."

"For 'Murder in the Cathedral' we made new front of house curtains in heavy blue velvet, and emblazoned across the front in gold braid were the initials MASP. We also gave performances at St Mary's Church in Morley and at Kirkstall Congregational Church."

"In 'She passed through Lorraine' I played Joan of Arc and had to wear armour, but mostly I looked forward to being given a part which required the issue of a fashionable new dress, as in 'When We Are Married'. This was perhaps the most enjoyable and memorable show for both the Players and the audiences. Up until quite recently, people have told me of their happy memories of all these shows, but as most of the productions took place in the 1930's, there are very few of us left. George and Martha Atkinson, were always in the cast and Martha's most memorable role was in 'Candida' when she took the lead, and gained some memorable press reviews."

"I see Norrie Ward at our Tuesday discussion group in the Baker Room at Morley Public Library. He was a reporter for the Morley Observer along with Robert Stead during the time of our pre-war shows."

(As we put the final touches to this book in May 2002, we are sad to note the passing of **Norrie Ward**, one time Mayor of Morley and a noted author and Yorkshire Historian).

Plays performed by the Morley Adult School Players:-

Date	Play	Producer
1929	The Price of Coal	John T. Kirk
1929	Moonshine	John T. Kirk
1929	The Private Life of P.C. Pettifer	John T. Kirk
1930	Hindle Wakes	John T. Kirk
1930	The Return of the Prodigal	John T. Kirk
1931	Yellow Sands	John T. Kirk
1931	The Passing of the Third Floor Back	Hedley Marwood
1932	A Bill of Divorcement	George W. Atkinson
1932	Sar' Alice	Stephen Stafford
1933	Hobson's Choice	George W. Atkinson
1933	Misalliance	John T. Kirk
1934	Ebb Tide	George W. Atkinson
1934	Exhibition (written by John T. Kirk)	George W. Atkinson
1934	Outward Bound	Hedley Marwood
1935	Black 'Ell	John T. Kirk
1935	She Passed Through Lorraine	John T. Kirk
1936	Thread O'Scarlet	George W. Atkinson
1936	Altar Piece	Stephen Stafford
1936	The Late Christopher Bean	S. Kathleen Marwood
1937	Neighbourly Love	George W. Atkinson
1937	Meet Mrs. Beeton	George W. Atkinson
1937	Hay Fever	George W. Atkinson
1937	The Young Mrs. Greenshaw	George W. Atkinson
1938	Candida	John T. Kirk
1938	S.O.S.	George W. Atkinson
1938	A Turn for T'Better	George W. Atkinson
1939	The Prize Pigeon	George W. Atkinson
1939	Not What They Seem	George W. Atkinson
1939	A Collier's Friday Night	John T. Kirk
1939	Murder in the Cathedral Part 2	John T. Kirk
1940	Murder in the Cathedral Part 2	John T. Kirk
1946	Friend's Adult School Jubilee Pageant	George W. Atkinson
1948	Fumed Oak	George W. Atkinson
1948	The Linden Tree	Trevor Sowden
1950	The Light of Heart	John Anderson
1951	George and Margaret	George W. Atkinson
1951	When We Are Married	John T. Kirk
1957	The Secret Tent	George W. Atkinson

The Bethel Drama Group formed in 1958 and was part of the **Bethel Methodist Church,** and the majority of the players were church members. The Drama Group took part in all the church activities such as bazaars, concerts and anniversaries. One year the Group arranged a 'This is Your Life' about **George Rankin** who was a church member and patron of the Group. On another occasion the church had a Daffodil Fayre and our members decorated the whole Sunday School with daffodils carefully made with crepe paper. During its active years at the Bethel the Group also organised the café side at numerous efforts.

Over the years the Drama Group had 45 to 50 members, including the non-acting ones. Mostly we performed two plays per year, and always worked together with great enthusiasm. Each year there would be a Christmas party when partners and children came along.

At the end of 1969 the Bethel Church amalgamated with the Central Methodist Church and the name 'Central Drama Group' was adopted. The Group continued to produce plays and take part in the Church activities. The very last use of the Bethel Schoolroom was for the 21st anniversary production of 'Little Women'.

Once or twice at Easter we enacted the Trial and Crucifixion of Christ in the Sunday School and gave readings in the Church. In the final years of 1972 and 1973 the Group had difficulty in casting parts as people were moving away, getting married etc. In 1974 a committee was formed to arrange fortnightly meetings and have speakers, slide shows, musical evenings etc. From the first meetings of about eight or nine people, the numbers gradually grew and the Group became known as **'Thursday at Eight'** and over the years became very popular. It now meets in the afternoon under the title **'Thursday Group'** and the six or so people who run the meetings are all founder members of the **'Bethel Drama Group'.**

One very special production for the Bethel Drama Group was 'Little Women' by Louisa Alcott, which was the choice for the Group's 21st performance. The casting was excellent, the costumes, props, stage and acting were all first class and everyone played with great enthusiasm. In that year 1969, we were due to move to the Central Methodists, but it was arranged to keep the Bethel Schoolroom open just for the production of 'Little Women'. Everyone was pleased about this and gave of their best. The lady who was due to play 'Marmee' was taken ill only days before the performance, so the producer had to quickly improvise with the result that one lady read offstage and another mimed the part onstage. This arrangement worked beautifully and saved the day.

The authors are grateful to **Mrs Mary Armitage** *for her memories and for supplying the details that follow of the many and varied productions of this excellent group.*

1958 Curtain raiser (two plays OHMS & The Third Shot) The Happiest Days of Your Life

1959 Job for the Boy

1960 Man for the Job. The Whole Truth

1961 Running Riot. Mad about men

1962 A Murder has been arranged. See How They Run

1963 Caught Napping

1964 Freida. Pools Paradise

1965 Wanted One Body. The Gift

1966 Sailor Beware. Watch It Sailor

1967 Policy For Murder

1968 Sinbad The Sailor (Pantomime). Job for the Boy

1969 See How They Run. Little Women (21st production & last at Bethel)

1970 2 One Act Plays (The Sky is Overcast & Out Patients). Fish Out of Water

1971 Dr Brent's Household

1972 Caught Napping

1973 Honey Pot

The 'offcomed-un' has some fond memories of the **Bethel Chapel** for it was often talked of within the Hartley family. **Norman Hartley** and his wife **Linda (nee Dormer, daughter of 'Bobby Dormer'** paragon of the local constabulary) both attended the Bethel. Norman as active as ever on the piano, while Linda exercised her good trained soprano voice. The Bethel was always a friendly place to visit and one occasion stands out in my memory was when the choir presented a concert version of Edward German's 'Tom Jones'. I was asked to take the part of Tom Jones and sang my way through the role with some trepidation, for in the early 1950's my voice was still finding its feet in the upper registers of song. I am sure it was not one of my better performances. I would have been far happier singing the role of Squire Western ("on a January morning in

The Bethel Chapel on Commercial Street, Morley.

Summersetshire, two pretty maidens were walking along").

In a concert version, the costumes and makeup are missing; the scenery is non-existent and you cannot embrace the heroine – but I had a great time among such warm and friendly people.

4th March 1955.

What is significant about this date you may ask? For me the 'off-comed-un' it is full of relevance as I sit at my keyboard writing this piece, for in front of me is an aging full page from **The Morley Observer** dated 4th March of that year and I am working for the Barraclough/Reekie venture exactly 47 years later on the 4th March 2002.

Page seven devotes a three-column quarter page to the 'Amateur Stage'. The report covers a mini-biography of **'Leo' Leathley** (from whose scrapbook the page in question comes, courtesy of his son **Chris Leathley**); news of the Gildersome Parish Church Society preparing their very first play called 'The Paper Chain'; a J.B. Priestley play 'Mystery at Greenfingers' in production by **Queen Street Methodist Dramatic Society** under the direction of **George W Atkinson**; a report on two shows held at **The Ebenezer Methodist Church**; a note that the **OMADS 'Valentine's Revue'** had cleared their costs after the first night of a five night run at the Pavilion; **Morley Grammar School** pupils were about to start a full week's presentation of **'The Gondoliers'** in the School Hall under the direction of those two masters of the art **John Dews** and **Donald Webster**; immediately after the close of Gilbert & Sullivan's wonderful operetta, the **Technical Operatic Society** were performing a concert version of 'Il Trovatore' with the advice to book early because the ticket prices were subsidized as part of an ongoing education programme; the **Rehoboth Dramatic Society** were putting the finishing touches to 'The Young at Heart', having had to wait three months for the services of **George Atkinson** (it's that man again); two sections of **Morley Guides** were battling it out in the final of the Junior section of the Four Valleys Youth Festival of one-act plays held at **St Peter's Parish Church,** while in the senior section being competed at Huddersfield, the finalists were **St Peter's Youth Group** and **Drighlington Parish Church Youth Group**; and finally **Woodkirk Parish Church Youth Group** were in rehearsal for an operetta called 'The King of Sherwood'.

Not content with all the above, on the next page there is a three column, three inch deep headline and photograph, followed by a six inch single column report of the 'Snow White and the Seven Dwarfs' production by **Rehoboth Sunday School Scholars**; a reporter of the **Morley Observer** was active and present in order to give a first hand report.

Which poses the question, "would the **Morley Observer** send a reporter to such an event today"?

I hope that by recalling this old edition of what was considered to be

Morley's premier paper amply reflects the great strength of amateur entertainment in the town in the immediate post-war years. Of course it did not evolve by accident, but was built upon the tradition and guidance of previous generations.

On a recent visit to Morley I was told by a respected and long established local figure, and I quote *"The Morley Observer? With the exception of politics they are sadly no longer interested in local affairs; why they did not even bother to send a reporter for the Operatic Society's 2001 production"*.

How times have changed! I can think of at least three members of the Stead family, founders of The Morley Observer, who would thump the current Editor's desk were they able, and I cringe to think what that once great Fleet Street writer Vincent Mulchrone is saying as he writes his feature column in even higher circles.

The Mayor of Morley, James Askey, on stage with Harold (Leo) Leathley in 1937.

It's a Small World.

During our researches, much use was made of the internet, with electronic mail flying between Churwell and Bedale almost daily. The World Wide Web came up trumps on occasion, and it was while visiting the Reading University site in search of **Professor John Barstow,** that an e-mail was sent to **Christopher Cipkin**, at the University's Library. By return came a reply... *"Good luck with your book, I used to be a member of the Morley Music Society and my parents live in Heckmondwike".*
We immediately responded with the question *"where's Heckmondwike?"*

They say a rolling stone gathers no moss, but did you know that **Mick Jagger's** antecedents settled in Morley in the early 1700's? They were engaged in the clothing trade and were tenants of the **Earls of Dartmouth** and the family was among the early converts to Wesleyan Methodism. Mick's Great Grandfather was born in Morley Bottoms in 1845, and it was he who moved away from the town saying, *" I can't get no satisfaction".*

It was a wet October Sunday morning in Bedale. The Dales can be as miserable as anywhere on such a day, so I headed for an Antique Book Fair being held in Bedale Hall. This took tremendous effort on my part, because the Market Place is a good ten-minute walk, if I go really slowly and drag my feet. That morning several hundred people had also dragged their feet into the ballroom where the Duke of Wellington had once dined, and most of them were wearing his boots. A wet and wasted journey, or so I thought, until I spotted a chap thumbing through a selection of picture postcards relating to Morley, *"Are you particularly interested in Morley?"* asked I, *"Do you know it?"*

"I ought to do, I was born there." And so the conversation flowed, neither of us recognizing the other.

He told me of his interest in Bradford Museum and old printing machinery, and still the penny didn't drop. Then we exchanged cards.

"Good heavens" says he, *"Well I be blowed,"* said I.

It was **Brian Aldred** proprietor of Derdlab Press, print historian & collector of memorabilia and ephemera, who now lives at Addingham, Ilkley.

It turned out we used to be in **Queen Street Methodist Choir** together in the days when **Charles Brearley** was organist and choirmaster.

"Do you remember", says Brian *"when I was thrown out of choir practice for being drunk?"* My jaw must have dropped somewhat, because he hastened to add, *"well I wasn't drunk really. In those days I was a press minder at Petty's in Leeds and the process required the sheets coming off*

the presses to be sprayed with a Gum Arabic solution that contained alcohol. Each half hour we had to go to the small boys room to wash the residue from our faces in order to avoid intoxication. I had gone straight from work to the practice without washing down, and it caught up with me."

Brian's father, **Jack Aldred**, was Norman Hartley's boss when my pa-in-law worked for **Tillotson and Firth**.

The next morning **Ronnie Barraclough** called to see **David Atkinson** to tell him of the chance meeting. *"Yes I know all about it"*, said David, *"Brian's brother, **Peter Aldred** telephoned me a few minutes ago."*

I'll tell you what; they have got some fast pigeons in Addingham.

Colin Crabtree who has been of invaluable assistance in researching the histories of **The Morley Vocal Union and The Morley Music Society** confesses that he has become hooked on delving into the back numbers of local newspapers in Morley Public Library.

In a letter to **David Reekie** dated 11 March 2002 he wrote, *"I was in the local history room last week and got into conversation with a man who was looking at family history on the microfiche reader. When I said that I was looking for Vocal Union information, he immediately said that his father had been a member in past years and I soon realized that he was talking of Kenneth Scarth, whom we both knew and sang with during our time with the Union. It was Kenneth's son Kevin, a retired Fire Officer, and we have arranged to meet again to compare notes and photographs."*

David Atkinson an early source of inspiration and help for this book was asked one day for **David Reekie's** telephone number. Seeing that the enquiry came from a lady, **Mr Atkinson** must have thought *"hello, hello, the lad's past is catching up with him"*. and discreetly referred the matter to an intermediary in the shape of **Ronnie Barraclough**. You will be well aware of how long things take once diplomacy takes hold, so it was some weeks later that curiosity overcame a certain reluctance and the said **Reekie** telephoned the lady in question. **Edna Clough** turned out to be a distant relation of my wife and we had a most enjoyable conversation, which hopefully will lead to an exchange of information for our respective family histories. **Edna** married **Ronald Clough** way back during my early days in Morley and had called at 174 Britannia Road to enlist the help of **Jim Hodgson** to provision a modest 'wedding feast' for her nuptials. **Edna** said *"don't you remember? You sang for us with Stella at the piano."* My past had caught up with me!

The Morley Music Society.

(We are indebted to Colin Crabtree, Hon Librarian, for use of his archived material and for his contribution towards this particular story).

The seeds were sown for the formation of the present society on Thursday 27th May 1943, when **Mr Harry Hardy** chaired a meeting in the Ebenezer Chapel Schoolroom Morley, at which it was resolved *"that a concert version of 'Merrie England'be given in the Town Hall on July 27th and 28th 1943"*.

That year marked the 21st anniversary of the Morley Medical Charities Fund, and the intention was to raise monies and to brighten the lives of a war weary community. The Mayor of Morley, **Alderman David Dickinson** conceived the idea, for he had been actively involved with the charity since its inauguration, and with the help of a few like-minded friends, drew together members of local church and chapel choirs along with other interested helpers. So it was that a 'scratch' choir was formed.

The venture proved so successful that a General Meeting was arranged back in the group's birthplace on 23rd August 1943, and the **Morley Musical Society** was born.

Harry Hardy (later to become **Sir Harry Hardy**) was elected President, **Councillor Allen H. Jowett** the Hon Secretary & Treasurer, and **Fred Butterfield** who had conducted the recent first performances became the Hon Musical Director.

Jerry Pashley was soon to be appointed Hon. Deputy Musical Director, and together with Fred Butterfield shared the direction for the first six

Morley Music Society's first public performance in the Town Hall in 1944.

213

seasons until 1949. That year saw the engagement of the first in a long line of professional Musical Directors by the arrival of **Clifford W. Towlson**, the then Headmaster of Woodhouse Grove School in Leeds. Later to become Dr Towlson, he stayed with the Society for eight years until he was forced to retire due to ill health in 1957.

Donald F. Webster, who unfortunately died on 26th March 2002, came to the Society in 1957 during the time of his service to music at the Morley Grammar School, and like his predecessor was later to achieve his Doctorate. He held the baton for six years until succeeded in 1963 by another Music Master **David Bryan** who taught at Salt Grammar School. David served for seven years before handing over to the third in a line of music teachers, with the arrival of **Anthony Norcliffe** in 1970. Anthony taught at both Batley and Morley Grammar Schools and was to stay with the Society until 1977. It was his proposal that the name of the Society be changed to that of **Morley Music Society.**

Over the next four years three MD's came and went. **Richard Bloodworth** 1977-80, **David Lennox** 1980-81 and **Howard Lorriman** 1981-82, until the appointment of **Susan Wanless** in 1982 introduced a five-year period of stability. Susan's successor **Stephen Williams** stayed for three years before **Elizabeth Jill Wild** took control for a further three years in 1990. **Sean Farrell** took the reins in 1993 while Assistant Organist at Wakefield Cathedral, before leaving Morley to take the Assistant's post at Ely Cathedral under **Paul Trepte** in 1996. (Paul Trepte was born and raised in Morley).

The present day Musical Director **Christopher Rathbone**, now in his sixth season, is also Organist and Choirmaster at Meanwood Parish Church and a Supernumery Tenor and regular organ recitalist at Leeds Parish Church. He is currently (November 2001) the President of the Leeds Organists Association and is a composer of note with 84 works to his credit, seven of which were recently recorded on an Amphion CD. At present he is working on the major commission of a cantata for Otley Choral Society's Diamond Jubilee in 2003. Christopher's earlier career saw him Assistant Organist at Carlisle Cathedral and Organist of Marlborough College Wiltshire.

Whilst those personalities leading the choir from the rostrum have come and gone following career moves and departure from the area, the stability given to the Society by those holding Presidential office has been remarkable.

Sir Harry Hardy	1943 - 1958
Dr James Roche	1958 - 1966
J Ralph Carr	1966 - 1982
A Hugh Smith	1982 – present day

Only two people have held the title of accompanist over all these years. **Edna H Firth** being the first to serve at the keyboard, was joined in 1958 by **Geoffrey Dunn** acting as deputy accompanist and organist. Geoffrey took over from Mrs Firth in 1962, and his personal musical (sorry Mr Norcliffe) marathon continues as we 'segue' to the 21st century. After the April 1998 concert, the President **Hugh Smith** was pleased to announce *"a historic event in the life of the Morley Music Society in the 40^h anniversary of Geoffrey Dunn's appointment as Hon. Deputy Accompanist at the AGM dated 5th May 1958"*. An autograph book containing the signatures and contributions of members and friends accompanied the presentation of a book entitled 'The Making of the Victorian Organ'.

The Golden Jubilee, was marked by a concert in April 1993, which was a repeat performance of 'Merrie England', echoing that first intended 'one-off' venture back in the dark days of World War 2, and appropriately nearly sixty years later during a 'Celebration of British Music' for the Millenium, there was again a faint echo of those early days. The introduction and chorus to Part 2 of 'Merrie England' is entitled *"The Month of May"*, and so it was in the month of May 2000 that the choir was joined in a joint concert at Morley Town Hall, by new found friends in the **Drighlington Brass Band**.

During the immediate postwar years there were over one hundred singing members and as many non-singing supporters. Concerts were held in Morley Town Hall, which was usually full to hear the many nationally famous Principals, such as Bessie Collins, Robert Easton, Walter Widdop, Ada Alsop and Norma Procter.

In common with other Choral and Music Societies the numbers of members and audiences have generally fallen. Economic conditions have meant that venues other than the Town Hall have had to be explored and alternative ways of financing the Society have had to be pursued to keep it viable. Orchestras could not be used as often, and the use of young and promising singers as soloists was adopted.

Whilst the firm base of choral music has been sustained, a much wider range of music has been introduced into the repertoire under the influences of succeeding Musical Directors. Composers such as Monteverdi, Purcell, Britten, Kodaly, Poulenc, Malcolm Williamson, John Gardner and John Rutter have all added to a rich tapestry of experience, but on a few occasions the importance of Victorian and Edwardian parlour music has not been ignored, with musical comedy and The Beatles enjoying acceptance at times.

Celebrity Recitals have included such names as Marisa Robles, Archie Camden and Anthony Hopkins. At other times instrumentalists have performed alongside the choir, with such noted names as Keith Swallow,

Joan & Valerie Trimble, Maurice Murphy, **John Barstow**, the Black Dyke Mills Octet, and most unusually Elton Hayes and his 'small guitar'. **Professor John Barstow** is one of Morley's own, and in October 2000 he gave a Celebrity Recital with his friends The Emiro Ensemble. In earlier times he had appeared with the Union on these occasions:-

Date	Event	Venue
21st April 1951	Morley Co-operative Society Festival Concert.	Morley Town Hall.
28th October 1952	'Merrie England'and other items.	-do-
3rd May 1960	Recital (last appearance in Morley before studying overseas.)	-do-
13th October 1968	Recital.	Morley Grammar School. New Hall.
17th October 1972	Recital	-do-

The Society during the latter part of the 20th century has made use of varied concert venues. The Central Methodist Chapel, St Peter's Parish Church Morley, Morley High School Hall (both the one later destroyed by fire, and the rebuilt one), Wakefield Cathedral, St Paul's Church, Morley, St Peter's Church, Gildersome, St Andrew's Church, Bruntcliffe, and Holy Trinity Church, Meanwood.

The Society is now approaching its Diamond Jubilee, a milestone marked by highs and lows. What is written here is of necessity only the briefest outline of events. We have chosen to record one milestone from each of the two centuries that now stride this Society's proud history.

Morley Observer: 29th June 1951: -

They Sang to Audience of 5,000.

Before an audience of nearly 5,000 in the Albert Hall, London on Sunday 24th June, forty-three members of the Morley Musical Society took part with a chorus of 1,000 Yorkshire voices in a Festival of Britain concert of Handel's music, organised by the Henry Wood Concert Society.

The choirs, conducted by Sir Malcom Sargent and accompanied by the Philharmonia Orchestra, were heard in part II of 'Israel in Egypt' by the same composer. Soloists were Isobel Baillie, Mary Jarred, Heddle Nash and Harold Williams.

The Morley party travelled to Leeds by motor-coach to catch the 7.0 am train on Sunday, arriving back on Monday morning. The president, Cty. Ald. Harry Hardy JP was unable to travel, as was the musical director, Mr. Clifford W. Towlson.

Choirs were represented from Barnsley, Bradford, Castleford, Doncaster, Halifax, Harrogate, Heckmondwike, Holmfirth, Huddersfield, Hull, Leeds,

Middlesbrough, Pudsey, Rotherham, Wakefield and York.

Massed in three banks on either side of the organ, and with the women wearing white, they made an impressive spectacle.

Equally impressive, an Observer reporter was told, was the tremendous vigour with which the great plague choruses in 'Israel in Egypt' and the Hallelujah chorus from the 'Messiah' were sung. The clear beat and firm control exercised by the conductor were major factors in the choir's undoubted success.

The performance was warmly applauded and there were cheers for Sir Malcolm from choir members, for whom the experience was one of the most memorable of their lives

26ᵗʰ February 2000 A Magical Evening with Arthur.

Thanks to a grant under the Millenium Festival *'Awards for All'* Scheme, operated by the National Lottery, the society was able mount a highly successful performance of Henry Purcell's 'King Arthur' in the new hall of Morley High School.

Sheila Wainwright the then Hon Joint Secretary was quoted at the time; *"We are a small society, with no outside support save that of our faithful patrons, which means that finance is always a major consideration – so to put on 'King Arthur' as authentically as possible, which was always our intention, never seemed likely. However earlier in the year we obtained an application form for the awards scheme, and after hours of work spent in writing and rewriting our submission, and projecting our current season's financial position, we finally sent off the many pages of the form, and all the back-up material required, with (I must confess) very little confidence. Imagine our surprise when, a couple of months later, we heard we had been awarded a grant for the amount we had requested (which is actually half the projected cost of the performance), and that money would be in our bank a month later.*

What a joy it has been to choose soloists we thought we couldn't afford, and to engage an orchestra of the size required – plus harpsichord. The only problem is that this might give us the taste for the 'good life'."

In the presence of the Lord Mayor and the Lady Mayoress of Leeds, this great work was performed in the impressive new assembly hall of Morley High School, with resounding success. Under the direction of **Christopher Rathbone**, the St Peter's Chamber Orchestra (leader David Salinger), Sean Ward, (harpsichord), with soloist sopranos: Sasha Johnson-Manning & Joanne Boddison, Daniel Wellings, alto, Roy Hirst, tenor, Stephen Williams, bass and with the Society Chorus (chorus master **Warwick Wainwright**). The narrators were: **Sarah Foxwell** and **Kevin Richardson**, while the dances were performed by **The Rachael Swann School of Dancing.**

The narration was in the hands of two scholars attending the High School then in the midst of their GCSE studies, and the pupils of the school of dancing are based at the nearby St Andrew's Church Hall. The two storytellers together with the choreographed movement of the dancers brought a theatrical air to this great piece of 'almost opera'.

There are some music buffs that close their eyes to enjoy great music, but this was not the way to enjoy this performance, for the visual delights went hand in glove with Purcell's magic. The society can justly place another feather in its already much decorated hat.

The Morley Music Society is fortunate to have many faithful and long serving members, without whose loyalty the choir would not have survived. The diversions of home entertainment and the impact of changing social habits have erased much that was the face of Morley in 1943. Other societies have wilted in these keen winds of change and it is appropriate that tribute be paid to the singing membership. It is always invidious to name individuals, but it seems proper that the names of all current members (at Sept/Oct 2001) be recorded here at the start of the new millennium.

The ladies and gentlemen of the chorus of The Morley Music Society

Sopranos	Altos	Tenors	Basses
Margaret Aldred	Sheila Barrass	Ray Cawsey	Colin Crabtree
Michelle Aldridge	Sylvia Bartle	John Hornby	Peter Graham
Carol Allen	Joan Cole	Alan Howarth	David Hinkley
Helen Allen	Joan Gaunt	Andrew Pinnock	David Hirst
Mary Armitage	Marilyn Harrop	Brian Robertshaw	Stephen Leigh
Diane Barnes	Joan Hepworth	Ian Russell	Malcolm Rennison
Pauline Cowan	Hilary Howarth	Warwick Wainwright	Alan Schofield
Helen Darbyshire	Trish Law	Jason Whiteley	Donald Taylor
Mary Dougherty	Catherine Lee	Peter Wrigley	Malcolm Warburton
Elma Dowson	Angela Leigh		Clifford Wood
Dorothy Dunn	Joan Poole		
Dorothy Earnshaw	Margaret Raby		
Liz Foxwell	Carol Russell		
Susan Galvin	Hazel Rennison		
Margaret Gower	Margaret Smith		
Margaret Hampshire	Philippa Stevens		
Jackie Hudson	Sheila Wainwright		
Gill Lockwood			
Margaret Lynn			
Joyce Moorhouse			
Jean Naylor			
Shelagh Senior			
Christine Smith			
Brenda Sykes			
Mary Sykes			
Deborah Warner			
Jan Webster			
Beth Wildsmith			
Janet Wood			

Epilogue.

It is with design and intent that the authors have placed The Morley Music Society as the closing chapter to this anthology. Ronnie Barraclough has allowed me as the 'off-comed-un' to write this postscript, for it could be described as self-indulgence were it to be penned by a true bred Morleian.

This choir has long held a prestigious position within the musical heritage of the 'Old Borough'. While other organized groups have folded or been forced from the town, The Morley Music Society remains firm and true to its roots. Much may be due to shrewd management and the loyalty of its members, but there is another hidden factor that shouts from between the lines. That secret is TRADITION.

A long hard look at the names appearing in the November 2001 concert programme is to enter upon a genealogical ride through the history of Morley. The members themselves will know what the authors mean, for there are connotations to be found at every turn; if they themselves do not carry the link, then their parents or grandparents do. Echoes resound of the Morley Vocal Union, churches and chapels, the Operatic Society, the Tingley Sylvians, the West Riding Singers, the OMADS and many more.

Back in the 18th century Morley had its own 'fiddler on the roof', in the form of one David Hirst who helped found the very tradition so proudly carried by the Morley Music Society nearly three hundred years later, and his namesake still sings in the bass section. This is no coincidence, for the modern David Hirst, can trace his family back to that emerging village once transformed by the Industrial Revolution, and later to be transfixed by the motorways and annexed by the City of Leeds.

The people that matter are still here and still making music, but you see, that is TRADITION.

NOT THE END

Subscribers

Pamela J Alderson, Morley
Mary Armitage, Morley
David K. Atkinson, Morley
Freda Austin, Morley
Peter C. Aveyard, Morley
Margarita Mary Barraclough, Churwell
Jim Barry, Heckmondwike
Horace & Edith Bastow, Churwell
Jackie Batten, Australia
Delia Batty, Bakewell
Hilda Bell, Morley
Joan Blakeley, Morley
Helen Bond, Richmond
Connie Booth, Tingley
Catherine & John Botting, Otley
Eileen Botting, Huttons Ambo
Kenneth & Betty Bradley, Morley
Jean & Tony Brook, Tingley
Margaret & Gordon Bunney, Woodlesford
Renee Burrow, Tingley
Trevor & Jean Carr, Bushey
Andrew Castle, Woolley
J. Clark, Wakefield
K.W. Clark, Moortown
Edna & Ronald Clough, Morley
Betty Collinson, Morley
Colin Crabtree, Morley
Audrey Dale, Morley
Ronald Darrington, OBE, Tingley
E.M. Davies, Bromsgrove
Trevor Dawson, Churwell
Violet Dixon, Churwell

Shirley Downes, Churwell
Mary Eames, Morley
Judith M. Elliott, Mayor of Morley
Terry Elliott J.P., Tingley
Roy & Betty Fatkin, Morley
John & Mrs. Finnigan, Tingley
Phil Fryer, Churwell
Tony & Mrs. Garritt, Tingley
Tom Gomersal & Carol, Embsay
Margaret Gower, Gildersome
Rhoda Gray, Tingley
Kathleen Gray M.B.E., Morley
Bill Grimes, Morley
Marjorie & Fred Hall, Wigginton
Marilyn & Michael Harrop, Morley
Simon Hayes, Bexley Heath
John & June Heywood, Morley
David & Millie Hirst, Morley
Barbara Holliday, Morley
Steven Holt, Morley
Celia Hopkinson, Radcliffe on Trent
Derek & Mary Hudson, Morley
Peter & Beryl Jackson, Morley
Cllrs. Paul & Keely Jamieson, Morley
Michelle Le M. Jenkins, Seaford
Frances Jones, East Ardsley
S.M. Kiernan, St Annes on Sea
Joyce King, Morley
H.C.J. Leathley, Morley
Rene Lamb, Morley
David Mason, Morley
Andrew & Jenni Mason, Bedale
Stewart McArdle, Churwell

Margaret McCutcheon, Wrenthorpe
Clive McManus, Morley
Hazel Noble, Morley
John & Ellie Ormonroyd,
Brookmans Park
Julia Pearson, Snape
Lucy Piercy, Ewell
David Poole & Lizzie Lowe,
Morley
Peter Powell, Churwell
Ann & James Poyner, Tingley
Chris & Liz, Reekie, Kirkby
Fleetham
Mavis Reekie, Bedale
John Rhodes, Morley
John & Molly Richards,
Northallerton
Keith Richardson, Morley
M. Elaine Rickman, Timperley
Sheila Roberts, Lyme Regis
J. Robinson, Morley
A. Margaret Saunders, Thirsk
Martyn L. Scargill, Kilham
Mary Scargill, Morley
Shelagh Senior, Liversedge
Jocelyn Simons, Aylesbury
Muriel & Allan Smith, Bramley
Christine A. Smith, Morley
Kevin Smithson, Batley
Geoff & Joan Snowden, Morley
Jean E. Spruce, Morley
Keith & Christine Spruce, Morley
Margaret Stegeman, Richmond
Norman Stevenson, Morley

Anne Stevenson, Morley
Derek Summers, Ingleby Barwick
Dr. Vernon C. Sykes, Morley
Reg & Barbara Taylor, Morley
Robert Tempest, Morley
Joseph E. Tetley, Churwell
Ruth Trepte, Morley
Marjorie Trowsdale, Morley
Ian Tugwell, Hunton
Peter & Margaret Wilcock J.P.,
Batley
Sheila Williamson, Dewsbury
Clifford & Janet Wood, Gildersome

Index.

1944 Co-operative Society Pageant
    many organisations & societies take part   126
7th Morley (Grammar School) Boy Scout Troop   188
A 4.0 am Queue in Morley
    a Morley Observer headline in November 1938   156
A Day in the Life Of....
    a Popplewell play   67
a Reform meeting in York
    attended by The Morley Reed Band   77
Abbey, Carine
    tap dancer   74
Adult School Players   58, 125
    post war improvement to their stage facilities   127
Ainley Richard
    father to Henry Ainley   10, 11
Ainley, Anthony
    Henry Ainley's Grandson   18
Ainley, Henry
    a silent film of his Hamlet shown in Morley 1912   109
    details of his English Film Appearances   23
    details of his London Stage Appearances   19
    his death in West Acton Middlesex   15, 16
Ainley, Henry Hinchliffe
    Actor of Stage, Screen & Radio   10
Ainley, Henry Junior
    Henry Ainley's second son   18
Ainley, Richard
    Henry Ainley's eldest son   17
Akeroyd, Bob
    Morley Area Administrator   124
Akroyd, H
    one of the last remaining nine members of The Morely Vocal Union in 1970   128
Albert Hall   56
Alderson, Katie
    part of the Four Generations   152
Aldred, Brian
    prop of Derdlab Press and print historian   211
Aldred, Jack   212
Aldred, Peter   138, 212
Alexander Sir George   11
Alexandra Hall, The
    wartime dances   126
Alexandra Palace Theatre   110, 113
    situated within yards of the Town Hall   107
Alexandra Picture Palace, The
    a new name for The Alexandra Palace Theatre   113
Alhambra Theatre
    a programme of events   101
    a travelling theatre   101

Alhambra Theatre, Bradford	47
Alick McLean's band	52
Alliance Hotel	108
American Theatre Hall of Fame	29
And Suddenly its Spring	
a 1959 Popplewell play	67
Anderson, Noel	
founder of The West Riding Singers	128, 133, 134
Anglia Television	60
Annual Speech Day at MGS in 1951	
a musical programme of note	147
Anti-Aircraft Battery at Wellington Hill	
The Revellers in action 7th Nov 1939	181
Armitage, Mary	207, 218
Armley Jail	31, 131, 135
Arnold, H B	191
Arthur Spencer	90, 117
Asquith, H H the Right Honourable QC MP	
opens The Town Hall on 16th Ocyober 1895	110
Asquith, Henry Herbert	
Morley's most famous son	23
Associated Newspapers Group Ltd	65
Atha, Bernard OBE	
Councillor & a Lord Mayor of Leeds	161
Atha. Bernard	
Lord Mayor of Leeds	43
Atkinson David K	
Morley Historian	6, 8
Atkinson, David	204, 212
Atkinson, David K	125, 227
a fount of all local knowledge	84
Atkinson, G W	190, 206, 209
Atkinson, George	
a renowned local historian & supporter of the Arts	84, 124, 126, 198
directs The Rehoboth Dramatic Society	208
Atkinson, George W	
founder member of The Adult School Players	124
involved from the start with our World Premiere	123
Atkinson, Gilbert & Ethel	
celebrate their Diamond wedding in 2000	125
Atkinson, J Mrs	
music teacher at Cross Hall School	200
Atkinson, Martha & George	
Adult School Players	206
Aycliffe Chronicle	30
Back Green Methodist Chapel, Churwell	32
Baines, G E	
President of The Vocal Union in 1914	130
Baines, George Edwin	
patron to many local societies	85
Baines, James Edwin	
Musician & hero	25

Baker Room, Morley Library   206
    a memorial to Harry Baker   131
Baker, Harry
    remembered today by The Baker Room at Morley Public Library   131
Balchin, Fred   191
Baptist Tabernacle   79, 126
Barker, Richard (Dicky)
    a worthy servant of Morley's brass band   79
Barracks, The
    1913 old cottages demolished   116
    Albion St, new home of the Salvationists in 1883   112
Barras, Clifford   137, 160
Top Town Committee Member   192
Barrass, Clifford   170
    as Francois Villon   157
    Tenor   95
Barron, Sam   181
Barry, George
    acting manager of Excelsior Animated Picture Co   110
    appointed Manager of The New Pavilion   113
    first manager of the New Pavilion Theatre   104
Barstow, Professor John   91
    An early concert   147
    A celebrity concert in 2000 for Morley Musical Socy   216
    When at Reading University   211
Bartholomew, Eric
    of Morcambe & Wise fame   74
Bastow, Horace & Edith
    parents'of two famous sons   26
Bastow, Trevor & Geoffrey
    Musicians of International Renown   26, 91
Batley Cooperative Society   50
Batley Grammar School.   26, 30, 151, 197
Batley Variety Club   43
Batten, Jean
    a correspondent from Australia   198
Batty, Delia   168
Batty, John   164
BBC Children-in-Need competition
    'Bears in their Eyes'   43
BBC Salon Orchestra   53
BBC Studio Players   54
BBC Television series 'An Age of Kings'   40
BBC Television's 'Spread of the Eagle'series   41
Beaton, Betzi
    2nd wife if Richard Riddle Ainley   17
Beaumont, Baroness
    of Carlton Towers   31
Beaumont, Hubert
    MP for Batley & Morley   17
Bedford, Brian
    Shakespearean Actor & Director   28, 40

Beilby, Jean nee Lloyd 169
Benson, Frank R
    Shakespearean Impressario 11
Bentham, Mary 160
Bermont's
    London West End Costumiers 38
Bernard, Peter of Huddersfield Theatre Royal
    a Judge for Top Town Comp 192
Berry, Ralph
    one of the last remaining nine members of The Morley Vocal Union in 1970 128, 130
Bethel Drama Group 206, 207
Bethel Methodist Church, 134, 206
Bielby, Leslie 32
Billy Theaker & His Orchestra 90
Binks, J W. Alderman & Mrs
    Morely's Mayor & Mayoress in1974 64
Birdsall Bros. (late Wallis)
    Hatters & Hosiers, 85 Queen St Morley 111
Birmingham Repertory 40
Birmingham Repertory School 58
Black and White Minstrels 110
Black Diamond Minstrel Troupe 106
Black Dyke Mills Band 78, 133, 216
Blackie, Johnny
    the performing bear for thee Parrock Nook Prize Band 84
Blackpool Tower. 108
Blake, Fred
    the proprietor of the Alhambra Travelling Theatre 101, 102
Blake, Mrs F
    her funeral service at Morley Catholic Church 102
Blakeley, Tommy
    a close colleague of David Hirst 77
Blind Alley
    Jack Popplewell's 1st play 67
Bloodworth, Richard 214
Blythe, Doreen
    Ernie Wise's wife to be 105
Bombay Sunday Standard 54
Bombay Symphony Orchestra 54
Bond, Dorothy
    Coloratura soprano & Tom Jenkins second wife 55
Booth, Edward (Teddy) 159
Booth, John 30
Booth, Norman
    Organist 30
Boothroyd, Derrick
    Morley News & Obserfver Presents Top Town Trophy 197
Borough Arms (now the Slip Inn) 112
Bowes Lyon, Lady
    the late Queen Mother 13
Boy Choristers, The for Top Town Team
    a definitive list 195, 197

Boyd Neel Orchestra	55
Bradford Blue Imperial Band.	45
Bradford Civic Playhouse	40
Bradford Palace Theatre orchestra.	48
Brash-Grant, D R	
a Morley Dentist & The Revellers	181
Breakfast in Bed	
written in four weeks by Jack Popplewell	67
Brearley, Charles	121
Choirmaster, organist & singing teacher	211
Brenda and Barry	
Top Town Team's youngest members	192
Brewster, Anne & John	
children of The Mayor & Mayoress	187
Brewster, Harry & Jean, Mayor & Mayoress	
helping a celebration	187
Brian Bedford	28, 40
British Academy of Film & Television Arts Award	41
British Drama League Festival	125
British Legion, The	68, 78, 162
West Riding County Northern Area	181
British Thompson Houston Co. Ltd	
the installation of 'Talkie'equipment for The Picture House	116
Broadhead, Alan	130, 191
Broadley, Delia	33, 95, 167, 168, 169, 187
Broadley, Peter	176, 187
Brook, Christine (nee Smith)	
Soprano	95, 171
Brook, Geoff	174
Brook, Leslie	171
Brook, S H	181
Brooke, James	
song impressionist	74
Brooke, R	
a much sought after brass band musician	79
Brown, Olga	97, 173
Brunswick Chapel, The	120
Brunswick Hotel, The	
one time meeting place of The Vocal Union	132
Brunswick Primitive Methodist Chapel	30, 126
Bruntcliffe School	133, 172
Bryan, David	214
Bryant, Hope	144, 146, 184
Bundle's College	
Churwell	11
Bunney, Margaret nee Nowell	96, 160, 161
Burniston, Mr	181
Burrill, Donald	
Principal of the Joseph Priestley Institute in 1964	133, 148
Burrow Rene	7, 31, 71, 96, 159, 187
Burrow, Rene	
holder of NODA medal with Diamond bar	149

Burrow, Harry	31, 148, 169
baritone	95, 185
the Burgundian Herald	158
Burrow, Rene & Harry	31
Burton, Beryl	
Morley's World Champion Cyclist	30
Busybody'(1964)	
a Popplewell play that toured the world	67
Butlin's	26, 37
Butterfield, Fred	
1st musical director of The Morley Musical Society	213
Butterworth, E S	191
Butterworth, Eddie	
of Butterworth & Pilkington	122
Buttery, Hilda	
an Ebeneezer panto performer	161, 200
Bywater Jim	
Actor & Composer	34, 69, 197, 199
Bywater, Clifford	191
Father of Jimmy Bywater	34
C. Aubrey Smith	11
Callery, Claire	
another up & coming performer	149, 151
Callery, Jennifer	
a young experience of pantomime	149, 151
Callery, Victoria	
a young persons view of the performing arts	149
Canadian Broadcasting Corporation	29
Candlelighters Unit based at St. James's Hospital	42
Carr, Fred	48
Musician & orchestra leader	85
Carr, J Ralph Morley Music Society	
President 1966 - 1982	213
Carr, The Reverend Fred	164
Carr, Trevor	164, 171
Carr, Trevor & Jean	164
Carroll Levis'"Search for the Stars"	34, 121
1946	190
Carroll Levis (1910-1968)	190
Carroll Levis talent competition, A	
in 1946	121
Carson & Kid	
the young Ernie Wise on stage with his father	74
Carson, Ted	
the stage name of Harry Wiseman	73
Casson, Lewis	16
Castle, Harry	
the brass band's last permanent conductor	79
Cathleen Nesbitt	12, 15
CC41 Utility label	122
Cecil Moon Trio	52, 130
Celeste Octet	52

Central Drama Group   207
Chapman, Vincent Stanislaus
    Leader of the Alhambra Orchestra   101
Charity cricket match 26 May 1909
    between two travelling theatres   103
Cheesman, Winnie
    organiser of the Rockets Concert Party   91
Chew, Olwyn
    recalls a young Ernie Wise   75, 145
Chichester Festival Theatre   40
Choose 'Ow
    an Omads revue March 1938   72
Christian, Ken   42
Churwell Five Miler
    a Forget-me-not Charity event   42
Churwell Primary School   26, 151
Cipkin, Christopher
    librarian at Reading University   211
Citadel, The Acyroyd Street
    opened by Commissioner Hey in 1907   112
Civic Hall, Leeds   43
Clay, LG 1ˢᵗ Secy of Tingley Methodist Sylvians
    whose mother suggested the name   137
Clegg, Abraham
    founder of the Princess Theatre   100
Clegg, Charles
    Marie Clegg's brother   100
Clegg, Marie
    of the Princess Theatre   100
Clothing coupons
    another wartime joy   122
Clough, Edna & Ronald   212
Coats & Dale   25
Collins, David
    appointed Manager of The New Pavilion   115
Collins, David James
    Manager of The Pavilion & grandfather to many involved with this book   115, 162
Collins, Margaret   191
Collinson, Jim   166
Collinson's café in Leeds   45
Come Dancing   26
Commons, Billy`
    Parrock Nook's Dancing Donkey   84
Conservative Club
    Vocal Union offered free accommodation   99, 132
Consort of Musicke
    founded by Anthony Rooley   69
Cook, Harry (Nthn Opera & Drama Society
    a Top Town Comp Judge   193, 195
Cooke, Alistair
    one-time Fiance of Henrietta Riddle   17

Co-op Hall
    a grand soiree   79
Co-op Hall, The
    scene of auditions for Carroll Levis Discoveries   122
Cooper, Ernest
    Dame at St Peters Pantos   200
Coopers supermarket
    takes over the old Picture House building   117
Copenhagen Theatre, the
    a travelling theatre in 1908   104
Coronary Care Unit   42
Coronation New Pavilion Co. Ltd
    the Company set up to build The Pavilion   114, 162
Coronation of King George V   114
Coronation Street   34, 60
Cosmos Concert Party   170
Councillor Judith M. Elliott, The Mayor of Morley 2002/3   3
Court Players
    see Jean Kitson & Harry Hanson   59, 192
Crabtree, Bill
    a Bass singer with The Vocal Union   131
Crabtree, Colin
    a keen retainer of reference material   128
    Hon Librarian of Morley Music Society   212
    makes a chance meeting in Morley Public Library   213
Cragg Vale House   108
Crank Mill, Morley   10, 16
Croft House   23, 78, 197
Crosby, Luke
    landlord of The Cross Keys Hotel   84
Crosland, Frank (BBC)
    a Top Town Comp Judge   192
Cross Hall Boys School   62
Cross Hall Junior School Orchestra
    appear with Gilbert O'Sullivan for Yorkshire Television   199
Cross Hall Primary School
    Margaret Saunders recalls   199
Crystal Room
    ex Batley Variety Club   43
Currie, Elaine
    Professional Dancer   35, 194, 196
Daily Mail National Radio Award   55
Daily Mirror   30, 63
Dartmouth Arms   99
Dartmouth Park   85
David K. Atkinson   6
Dead on Nine
    Popplewell's massive West End success   67
Dean, Basil
    Impressario   14, 15
Dean, Joseph
    a blacksmith & founder of Morley Temperance Society   106

Dear Delinquent
    a 1957 Popplewell success   67
Denis Langfield Orchestra   26
Descriptive Writer of the Year in 1964
    a Vincent Mulchrone achievement   63
Dews, John
    Onetime Mayor of Morley & Father to Peter Dews   40
Dews, John Dews
    a show producer & Art Master   209
Dews, Peter
    TV & Theatre Producer   40, 198
Dewsbury Empire Theatre   48
Diacoff, Tom
    General Manager of The Alexandra Palace Theatre   110
Dickinson, David, Alderman & Mayor   213
Dickinson, Leonard
    bone soloist   74
Dixon, Winifred
    pianist at Collinsons Cafe   45
Don't Go Down the Mine Dad
    autobiography by David Reekie   8
Dougie Squires   38
Downes, Shirley nee Grimes   162
Dr Maxwell Telling   91
Drake, Clifford   191
Drighlington Brass Band   215
Drighlington Parish Church Youth Group   209
Drummer, H
    crooner   75
Drury Lane   15
Dunn, Geoffrey
    holds a record at the keyboard   91
Dunn, Geoffrey Morley Music Society
    Accompanist   215
Dunn, Harold
    Tenor   95
Durban Municipal Orchestra in South Africa   53
Durham Advertiser   30
East Ardsley Boys'school   73
Ebeneezer Methodist Church
    The Young People's Society   201
Ebeneezer Schoolroom   81
Ebenezer Methodist Chapel   173
Ebenezer Methodist Church   56, 208
Edward Maude's String Orchestra   51
Emily Fletcher   31, 68, 93, 171, 183, 184
Empire Palace Theatre, Edinburgh   25
Empire theatre
    New York   12
Empire Theatre, Leeds
    1939 Ernie Wise billed as Englands Mickey Rooney   49, 75, 146

Empress Palace Theatre
    opened in 1908   112
Encore
    an Omads revue February 1937   72
Ernie Wise   73, 105, 145, 146, 160
Evening Advertiser in Swindon   30
Excelsior Animated Picture Company, The
    a travelling cinematograph company in 1908   110
Excelsior Entertainers, The
    a travelling theatre in 1909   103
Farmer, Eileen   170
Farrell, Sean   214
Fatty Cake Row
    the site of a glue factory near Gildersome Crossroads   119
Fawcett, Jean   164
Fawcett, Jimmy
    part of the Four Generations   152
Fawcett, Pam   173
Fawcett, Pamela
    part of the Four Generations   196
Fearnley, Harry
    Alto   95
    alto & founder member of The West Riding Singers   133
Feature Writer of the Year in 1970
    a Vincent Mulchrone achievement   63
Fellow of the Royal Academy of Music
    Anthony Rooley   69
Festival of Britain   55
Festival of Britain concert of Handel's music   216
Field's Café   49
Films on Sundays   117
Financial Gazette in Harare   30
Financial News   30
First wireless broadcasting studio in Leeds
    designated 2LS by the BBC   130
Firth, Edna H Morley Music Society
    Accompanist   215
Firth, Marjorie   96, 197
Five Rascals, The
    Messrs Jim Hill, Albert & Willie Jowett, Tom Gill & Clifford Barras   137
Flesch, Carl
    violin tutor of world renown   52
Fletcher, Emily   31, 171, 168, 184, 185
    soprano   93
    'whence came you to this lonely place'   183
Forget-me-not charity   42
Forman, Rev G Eric   167
Foster, John
    the singing blacksmith   131, 187
Fountain pub, the
    the sceneshifters break   176
Fountain Street Working Mens'Club   86

Four Hands in Harmony.
    George Speight & Norman Hartley   87, 194
Four Martinis, The   191
Four Valleys Youth Festival   209
Fox, Cecil   144, 146, 160, 170
Fox, E D   181
Fox, H Cecil
    baritone   181, 187
Fox, Mr
    drummer for The Morley Reed Band   78
Franks Opticians in Queen Street
    the workplace of Harry Baker   131
Fred Carr's Premier Orchestra   85
Free Trade Hall, Manchester   56
French Foreign Legion   18
Frontier Club   43
Frudd, Willie
    conductor of Vocal Union in 1925   130
Fryer, Phil
    Churwell's 'Frank Sinatra'   42
Gagliano violin
    the disposal of Tom Jenkins greta violin   54
    Tom Jenkins first famous violin   53
Gardener's Question Time
    a Robert Stead production   72
Garrison theatre
    Leo Leathley recognised a long way from home   182, 191
Gaunt, Edith
    accordionist   74, 144
Geo. Glover's Famous Orchestra.   86
George Speight and his Orchestra
    dancing to in The Alexandra Hall   87, 88, 94, 120
George Speight Dance Band   47, 185, 191, 194
Gielgud, John
    later Sir John Gielgud   14, 28
Gilbertson, Harold   168
Gilbertson, Ted   160, 170
Glendinning, Ethel
    1st wife of Richard Riddle Ainley   17
Glover, George
    Insurance agent & orchestra leader   86
Gomersal, George
    accompanist & founder member of The West Riding Singers   133
Gomersal, Oliver
    up before the Bench   106
Gomersal, Tom   64, 188
Goodson, John
    sings with Jack Popplewell at the piano   68
Gower, Arthur   51
Graham Warner Orchestra   27
Granada T.V   43
Grand Hotel Orchestra, Eastbourne   50, 53

Grand Theatre, Leeds   14, 22, 35, 45, 58, 96, 127
Great illuminations of electric light
    by Excelsior Entertainers   104
Green, Alfred
    Morley's famous Pork Butcher   46
Green, John   170
Green, Phyllis
    Cellist   45
Green's Pork Butchers   63
Gurning through a horse-collar   98
H.M. the Queen   65
Haigh, Joseph Alderman & Mayor
    died in office before the opening of The New Pavilion   114
Haigh, Leonard
    singer   75
Haigh, Malcolm
    Top Town Committee Member   192
Haigh, Peggy   160, 191
Haigh, Verna
    Singer, Dancer & Accordianist   47, 85
Half & Half Appeal   42
Hall, Thomas H
    violinist & maternal grandfather of Tom Jenkins   50
Hallé Orchestra   45, 56
Handel's Messiah
    at The Brunswick Chapel   120
Hanson, Harry
    Producer & Director of The Court Players   59
Happy Landings   90
Hardy, Chiddy
    manager of the Imperial Picture House   107
Hardy, Donald   191
Hardy, Harry   78, 147, 159
    1st President of the Morley Musical Society   213
    chairs a meeting on 27 May 1943   213
Hardy, Sir Harry Morley Music Society
    President 1943 - 1958   213
Harewood House Convalescent Hospital for Officers   31, 182
Harmsworth, Vyvyan LVO
    Director of Corpate Affairs, The Daily Mail & General Holdings Ltd   65
Harold Fielding   38
Harris, Hetty
    ballet mistress to the Omads in 1938   76
    song & dance   75
Harrison, George
    Cashier at Hield Bros Mill   131
Harrison, Tom
    member of Vocal Union & Manager of Moerley'Labour |Exchange   130, 132
Harrogate Central Cinema Orchestra   52
Harrogate Prince of Wales Hotel   45
Harrogate String Orchestra   54

Harrop, Violet
    Phyllis Green's connection with Tom Jenkins 45
    Tom Jenkins first wife 52, 53
Harry Culpan 132
Hartley, Alice
    a memory the Adult School Players 127, 204
Hartley, Fred
    one of the last remaining nine members of the Morley Vocal Union in 1970 128
Hartley, Linda nee Dormer
    wife of Norman Harley 208
Hartley, Norman 169, 170, 185, 186, 191, 194
    accompanist for Vocal Union at first broadcast 128
    describing his VES lapel badge 181
    experience with singing hopefuls 122
    Morley's Mr Music Man 86, 94
    one of the last remaining nine members of The Morley Vocal Union 128
    Top Town Committee Member 192, 196
Hastings Municipal Orchestra 52
Hawkins, Brian 191
Headingley Test Match
    & Phyllis Green's meeting with Don Bradman 45
Heart Research 42
Heavy Woollen District Top Town Competition 119, 192
Help
    Omads first revue at Pavilion in 1934 115
Hemingway, G
    judge for Top Town Comp (Yorkshire Evening News) 192
Henry Hibbert's High Class Animated Pictures 111
Hirst, David Edward 168, 175, 219
    among his souvenirs 165
    an intro to the Operatic Society 152
Hirst, David 1779-1865
    a fiddler of great merit 78, 219
Hirst, George
    an organist of repute 201
Hirst, J
    a 19th century pianist 77, 79
Hirst, Joseph
    a member of the Morley Reed Band 79
Hirst, Millicent 61, 97, 160, 173, 163, 196
    choregrapher of Top Town shows 193, 197
    Top Town Committee Member 192
His Majesty's theatre 14
His Master's Voice 52
Hobson's Choice
    adapted into a musical 68, 204, 206
Hodgson family, The
    adopted a lonely Bevin Boy 121
Hodgson, Jim
    a man of provisions 212

Hodgson, Stella
    a boon companion   121
    song & impersonations   75
Holbeck Jungle Band   84
Holders of NODAMedal for 25 years service
    a definitive list   149
Holliday, Barbara   96, 148, 167, 168
Holliday, Joyce & Alf   171
Holmes, Janet
    vocalist   74, 144, 160
Holroyd, Joe
    a performer with the Parrock Nook Prize Band   84
Holt, Steven   148, 171, 172
Holy Trinity Church Meanwood   216
Hopkinson, Celia
    memories of H Cecil Fox   159
    recalls her father H Cecil Fox with the Omads   144
Hopwood, Arthur
    a principal cornetist   79
Horsfall, Lily
    Henry Ainley's aunt   10
Hot Spots   34, 162
Hotspots   90
Houldin, Betty
    daughter of Tom Harrison   130
Huddersfield Choral Society   49
Hudson, Derek   166
Hughie Green   35, 38
Hulbert, F H
    Grammar School Head   64, 143
Hull Musical Festival   51
I and the best pork pies in the world come from Morley
    Vincent Mulchrone   63
If I Should Fall in Love Again,
    a Jack Popplewell hit of the 1940's   67, 68, 185
Illingworth, Ananias
    the 18th century singer with perfect pitch   76
Imperial Electric Picture Company
    new tenants of the Temperance Hall   107
Imperial Picture House The
    as the Temperance Hall was known in 1912   107
Industria Omnia Vincit
    the motto from Morley's Coat of Arms   188
Industrial Revolution   76, 219
Ingle, Martin
    tenor & founder member of The West Riding Singers   133
Ingle, W L Alderman
    Mayor of Morley 1911   48, 115
Ingle, WL. Mayor of Morley
    officially opens The New Pavilion   115
Ingle's Leather Mill in Churwell   164

Inman, Alfred
  his association with Tom Jenkins 51
  professional violinist 86
  Violinist 48
Issue of petrol coupons
  for The Revellers 182
Iveson, Tony of Granada Television
  a Top Town Judge 192
J H Squire's Celeste Trio 52
Jack Popplewell 32, 67, 185
Jackson, Ceres
  a trumpeter of great merit 78
Jackson, Pat Miss
  Top Town Judge & Yorkshire Evening Post 192
Jackson, Phil
  reporter for The Morley Advertiser 130, 131
Jagger, Mick
  his family roots in Morley 211
Japa Paper Products Ltd of Churwell 90
Japa Service's Welfare Fund 90
Jarvis, Brian 190
Jelly, Noel
  tenor 95
Jenkins Michelle Le Mesurier
  Tom Jenkins widow 9, 57
Jenkins Tom 9
Jenkins, Albert Hilton
  Tom Jenkin's younger brother 50
Jenkins, George Hollins
  Tom Jenkin's older brother 50
Jenkins, Harry
  Tom Jenkins father 50
Jenkins, Henry
  supposedly Yorkshire's longest living man 118
Jenkins, Tom 9, 46, 86
  his association with Cecil Moon 130
  Violin Virtuoso 50, 51, 54
John Hopkins University School for Advanced International Studies 30
Johnny Howard Orchestra 26, 27
Johnson, Clifford
  Top Town Judge 192
Johnson, Herbert
  pianist 91
Johnson, Sidney
  organist 91
Joseph Priestley College Award evening
  Phil Fryer, guest speaker 43
Jowett, A H 190
Jowett, Albert
  founder member & recorder of Tingley Sylvian history 138
Jowett, Alderman W H
  Secy to Morley Tradesmen's Benevolent Association 105

Jowett, Allen H Councillor
1st Secretary & Treasurer for the Morley Musical Society   213
Joyce & Dorothy Dancing School   97, 184, 187
Just to be Frank
    a Yorkshire TV documentary   42
    Phil Fryer's CD   44
Keighley, Bertha of Leeds Art Group
    a Top Town Comp Judge   192
Kelly, Jimmy
    played a mock street gaslamp for the Parrock Nook   84
Kent, Allan   43
Killerby, Brian
    monologist   74
King Edward VII's Coronation in 1902,   11
King's Arms, The
    a hostelry at Gildersome Crossroads   119
Kirk, John T
    Actor, Producer & Theatre Manager   58
    turns professional after being demobbed   127
    a founder member of The Adult School Players   126
Kismet
    last amateur production at Pavilion 1967   115, 175
Kitson, Jean Heather
    Actress   59
L&Y Exclusive Picture Company, The
    a Town Hall showing in 1913   111
L.A. Drama Critics Award   28
Lacy, Joyce
    Landlady of The Needless   167
Ladley, Dorothy & Sydney
    producers of St Peters Pantos   200
Ladley, Sydney & Dorothy   171
Land, John
    female impersonator & bear attendant for the Parrock Nook   84
Laurie, John   23
Lawrence, DH
    novelist. poet & playwright   58, 124
Le Mesurier Croll, Michelle
    Tom Jenkins widow   55
Leathley, Leo   31, 144, 146, 171, 193, 195, 209
Leathley, Harold
    Secretary of the Omads in 1938   74
Leathley, Harold Councillor
    Top Town Committee Member   192
Leathley, Harold 'Leo'
    the driving force behind The Revellers   181, 184
    1932 produces a review for Morley Cricket Club   181
    co producer of Top Town Shows   192
Leathley, Walter
    a man always behind the scenes   185
Lee Fair Anthem   83
Leeds Amateurs   35

Leeds Chest Clinic 38
Leeds Church Institute 51
Leeds City Varieties 35
Leeds Civic Theatre 33
Leeds Coliseum 78, 110
Leeds General Infirmary 35, 159, 102
Leeds Grand Theatre 35, 45, 58
Leeds Irish Centre 43
Leeds Mecca Locarno Ballroom 26
Leeds Musical Competition Festival 51
Leeds Organists Association 213
Leeds Scala Orchestra, 49
Leeds Sylvians 90, 191
Leeds Symphony Orchestra 51
Leeds Town Hall 54
Leeds-Bradford Radio station 51
Lennox, David 214
Les Brown (and his band of renown) Orchestra. 27
Lessons, Phyllis 75
Lets
    18th February 1935 47
    an Omads revue of 1935 72
Lewis's Department Store 62
Lewisham Park
    land donated by Lord Dartmouth 114
Life Members of The Operatic Society
    a definitive list 149
Liley, George A 181
Lindley 143, 196, 197
Liverpool Repertory Company 28
Llandudno Pier Pavilion 38
Lloyd, Jean 33, 169
    soprano 94
Lloyd's List 30
Local rhubarb 67
Lockwood, W
    pianist 181
Lodge, Kathleen
    part of 'Four Generations' 152
London Bach Society 30
London Palladium 26, 38
London Philharmonic Orchestra 53, 56
London Theatre Orchestra
    Tom Jenkins final performances 56
Lord John Sanger's Circus and Variety 105
Lorriman, Howard 214
Loyd, Jean 191
Luscombe, Duel
    a Top Town Judge & Producer for The Court Players 192
Lyceum in London 27
Magic 828 43
Maharg 90, 191

Malton White Star Band	51
Manchester Evening News	63
Manor House	112
Marjorie, Will & The Two Dots	191
Mark Moon	130
Marshall, Tommy & Arthur Wilson	
the inebriated comedy duo	146
Maskell, John	191
Matthew,Beatrice & Elsa Riva	
song & dance artistes	74
Maude, Edward	
leader of Leeds Symphony Orchestra	51
Maude, Lily	191
Mayor's Rooms, The	
Norman Hartley's 70th Birthday celebrations	186
McCallum, David	
leader of LPO & vendor of Tom Jenkins Gagliano violin	53
McGough, Jocelyn	
now Mrs Simons	94, 159, 170
Mecca Locarno Ballroom in Bradford	26
Melton, June	191
Menston Hospital	182
Mercantile Club	132
Messiah, The	
a tradition	120
Metcalfe, Dorothy	97
"Mikado" at Morley Town Hall in 1927	85, 152
Miller, Gilbert	
associate of Henry Ainley	14
Miss World Contest	27
Mitchell, Ronnie	74
Moon, Cecil	
Mark Moon's famous son	130
renowed musician & son of Mark Moon	52
Moon, Mark	
renowned Bass soloist & member of The Morley Vocal Union	130
Morecambe & Wise	39, 73
Morely Technical Institute Operatic Society	
a concert version of Il Trovatore	209
Morley & District Corps of the St. John's Ambulance Brigade	51
Morley Adult School Players	58, 124, 125, 126, 204, 206
a delightful contribution by Alice Hartley just prior to her death	204
perform 'ACollier's Friday Night Out@	124
Morley Amateur Operatic Society	8, 31, 49, 85, 123, 148, 152, 173
Morley artistes appearing in Top Town	
a definitive review	193
Morley Borough	
25 years with a Royal Charter	114
Morley Borough Court in April 1909	102
Morley Bottoms	71, 80, 98, 99, 100, 211
Morley Brass Band	78, 101
successors of The Morley Reed Band	78

Morley Conservative Club.   99
Morley Corps of the Salvation Army
  founded in 1882 using a room in Morley Market   112
Morley Cricket Club   108, 181
Morley Cycling Club   30
Morley feast   98
Morley Fire Brigade
  attend a fire at The Alexandra Theatre   113
Morley Grammar School   27, 34, 46, 51, 58, 59, 62, 64, 68, 71, 138, 142, 162, 178
  the new school hall   178
Morley Grammar School pupils
  a presentation of 'The Gondoliers'   209
Morley Grange
  Churwell   11
Morley Guides   209
Morley High School   138, 217
Morley History Society
  the annual dinner in 1974   64
Morley Liberal Club   72
Morley Market.   108, 112
Morley medical charities in 1930
  a show to raise for on Tuesday 28th October   182
Morley Music Society   91, 95, 128, 145, 147, 211, 213, 218, 219
  a Festival of Britain Concert at the Albert Hall   213
  a roll call of members   218
Morley Nursing Association   48
Morley Observer   50, 62, 64, 71, 85, 124, 169, 182, 201, 206, 209, 216
  a cutting dated 24 March 1939   124
  article March 1923 re Tom Jenkins   50
  Vincent Mulchrone's first newspaper   62
Morley Observer 25th November 1938   156
Morley Observer 2nd December 1938   156
Morley Observer, The
  a question is put to today's management   209
Morley Pantomime   150, 185
Morley Parrock Nook Anthem Prize Band   81, 84
  an earley 20th cent delight   81
Morley Picture House Ltd, The
  build a cinema in the area known as The Barracks   116
Morley Reed Band   77
Morley Rugby Union Club   177
Morley Secondary School
  precursor of Morley Grammar in 1906   142
Morley Skating Rink
  a failed venture   116
Morley Technical Institute Amateur Operatic Society 31, 46, 115, 123, 127, 148, 157, 167
  1st post war production in 1947   157
  what a mouthful?   123
  contributions from around the country by ex members   148
Morley Temperance Hall   106
Morley Temperance Society   106
Morley Top Town Team, The   34, 69, 97, 152

a winning combination 192
Morley Town Council 71
    accept a portrai in oils of Benjamin Hale Worrall 109
Morley Town Hall   23, 44, 51, 64, 72, 88, 114, 124, 126, 167, 178, 181, 186, 215
Morley Township
    an increasing population 98
Morley Tradesmen's Benevolent Association
    President Mr R Metcalfe 105
Morley Vocal Union   85, 107, 128, 129, 130, 212, 219
    a once famous Male Voice Choir 126
    at Armley Jail 129
    one of the first to broadcast from the Leeds BBC Studios 128
    a 1948 quartet with a combined age of 298 years 130
    those travelling to Paris in 1914 128
Morley'Oil 99
Moss, Tom
    judge for Top Town Comp & retired comedian 192
Mountain, Willie
    ventriloquist 74
Mulchrone, Mrs & Mrs Patrick
    parents of Vincent Mulchrone 62
Mulchrone, Vincent
    reports on The Revellers 182
Mulchrone, Vincent J
    a great Journalist 62
    his report on a Rehoboth play 202
Mundy, Gloria
    celebrated her 21st with The Top Town Team 192, 195
Mundy, Gloria & Pauline
    prominent St Peters Panto performers 200
Murray's Cabaret Club 37
Musica Oscura, a record label
    est 1993 by Anthony Rooley 70
Nelson Cricket Club 108
Nelson's Arms 98
Nesbitt,Cathleen
    an Ainley leading lady 12, 15
New Century Picture Company in Leeds 88
New Inn Churwell, 78
New Pavilion Theatre   48, 102, 114, 143, 145, 153
    the demise of the travelling theatre in Morley 105
New York Drama Desk Awards 28
News Chronicle'£50 song contest winner
    Jack Popplewell 68
Newton, Peter 160
Niven, Joyce
    sciptwriter for St Peters Pantos 200
Noble, Hazel
    a remembered legacy 165
    holder of NODA medal for 50 years service 149
NODA 149

Norcliffe, Anthony
    he changed the name of the Morley Musical Society   214
Norman & George on Two Pianos   191
North View, Rooms Lane
    the Ainley family home   10, 17
Northallerton Jail
    a Revellers visit on Sunday 22 September 1957   185
Northern Commanders   90
Northern Philharmonic Orchestra   49, 54
Northern Spotlights   90
Nowell, Margaret & Barbara Kellet
    'Babes in the Wood'at Ebenezzer Panto   200
Nursing Association of Morley   10, 48
O'Sullivan, Gilbert
    singing with children of Cross Hall   199
Oakes A S (Arty)   190
Odds On
    1939 Omads Revue   53\
Old Manor House Bruntcliffe, The
    home of George Wilson   122
Old Morleian Amateur Dramatic Society
    The OMADS   142
Old Morleian Association, The
    a name change in 1912   142
Old Morleians Amateur Dramatic Society   58, 63, 67, 115, 145, 181
    the first society to book The Pavilion   115
Old Scholars Association
    founded around 1910 for The Secondary School   142
Old Templeton   99
Oliver Brooke Appeal   44
Olivier, Laurence
    later Sir Laurence Olivier   16, 23
OmaDarlings   31
OMADS revue
    a postwar revival   122
OMADS, The
    a 'Valentines Revue'   209
One hundred and eight signatories
    a list of those attending Norman Harley's reception   181
Orient Giant Electric Picture Company   111
Osborne, S
    a much sought after brass band musician   79
Palace Cinema, Morley   88
Palm Court Orchestra   54
Paris International Musical Festival   129
Paris Lido   37
Parker, Margaret   190
Parrock Nook Congregational Church at Rishworth, near Sowerby Bridge.
    possibly the inspiration for for Morley's Parrock Nook Band   82
Pashley, Beth   96, 178
Pashley, Eric   176
Pashley, Jerry   213

Pashley, Margaret   96
Past Presidents of The Operatic Society
    a definitive list   148
Pathé News   52
Pauline Taylor (nee Beveridge)   173
Pavilion Theatre   34, 46, 49, 50, 58, 63, 74, 90, 121, 122, 145, 152, 162, 173, 176, 182
Pavilion Theatre, The
    scene of The Revellers 150th show in 1942   182
    wartime Sunday evening concerts   121
Pearson, Ladley   181
Peel Robert 'Bobby   11
Peel Street Boys School   164
Peel, Annie
    actress & singer   96
Peel, Margaret   164
Peel, Sam   96
Penguin Book of Early Music
    1982 by Anthony Rooley   70
Percival, Arthur
    violinist at Collinsons Cafe   45
Performance: Revealing the Orpheus Within
    by Anthony Rooley   70
Pete Hurley Trio   26
Peter Dews   40
Picture House, The
    is sold & screens last programme in February 1960   116
Piercy, Lucy (nee Strickland)
    visit to Vincent Mulchrone's Fleet St memorial   66
Pirates of Penzance, The
    1st G & S by Tingley Sylvians in 1933   137
Pontefract Lane Cinema   45
Pontins, Blackpool   43
Poole, Joan Mrs
    daughter of Harry Culpan   132
Popplewell, Jack
    Songwriter & Playwright   32, 67, 185
Popplewell, Walter
    Rhubarb grower & father of Jack   67
Powell, Peter   160, 162
    comedian   96
    some memories   173
Prince of Wales Theatre in London   52
Princess Theatre in Blackpool   43, 99, 100
Pugh, Peter & Duncan Heath
    authors of 'The Tom Jenkins Story'   57
Pump Room Bath   56
Purcell's 'King Arthur' in the new hall of Morley High School
    a Morley Music Society's huge success   217
Puss in Boots
    the Pavilion cat   165
Queen Elizabeth Grammar School   40

Queen Hotel, The
    previously The Alliance Hotel & now home of the Victoria Music Hall   108
Queen Street Junior School   62
Queen Street Methodist Dramatic Society   209
Queen Street Wesleyan Mandolin & Banjo Band
    rehearsed in Harry Roebuck's furntiure shop in Morley Bottoms   80
Queen Street Wesleyan Methodist Chapel   93
Queen's Park   108
Queen's Theatre, Holbeck   88
Rachael Swann School of Dancing   152, 217
Radio Aire   43
RAF stations throughout the county
    The Revellers were there   68, 182
Raimond, Ada   190
Rains, Claude
    Hollywood star   14
Ralph Berry   128, 130, 131
Ranalow, Frederick   17
Rankin, George
    stalwart at The Bethel   206
Rathbone, Christopher
    Musical Director of Morley Music Society   214, 217
Rawicz and Landauer   39
Ray McVay Orchestra   27
Raymond's Revue bar   37
Reading University   30, 211
Redick T Alderman & Mrs,
    Mayor & Mayoress   190
Rehoboth Church Choir   145
Rehoboth Congregational Church
    a place of good music & excellent drama   200
Rehoboth Dramatic Society, The
    present 'Young at Heart'   209
Rehoboth Productions   202, 203
Rehoboth Sunday School Scholars   209
Rehoboth Young People's Society   201
Revel Girls, The
    a definitive list   185
Revellers Concert party, The
    was born out of a 1932 revue   181
Revellers, The
    a wartime concert party of note   181
    action at the outbreak of war in 1939   181
    early 1941 & their 100th show   182
    over 20,000 serving men entertained during the 1st year of war   182
Reviews earned by The Revellers
    a selection   187
Revubilee
    23rd March 1936   47
Rhodes & Vinces Royal Entertainers, The
    a travelling theatre in 1907   103

Rhodes, June   147
    contralto   92
Rhodes, S. Alderman & Mayor
    lays the foundation stone to The New Pavilion Theatre   115
Rhubarb
    How appropriate for an Actor & Politician   24
Riddle, Bettina
    see Baroness Bettina von Hutten   17
Riddle, Henrietta
    Henry Ainley's daughter   17
Riley, Moira   147
Roberts, Edgar & Willie
    Ebeneezer Panto Stars   200
Roberts, Jim Councillor & Mayor
    photgraphed with The Vocal Union   131
Roberts, Tony   172, 179
    tenor   95
Robertshaw, Brian   164, 218
Robertson, Fanny
    contralto   181
Roche, Dr James Morley Music Society
    President 1958 - 1966   214
Rockets   90
Rogerson, George Alderman & Mayor   167
Rogerson, Margaret, Mayoress   167
Rollinson, Paul   142, 174, 175, 180, 200
    an early conributor to this book   123
Rooley, Anthony   34
    Lutenist & authority on Early Music   69
    lutenist & early music specialist   91, 197
Rooley, Henry & Madge
    Anthony Rooley's parents   69
Rose, Thomas
    a member of The Morley Reed Band   77
Royal Academy of Dramatic Arts   28
Royal Academy of Music   69
Royal Animated Picture Company, The
    a travelling show in 1912   111
Royal Baths Quartet   52
Royal Festival Hall   55
Royal Hotel   95
Royal Magnets, The
    a travelling theatre in 1908   103
Royal National Theatre, The
    a tour under the Big Top in 1998   105
Royal Philharmonic Orchestra   56
Royalty Theatre in Chester   60
Rushforth, Joyce   97
Sadler Wells Orchestra   55
Sam Wild's 'Theatrical Booth'   99
Sanderson, Ann
    a brush with a guardroom sergeant   183, 184

Saunders, Derek& Mayla   199
Saunders, Margaret   198
Saynor, Anne   160
Scarborough Open Air Theatre   171
Scargill, Dennis
    entertainer   95
    Top Town Committee Member   192
Scargill, Mary   171
Scargill, Stella   142, 166, 170, 174, 196
    a performer of all-round talent   95
Scargill, Stella & Dennis   186, 193
Scarth, Charles JP
    opening the Temperance Hall as Mayor in 1895   106
Scarth, Kenneth late of The Vocal Union
    his son Kevin makes a chance meeting   212
Scatcherd Alice Cliff   10
Scatcherd Lane Athletic Grounds   99, 103
Scatcherd Lane Cricket ground   103
Scatcherd, Oliver
    the park named after him is opened   114
Schofield, Harold
    comedy roles with Ebeneezer Pantos   200
Schofield, W P Architect
    The Picture House Morley   116
Schwarze, Hans Doctor
    University of Tubingen   124, 127
Scott, David
    a member of The Morley Reed Band   77
Scott, Jean
    contralto   92, 171
Scottish Orchestra   49
Scottish Theatre Company   40
Senior, Shelagh nee Woodcock   160
Sheard, Ralph W
    Manager of both the L&Y Exclusive Pi Co & the Alexandra Palace   111
Sheldon, Susanne
    Henry Ainley's 1st wife   17
Shelly, Betty nee Briggs   160
Sibley, Willie
    violinist   90
Siegen (Morley's Twin Town in Germany)   42
Simons, Jocelyn nee McGough   159, 170
Sinatra, Frank Junior
    Phil Fryer's meeting with   42
Slater, Robert
    a violinist of Morley   51
Sleight, Elizabeth
    soprano & founder member of The West Riding Singers   133
Smilers   90
Smith, A Hugh Morley Music Society
    President 1982 - present day   214

Smith, Alan
    one of the finest crown green bowlers in Yorkshire   131
Smith, Aubrey C
    Hollywood film star   11
Smith, H Malcolm, Alderman & Mayor
    reopens The Picture House in 1956 after installation of Cinemascope   116
Smith, Margaret   185, 190
Smith, R W   181
Smith, Roland
    one of the last remaining nine members of The Morley Vocal Union in 1970   128
    tenor   95
Smith, Sam
    Conductor of The Vocal Union in Paris   129, 130
Smith, William
    comments on The Philharmonic Society   79
    gives a lecture on musical matters   79
    the great 19th century historian   77
Sotheby's in New Bond Street, London
    the sale of Tom Jenkins Strad violin   57
Spa Orchestra   56
Spark, Dr William
    organist & friend of S S Wesley   201
Speight, George
    pianist & dance band leader   87, 120, 185, 191
Spencer, Arthur
    Manager of Morley's two cinemas   117
    Manager of the Picture House & Pavilion   90
Spencer, Lavinia
    confidante to Lady Bowes-Lyon   13
Spread Eagle, The
    a large inn on Gildersome Crossroads   119
Spring Fever
    Omads revue in April 1948   63, 143
Spruce, Jean   97
Spruce, Keith   162
Spurr, John Willie
    conductor of the Parrock Nook Prize Band   84
Spurr, Maureen   147
St Andrew's Church Bruntcliffe   216
St James'Theatre in London   14
St Mary's Congregational   119, 164
St Mary's first organ
    in 1798   76
St Mary's in the Wood
    in the early 18th Century   76
St. Mary's Players   171
St Paul's Church Morley   216
St Paul's Church vestry   174
St Paul's Sunday School   155
St Paul's Youth Group
    recalled by Jean Batten from her Queensland home   198
St Peter's Church Gildersome   216

St Peter's New School	11
St Peter's Parish Church	77, 209, 216
Paul Rollinson recalls his boyhood visits	200
St Peter's Youth Group	200, 209
St. Martin-in-the-Fields	16, 57
Henry Ainley's Memorial Service	16
Stacey, Matt	
Phil Fryer's Musical Director	44
Stage magazine	43
Stakes, J W	
Hon Secy of The Vocal Union in 1914	129, 130
Staniforth & Hall	
Sheffield Brokers	11
Stead, G H	
secretary to the Morley Philharmonic Society	79
Stead, Horatio	
an Alto voice like a bell	131, 132
Stead, Robert	181
Journalist & BBC Producer	71
Stead, Samuel	
established Morley's 1st printing press in 1854	71
launched the Morley Observer in 1871	71
Steel, J W	
organiser for the Parrock Nook Prize Band	84
Sterling, Louis	
pre-war Managing Director of HMV	52
Stevenson, Norman	
co producer of Top Town shows	197
Top Town Copmmitte Member	192
Stockdale, Geoff	164
Stokes, Fred	170
Stonehouse, George	191
Storr, Richard	
bass & founder member of The West Riding Singers	133
Stradivarius violin	54, 57
a major acquisition for Tom Jenkins	54
Stratford Festival in Ontario	40
Stratford Festival of Canada	28
Stratford Memorial Theatre	58
Sun newspaper	
'The New Frank'by Christa Akroyd	43
Sunday People	166
Sunderland Mrs	
Yorkshire's Queen of song in 1862	201
Sykes (nee Slater)Kathleen	
a principal girl at Ebeneezer Pantos	200
Sykes, Frank, Alderman & Mayor	
Top Town committee member	192
Sykes, John	
'Drum Hugger' to the Morley Reed Band	78, 79
Sykes, Nancy	186, 195
contralto	92

Talented children of Cross Hall
    the cast of those appearing with Gilbert O'Sullivan   199
Taylor, John
    tune striker, bell ringer & grave digger   76
Taylor, Pauline nee Beveridge   173
Taylor, Reg   173, 200
Teale, Gilead
    one time President of The Vocal Union   132
Teale, John
    remembers his father Gilead   132
Technical Operatic Society   209
Teenage Ramblers Skiffle Group   34, 69, 194,197
Tempest, Stanley
    one of the last nine remaining Members of The Vocal Union in 1970   128
Terpstra, Arjen
    Anthony Rooley's partner in 'Musica Obscura'   70
Tetley shire horses   168
Tetley, Joe
    a member of Billy Theakers orchestras   90
Thackray, David. County Alderman JP
    a filmed report of his funeral in 1912   111
The 'ATC 's   90
The 'OK's   90
The Best of Vincent Mulchrone
    a Daily Mail publication   65
The Cliff Adam's Singers   92
The Cross Keys Hotel in Britannia Road
    home of the Parrock Nook Anthem Prize Band   84
The Daily Mirror   30, 63
The Desert Song
    MTIAOS first production at Pavilion 1938   115, 155, 165, 175, 185
The European   30
The Filey Fishermens'Choir   95
The Grand Theatre Leeds   96
The Great Lafayette
    Illusionist   25
The Guardian   30
The History & Antiquities of Morley'
    by William Smith 1876   77
The History of the New Pavilion
    by Ronald Barraclough   8, 160
The London Symphony Orchestra   26
The lying in state of Sir Winston Churchill
    Vincent Mulchrone reports   63
The Magnets
    16th January 1944   47, 68
The Morley Amateur Operatic Society   8, 49, 123, 148, 152
    the earliest mention found   85
The Morley Concertina Band
    a family affair, including the Sharps, the Mitchells and the Hawkins   79
The Morley Harmonic Society
    formed in the early 1870's   79

The Morley Juvenile Band
    formed in 1910 by Jim Issacs   84
The Morley Private String Band   79
The National School   77
The Observer   30, 156
The OK Concert party   31
The OMADS   31
The Pavilion Orchestra of Talented Musicians   48, 86
The Princess Theatre   99
The Revellers   31, 47, 63, 68, 92, 97, 181, 187
The Tom Jenkins Quintet   56
The Tom Jenkins Story
    a biography by Peter Pugh & Duncan Heath   57
The Tom Jenkins Orchestra
    or The Winter Garden Orchestra   56
The Town Hall   110
The Trumpet Shall Sound
    Ceres Jackson at the Albert Hall   79
The Vincent Mulchrone Room
    at The Harrow, just off Fleet Street   66
The Way It Is
    a Daily Mail article in 2001   65
The West Riding Band Contest at Knottingley Town Hall
    won by The Morley Brass Band   79
The Workpeople's Treat   79
Theatre Royal and Opera House in Wakefield   138
Theatre Royal in Leeds   59
Thorpe Junior and Infant school   73
Those holding Presidential office   214
Thursday Group   207
Tiffany, James William
    Phyllis Green's father   45
Tillotson & Firth   88
Tillotson and Firth   212
Times Educational Supplement   30
Tingley Methodist Sylvians   137
Tingley Sylvians Amateur Operatic Society.   91, 94, 137, 219
Tinner Taylors
    a long established hardware shop   82
Tipling, Lorna   163, 164
Titus-Fearon, Elaine
    Henry Ainley's 2nd wife   17
Tolson Brothers, The   186
Tom Jenkins   50
Tony Award   28, 40
Tony Hopkin's North Pier Orchestra   52
Top Town Team   34, 69, 92, 152, 192
Top Town Trophy
    a tribute to the late Major Norman Stevenson   197
Towlson, Clifford W   147, 214
Towlson, Dr Clifford
    a Top Town Comp Judge   193

Town Hall, The
    built at a cost of £41,227   110
Townend, Stan   166
Tread Softly Stranger
    a film version of Blind Alley   67
Trepte, Paul   214
    organist at Ely Cathedral   91
Trouble is tha were stillborn
    an old collier's comment   119
Trowsdale, Marjorie
Tullett, Jack   198
Turner, Alec E
    Hon Secy for the Operatic Society   156
Twenty-Four Hour Luncheon Club.   72
VES
    entertainers under the direction of Northern Command   181
Victoria Music Hall, The
    until 1896, charging 2d, 4d, & 6d for admission   108
Victoria Road School   48, 93
Victory   90
Vincent Mulchrone   62
Voluntary Entertainment Services of the Northern Command   31
Voluntary Entertainment Services, The
    or VES for short   181
von Hutten, Bettina, Baroness
    born Bettina Riddle & mother to Henry Ainley's daughter Henrietta   17
Wade, Samuel
    a member of the Morley Reed Band   77
Wainwright, Sheila   217
Wakefield Cathedral   214
Wakefield College Choir   43
Wakefield Opera House   138, 150
Wakefield Prison   92
Wakefield Theatre Club   26, 166
Wakefield, Olga   190
Walker, Harold
    one of the last remaining members of The Morley Vocal Union in 1970   128
Walsh, Horace
    the last President of The Vocal Union   128
Walsh, Mavis   191
Walton, Blanche
    celebrated her 21st with The Top Town Team   192, 193
    soprano   94
Waltz Without End
    the Observer story in 1957   32, 169
Wanless, Susan   214
Ward, Norrie   206
Washington Post   30
Watkins, June   96
Watson, T L Mrs
    violinist   181

Webster, Donald
    early days at the Grammar School   209
Webster, Donald F   214
    music master at MGS in 1951   147
Webster, Samuel
    a bass trombonist of great girth, known as Bunkus   79
    a member of The Morley Reed Band   77
West Ardsley Male Voice Choir, The
    appeal for new members in 1970   128, 138, 145
West Riding County Council   51, 112, 153
West Riding Singers, The
    founded by Noel Anderson   133, 219
    issue their first LP   128
    only three conductors in the choir's history   134
Westerton School   51
Westminster Theatre, London
    the venue for nearly 200 performances of 'Dead on Nine'   67
Westmoreland, V   181
What Now?   122
    an Omads 1946 revue   122, 146
Whirlem & Twirlem
    acrobats (ASykes & J Ackroyd)   75
Whitaker, William
    a master plumber of Chapel Hill   108
Whitby Municipal Orchestra   52
Wilcock, Mary   191
Wild, Elizabeth Jill   214
Wildman, Harry
    Vocal Union member & master decorator for the Co-op   131, 132
Wilkinson, Arhtur
    editor of the Morley Observer in 1939   124
Williams, Stephen   214
Williams, Thomas R (Taffy)   191
Wilson, George   146
    producer of 'What Now?   122
Wilson, John
    Musical director for the Omads   144
Wilson, Kepple, and Betty, a wellknown sand dance
    & their imitators Leo Leathley, Cecil Fox & Hope Bryant   146
Wise, Ernie
    a local success in 1938   145
    an eraly post-war tour with Eric Morecambe   105
    the Morley half of Morecambe & Wise   39, 73, 74
Wiseman, Ernest aged 12
    comedian   75
Wiseman, Harry
    the father of Ernie Wise   73
Withens Clough reservoir   108
Wood, Clifford
    our source for The Rehoboth Drama Group story   202
Wood, Janet nee Holmes
    recalls The Omads in 1938   75, 144, 146

Woodfield, Eunice of Doncaster
    a Top Town Comp Judge 193
Woodkirk church 25
Woodkirk Parish Church Youth Group 209
Woodkirk Secondary School 138
    Tingley Sylvians move in 1964 138
Woodward, Capper
    understudy Donkey to Billy Commons 84
Woolf, Rowena
    3rd wife of Richard Riddle Ainley 17
Woollin, Bill 190
World Premiere in Morley, A
    an achievement at The Friends Adult School 124
Worrall, Benjamin Hale
    entrepreneur 108
YMCAin Albion Street Leeds 181
Yorkshire amateur premiere of Pickwick 179
Yorkshire Animated Picture Company
    using the Temperance Hall in 1911 106
Yorkshire Electricity Players 31
Yorkshire Evening News 63, 192
Yorkshire Evening Post, The
    an advert calls for volunteers to entertain 181, 192
Yorkshire Post 30, 166
    merry hell over The Merry Widow 167
Yorkshire Television
    a 1976 production 199
Yorkshire TV 43
Young Men's Improvement Society 11
Zion Methodist Church, Batley 50

Printed in the United Kingdom
by Lightning Source UK Ltd.
9469900001B